InvestBeyond.com

InvestBeyond.com

A new look at investing in today's changing markets

Victoria Collins Ph.D., CFP

Foreword by
Charles R. Schwab

This publication is designed to provide accurate and authoritative information in regard to the subject matter covered. It is sold with the understanding that the publisher is not engaged in rendering legal, accounting, or other professional service. If legal advice or other expert assistance is required, the services of a competent professional should be sought.

Associate Publisher: Cynthia Zigmund
Managing Editor: Jack Kiburz
Project Editor: Trey Thoelcke
Interior Design: Lucy Jenkins
Cover Design: Elizandro Carrington
Typesetting: the dotted i

Library of Congress Cataloging-in-Publication Data
Collins, Victoria F. (Victoria Felton), 1942–
    InvestBeyond.com : a new look at investing in today's changing markets / Victoria Collins.
        p.   cm.
    Includes index.
    ISBN 0-7931-3817-5 (6x9 pbk.)
    1. Investments—Computer network resources.   2. Stocks.   3. Speculation.
I. Title.
HG4515.95.C65 2000
332.6–dc21   00-022740

Dearborn books are available at special quantity discounts to use as premiums and sales promotions, or for use in corporate training programs. For more information, please call the Special Sales Manager at 800-621-9621, ext. 4514, or write to Dearborn Financial Publishing, Inc., 155 N. Wacker Drive, Chicago, IL 60606-1719.

Advanced Praise for *InvestBeyond.com*

"*InvestBeyond.com* is brilliant! I haven't read anything like it. This is truly a book whose time has come. Finally, someone not only explains this New Economy clearly and simply, but tells me exactly how to navigate these new, and unfamiliar waters with specific investment strategies. It's a fascinating book written in such a lively, fast-paced style that I couldn't put it down. Really. I read it like a novel. I want everyone I know to read this book before they put another dime in the market. I know I'm glad I did."

Barbara Stanny
Author of *Prince Charming Isn't Coming: How Women Get Smart about Money*

"Victoria Collins' *InvestBeyond.com* should be required reading for all investors. She dispels many investment myths, replacing them with sound and sage advice."

James P. O'Shaughnessy
Chairman & CEO, Netfolio, Inc.

"When stock market madness tempts you to lose your head, Collins will keep you well grounded with advice on investment portfolios for the 21st century."

Janet Bodnar
Senior Editor, *Kiplinger's Personal Finance*

"A must-read for the new investor dying to jump into the markets by jumping into the latest dot-com. Victoria Collins offers a specific, easy-to-understand investment approach that will help prevent you from losing it all."

Jennifer Openshaw
CEO, WFN Women's Financial Network <www.wfn.com>

"Just when investors needed it most, Victoria Collins has written *Invest-Beyond.com*. Successful investing in the New Economy requires taking a different look at asset allocation. This timely, clearly written and thoughtful book helps readers incorporate technology into their portfolios without taking undue risk. A must read for investors (and advisors)—implementing these recommendations may change your life!"

Alexandra Armstrong CFP, CMFC
Author of *On Your Own: A Widow's Passage to Emotional and Financial Well-Being*

"Essential reading for every woman—and man—confused by the volatility in today's markets."

Dr. Judy B. Rosener
Graduate School of Management, UC Irvine

Dedication

This book is dedicated to my clients whose thoughtful questions on the changing investment world challenged me to develop a new perspective on traditional strategies.

Contents

Foreword

The world is changing before our eyes, sometimes startlingly so. And nowhere is this more apparent, or more dramatic, than in the world of investing. In the last few years, the Internet has come front and center, and as a result, the financial world is a different place than it was a few years ago. So while the path for individual investors has been paved for decades, it's become a well-traveled road only recently.

What's changing? Access to information, for one thing. Today the information available to individual investors is astonishing, in both quality and quantity. Everyone can learn to become better investors—to take control of their financial lives. The tools are abundant, the stage is set, the knowledge is here for the taking.

All of which is wonderful. Learning to invest and becoming a wise investor is empowering, and you can get started investing in a remarkably short time. Yet, sometimes you hit a snag. The very thing that's empowered people can also intimidate them: all that information, all that easy access. The world of independent investing can feel like a complicated place, a maze that's tough to get through on your own.

What's needed, of course, is guidance, someone to hold your hand or look over your shoulder. You may not need someone to take over; you probably just need some help. And that's what this book is: 225 pages of valuable guidance.

Victoria Collins is one of the top money managers in the country. *Worth* magazine has included her among the best financial advisors around for four years running, and she's been a financial advisor for 20 years. That experience has served her well—start reading and take control of your financial future.

Charles R. Schwab

Acknowledgments

It's true that no book is ever written solely by the person called the author. As you read this one, I would like you to be aware of the many exceptional people who played a part in making it happen. My special thanks go to:

First and foremost, Elaine Floyd, whose research and writing gave life to my thoughts, ideas, theories, and words. Her style is crisp, clear, warm, and contemporary. She integrated vast amounts of information, teased out elusive concepts, and brought clarity and focus to all. Elaine worked tirelessly with me to complete the manuscript in a very short period of time and it could never have been done without her. It is always a pleasure working with a true professional.

Cynthia Zigmund, my editor at Dearborn, whose astute input, challenging questions, and unflagging encouragement and support all went toward making this book the best it could be.

My partners and colleagues at the Keller Group Investment Management Inc. who supported my sabbatical and cheered me along the way. Rick Keller, John Hakopian, Rick Tarlos, and Bates Reese shared ideas, insights, and research about the changing investment world and special thanks go to them.

David, my husband, mentor, sounding board, and closest friend. His perceptive insights, constructive ideas, and never-ending support were true gifts to me personally and to the completion of this book.

PART ONE

How Investing Is Different Today

The Internet
Changes Everything

Wall Street legend has it that when people start saying "it's different this time," the market is doomed. That's because the contrarian philosophy of investing holds that when *everybody* thinks the market will go higher, then presumably *everybody* is already fully invested in stocks. With nobody left to buy, the market consists only of sellers, which means there's only one way for stock prices to go: down. In theory, the philosophy makes sense. In practice, the markets are never as rational or predictable as one expects them to be. Still, the phrase "it's different this time" sends chills down the spines of longtime market watchers who have lived through a bear market or two and know how devastating it can be to witness a prolonged decline in stock prices.

Why does the phrase "it's different this time" create such anxiety on Wall Street? Because people use it to justify paying more for a stock when all manner of reason says the stock is already priced too high. Continued buying at higher prices raises the alarm that once investors come to their senses they'll start selling en masse and valuations will return to more traditional levels, as measured by price/earnings (P/E) ratios and other traditional measures of value. Investors who say "it's different this time" give themselves permission to buy stocks with P/E ratios of 50 or 100 or N/A (because the company has no earnings) or otherwise pay more for a stock than they normally would because, well, things are different now. They say traditional valuation methods are outdated because (1) companies are growing faster now; (2) earnings don't matter anymore; or (3) just because. That's when the market traditionalists cringe, shake their heads, and say "watch out!"

What really is different today is that even the people who recoil at the phrase "it's different this time" are starting to say it themselves (often in private—nobody wants to admit that they've caved). They're watching young investors who have never seen a bear market blithely pay what seem like outrageous prices for fledgling companies with good stories but no earnings—and they're making money at it! This really steams some of the oldtimers who cling to the traditional methods of valuing stocks, and who these days are running out of stocks to buy. To stay in the game, they're being forced to cast aside old beliefs and pay more for stocks than they ever would have thought reasonable. They justify it by joining in the chorus (with a whisper, if they can't bring themselves to utter the words aloud), "it's different this time."

But Investing Really Is Different Today

Really. And I'm not just saying that because I want to pay high prices for the stocks I like. When I step back and look at how investing used to be compared to what it's like now, I have no choice but to marvel at the differences. Traditionalists know the past very well, and in some ways this previous knowledge hampers their acceptance of the present. Today's new investors, on the other hand, lack the experience that produces caution in people who have witnessed the past. In this book I propose a middle ground, drawing from the past while keeping an open mind about where investing is likely to go in the future. Let's take a look at what has changed.

Securities Trading Has Evolved

The stock market has come a long way from the days when brokers and merchants traded securities face to face in downtown Manhattan in the late 1700s. With no central meeting place, they had to search all over town to find someone to trade with. And with no written guidelines, they had to trust each other to comply with the group's implicit rules of conduct. So on May 17, 1792, a group of brokers signed the famous Buttonwood Agreement specifying that they would meet at one location—under the buttonwood tree at 68 Wall Street—and trade only with each other. This two-sentence agreement set in motion a formalized process for trading that has evolved into the bustling, rapid-fire systems that now exchange millions of shares each day among buyers and sellers who don't know each other, never see each other, and are trading from locations all around the world.

Why should we care about how securities trading has evolved? Because it's only by understanding the present within the context of the past that we can appreciate just how different the market is today and how the changes are impacting us as investors. Looking at how the markets have developed explains why some people and institutions are being dragged kicking and screaming into the twenty-first century, while others are welcoming the changes with open arms.

The Venerable New York Stock Exchange
Initially Set the Tone for Trading

The elite, clubby nature of the Buttonwood group, which later grew into the New York Stock Exchange (NYSE), set the tone for investing during most of the twentieth century. Although the formation of the exchange was designed to give more people access to the securities markets, it has not exactly been an open society. Only firms and individuals meeting rigorous personal and financial standards are allowed to trade there. Membership is limited to 1,366 seats, and one can buy a seat only if someone else is willing to sell. The price is based on supply and demand and now costs over $2 million. Membership in the exchange was exclusively male until 1967, when Muriel Siebert became the first woman to buy a seat. (Even female employees weren't allowed on the trading floor until 1943.) The first African-American, Joseph L. Searles III, was admitted into membership in 1970. The public is not admitted on the trading floor except during VIP tours, but anyone can watch the activity from a glass-enclosed gallery high above.

You can only buy or sell a stock listed on the NYSE through a member firm. You can't just call up the exchange and tell them you want to buy 100 shares of IBM. Instead, you must call a *registered representative* of a brokerage firm that owns a seat on the exchange and tell him or her what you want to buy. Your order is then transmitted over the brokerage firm's wire system (an electronic version of the old teletype system) to the floor of the exchange. From there, a *floor broker* picks it up and physically takes it to the post where the stock is traded. There are 17 posts on the exchange floor; each post trades more than 150 stocks. For each stock, a *specialist* matches up all the buy and sell orders and finalizes the transactions. When your order to buy 100 shares of IBM is brought to the specialist, he immediately finds a matching sell order and completes the trade. The floor broker sends this information back to your registered representative, who calls you and tells you that your order has been filled. All of this generally happens within a few minutes.

The member firm that executes your order will charge you a fee—called a *commission*—for handling the trade. Prior to 1975, commissions were regulated by the government which meant all the brokerage firms charged roughly the same amount. Deregulation was a major milestone in the history of stock trading and for the first time opened up competition in the commission arena. Discount brokers popped up, creating a two-tier brokerage system, with so-called full-service brokers continuing to charge preregulation commissions and discount firms catering to do-it-yourself investors charging substantially less.

Of the many thousands of public companies in the United States, only about 3,000 trade on the NYSE. These are generally the larger, more established companies that are able to meet the exchange's requirements for financial strength, trading volume, and public disclosure of financial information. The rest of the nation's public companies trade somewhere else—and you'll never know where because there are no physical trading posts, just electrons that zip around the world in an invisible network that connects dealers sitting in front of computer terminals from Fairbanks to Miami.

The High-Tech Nasdaq Opens Up Trading to Include Many More Companies

In contrast to the deep roots and majestic presence on Wall Street of the venerable New York Stock Exchange, the over-the-counter (OTC) market grew up as a scrappy, alternative trading system for stocks that couldn't qualify for listing on the Big Board. In its early days, the OTC market consisted of dealers who spent a lot of time on the phone, calling each other and buying and selling stocks for themselves and their customers. These stocks ranged from established companies that fell just short of NYSE listing requirements, to outright shady companies selling for pennies per share. Trades didn't have to be reported, so the only people who knew about them were the buyers and sellers involved in the specific transactions. The only way to find out the price of a stock was to call a dealer and get a *quotation,* which consisted of two numbers: (1) the price at which the dealer would be willing to sell 100 shares of stock (the *ask price*) and (2) the price at which the dealer would be willing to buy (the *bid price*). The difference between these two prices— called the *spread*—is how dealers make their money. By buying a stock at the bid price and turning around and selling it at the ask price, the dealer could capture a profit of 50 cents a share or more. With no public display of trading activity, there were plenty of opportunities for dealers to manipulate prices and take advantage of investors.

In 1963, the OTC market began to get its act together. The Securities and Exchange Commission (SEC) issued a report saying the OTC market was fragmented and obscure and appointed the National Association of Securities Dealers (NASD) to create an automated system for about 2,500 OTC stocks. This was the beginning of Nasdaq, or the National Association of Securities Dealers Automated Quotation System. Brokers who were members of the NASD could now access information on these 2,500 stocks through their desktop terminals. If you wanted to buy a Nasdaq stock, you would call your NASD-member firm representative, who would check his screen and give you the current bid and ask prices. If you wanted to go ahead and buy the stock, the rep would send the order to the firm's OTC desk. If the firm made a market in the stock, it would sell you stock out of inventory; if not, it would call another firm that did make a market in it and buy the stock on your behalf, charging you a commission for the trade.

Although automation greatly legitimized the OTC market, at least for the 2,500 stocks that were part of Nasdaq, spreads were still wide and it was hard for investors to know if they were getting the best deal. So in 1980, Nasdaq began displaying inside quotations, or the best bid and ask prices, on screen. This kept dealers honest and narrowed spreads considerably. Then in 1997, Nasdaq took a big leap toward leveling the playing field by including investor limit orders in quotations. This meant that if an individual investor were willing to pay more for a security than a dealer's best bid, the world would know about it. Spreads narrowed from 50 cents a share to as little as 3 cents a share. Dealers' profits were slashed virtually overnight. But trading became much more efficient and fair, and investors could now expect the same above-board dealings in the smaller Nasdaq stocks that they had become accustomed to on the Big Board.

Speaking of smaller Nasdaq stocks, many of them aren't so small anymore. It used to be that a company traded on Nasdaq only if it couldn't meet NYSE listing requirements. As a company grew, it would move up to the Big Board to show off its new financial status and generate more interest in its stock. But as the Nasdaq has become more legitimate, many companies are happy to stay there. Microsoft, for example, could have moved to the NYSE a long time ago but chose to remain on the Nasdaq, and many other companies have done the same. It's unlikely the higher cost of NYSE listing was a factor in Microsoft's decision but rather the Nasdaq's method of trading, which utilizes technology rather than requiring a physical presence on an exchange floor. Indeed, technology is what has brought stock trading from its elitist origins under the buttonwood tree to its egalitarian present, where markets are made by free-thinking individuals and securities trading is fast, fair, and efficient.

The Internet Has Opened up Access to the Markets

Even as commissions fell and spreads narrowed, for a long time access to securities prices was restricted to brokers who could afford to pay $800 or $1,000 a month for a Quotron terminal. If you wanted to know the price of a stock and didn't want to wait for the evening newspaper, you had to call a broker for the information. So even though the securities markets had come a long way in promoting full disclosure, the information flow pretty much stopped at the broker's desk, to be selectively dispensed to individuals who either took the initiative to call the broker themselves or were big enough clients to be included on the broker's call list.

Then the Internet happened. There's no other way to describe its beginnings. Nobody planned it. Nobody created it. And nobody is responsible for managing it (although a lot of people would like to try). In fact, the Internet had its origins back in the 1960s when the United States Department of Defense wanted to form a communications network that would continue to function following a nuclear invasion. Creating one central authority was out of the question because that would be the first target of an enemy missile. So the network was built on a series of nodes, from which data would bounce around until it reached its destination. If one of the nodes became incapacitated, the data would simply find another node and eventually find its way to the recipient. New nodes were added all the time, and there was no one person or institution regulating either the creation of the nodes or the flow of information.

In the 1970s and 1980s the Internet was used primarily by the government and academia. Text files traveled to destinations ending in *.gov* or *.edu,* and the general public was largely unaware of this growing information network. Then in the mid-1990s commercial interests discovered the Internet and the World Wide Web took off. Graphics were added, modems picked up speed, Internet service providers proliferated, and the public plugged into the richest source of information imaginable. Millions of new destinations were added, most of them ending in *.com.*

The Internet's impact upon investors is twofold. First, it changes the way people invest, allowing them to be less dependent on gatekeepers/brokers for information and trade executions. Second, it changes the behavior of the markets, as more individuals invest on their own and apply different thinking to their buy/sell decisions as compared to some of the more traditional investors and longtime Wall Street professionals. We will explore these two phenomena in more depth and attempt to answer some of the questions spawned by the growing realization that, yes, investing really is different today.

How the Internet Changes the Way People Invest

If the deregulation of commissions in 1975 opened up competition in the brokerage industry, the Internet has blown the cover off of it. With no need to build fancy offices and hire armies of brokers, it is now easy and inexpensive for brokerage firms to get clients and execute trades. So easy, in fact, that they can lower commissions dramatically and still make a profit. At last count there were some 100 online brokers offering trade executions as low as $5 per transaction. This compares to several hundred dollars often charged by the big Wall Street firms. If you want to find out the price of a stock, you no longer have to call a broker sitting in front of an expensive desktop terminal. All you need to do is log onto the Internet, type in the stock symbol (or use one of the many available symbol search devices), and the price, as reported by the NYSE or Nasdaq, pops up on your screen. (Prices on many sites are delayed by 20 minutes as a vestige of Wall Street control. Brokerage firms must still pay for real-time quotes, but online brokers usually provide them on their Web sites for free as a way to attract customers.)

Buying and selling are quick and easy.   If you want to buy a stock, you don't need to call a broker during market hours and spend precious minutes chatting pleasantries and explaining to the broker why you want to buy this stock. All you have to do is enter a few keystrokes on your home or office computer and your order is on its way. Right now, the mechanics of order execution are still pretty much the same. If you're buying an NYSE-listed stock, your online broker will transmit the order to a floor broker, who will take it to the proper post on the trading floor and have the specialist match it up to a corresponding sell order. If you're buying a Nasdaq stock, your order will eventually find its way to a market maker who will sell the stock to you out of inventory. However, it won't be long before your order may bypass the big exchanges and be executed through one of the new electronic communications networks, or ECNs. These networks function similarly to the way online auctioneer eBay brings together traders of collectibles and other items. They use the power of the Internet to hook up buyers and sellers and can do so at any time of the day or night at very little cost. ECNs, in fact, are beginning to threaten the very existence of the NYSE and Nasdaq. As the CEO of one ECN put it, "The New York Stock Exchange has more people smoking outside at any point in the day than it takes to run our system." At the very least, the traditional exchanges will need to become more competitive in their pricing and get rid of the rules designed to keep people out.

What all these changes mean for you, the investor, is that you can invest anytime you want, anywhere you want, and it will cost you a lot less than it did before. Just punch in your order and the investment is yours. No hassle. No waiting. No explaining to do.

What you may be missing.   When you invest online, no one will ask you if the investment you have chosen is suitable for you given your risk tolerance, time horizon, and tax situation. That's not their job. Their job is to execute orders for people who know what they're doing. And to get more customers and more business, the online brokers are working very hard to help people think they know what they're doing. This is a key point: the online brokers' success is directly related to the amount of self-confidence that they can instill in their customers. They provide lots of information about securities and investments while emphasizing that it's all so easy. Just a few clicks and you're there. As a result, more people are firing off trades without consulting anyone—except maybe their favorite online chat group.

Some of these new electronic do-it-yourself investors really do know what they're doing, often as a result of having moved through the ranks from full-service broker to discount broker to today's online discount broker. These longtime investors who have recently embraced the Internet say that the Web has greatly facilitated investing. It has removed many of the obstacles, most notably the high commissions that can chip away at investment returns, and provided a direct link to the markets along with vast amounts of information never before available through a single broker no matter how full-service that broker was. These experienced investors have great confidence in their decision-making ability and are grateful for the many tools available to them today. They appreciate the fact that each time they want to trade they can do it virtually anonymously and not have to talk to a gatekeeper/broker who may have different ideas from theirs.

At the other end of the experience spectrum lie the new investors who only recently acquired enough assets to invest in stocks or mutual funds. The idea of consulting a full-service broker or other professional for investment advice seems strange to them, partly because they're not sure what kind of advice they'd get (commission brokers try to sell you stuff, right?) and partly because they're used to being independent in other areas of their life. Unlike members of the World War II generation, who have always relied on professionals (and salespeople passing as professionals) for advice in areas ranging from taxes to life insurance, today's baby boomers and members of Generation X are used to making their own decisions based on their own research and gathering of unbiased information. After buying cars, houses, and insurance this way, they're now moving into investing. They see the body of knowledge connected with investing as just another research project, no different from learning about the difference between term and whole life insurance. Some are facing the assignment with diligence, reading everything they can get their hands on and quickly increasing their understanding of the way investments work. Others are taking the easy route and believing the online brokers when they say investing doesn't have to be complicated. These impatient investors jump right in, preferring to let real-world experience be their teacher.

What seems to be missing from all the hoopla about online investing is the groundwork that needs to be laid before a stock or mutual fund is ever bought. In the rush to get in on the latest dot-com stock using the latest dot-com tools, the concept of personal financial management seems to have gotten lost. Without financial advisors asking such questions as "Why are you investing?" "What are your financial goals?" and "What is your risk tolerance?" people aren't stopping to think about these important personal issues that have always guided long-term investing in the past. Instead, people have become focused on finding the next big stock, never mind the risk potential or tax consequences. It's all about making money today.

By titling this book *InvestBeyond.com,* I don't mean to imply that the Internet is bad as an investment medium or that there aren't tremendous opportunities in Internet-related stocks. I just want people to realize that there is more to investing than picking a good stock and saving on commissions by trading through an online broker. Investing should encompass your whole financial situation and should serve as a means to an end, such as college for your kids or retirement for yourself; it is not an end in itself. I worry that when people go online they become so consumed with hitting it big that they are ignoring the concept of asset allocation, which involves spreading money among different market sectors in case the stock you like the best suddenly falls out of favor. The purpose of this book, therefore, is to encourage investors to take advantage of all that technology has to offer without ignoring some of the sound investing principles that financial planners and gatekeepers/ brokers would force you to think about if you didn't have this direct link to the markets.

At the same time, I recognize that the profound changes brought about by the Internet mean that the old concept of asset allocation deserves a new look. It was once considered gospel among investment professionals to spread a client's portfolio among different areas of the market—even when they knew some of those areas would underperform—because one could never know which areas would be the top performers. As a result, investment returns for a broadly diversified portfolio would always be lower than for a portfolio which was concentrated in the best-performing sector (but higher, of course, than a portfolio concentrated in the wrong sector).

As it turns out, investment professionals have had some explaining to do when their clients have come back at them after investing a portion of their money on their own in the latest hot sectors and beating the performance of the professionals! Some people have talked about abandoning the idea of asset allocation, while others still strictly adhere to it. I dare to say that it's possible to find a middle ground, and in this book I suggest some ways to tweak the concept of asset allocation so that it retains its validity while taking into account the indisputable fact that in business and in life, the Internet changes everything.

How the Internet Changes the Way Markets Behave

Think for a moment about what it means to invest. When you make an investment you exchange cash for something else in the hope of seeing a return on your investment, or somehow ending up with more money than you started with. Now, there are lots of things you can invest in—stocks, bonds, mutual funds (which are collections of stocks and bonds), real estate, pork bellies, Beanie Babies—but for the moment we'll limit our discussion to stocks. When you buy stock, you become part owner of a company whose principal business may be anything from building railroads (not very common today) to manufacturing the latest genetic drugs. As a holder of common stock you are entitled to certain financial rights. The one most clearly spelled out in a company's charter relates to the unlikely event of the company's liquidation: if the company goes out of business common stockholders will receive their respective share of the company's assets after all debts have been paid. While the company is operating, however, and as long as you hold your shares, you won't see much of a return on your investment—unless the company pays dividends.

Long, long ago, dividends were considered the primary reason to buy stock in a company, at least among ordinary investors who weren't speculators. People would buy stock in General Motors or AT&T, stash the certificates in their safe-deposit box, and sit back and collect their quarterly dividend checks. As the company's earnings grew over the years, it would generally raise its dividends, rewarding loyal shareholders and providing a nice return on investment. If a stock's price rose high enough, the company would often decide to *split* the stock in order to lower the price and attract new investors. If it was a two-for-one split, it gave the existing shareholders twice as many shares as they had before (although it didn't change the value of their holdings because the price of the stock dropped by half when the new shares were issued). Nevertheless, over the years the stock price would eventually work its way back up again, whereupon it would split again—and again and again and again. After a few decades (people had lots of patience back then and often passed stock to the next generation when the original shareholder died) the dividends had been raised many times and were now being paid on many more shares. Those quarterly dividend checks had reached sizable proportions and often supported loyal shareholders in their old age.

Yes, owning stock in a big corporation was definitely a good investment—as long as the company had increasing earnings. After all, it was out of earnings that dividends were paid. If earnings slipped, the dividend might be in jeopardy, and if the dividend was cut or eliminated, there wasn't much reason to own the stock anymore. Or so investors thought at the time.

Earnings tell the whole story . . . or do they?   Soon companies realized that if they didn't have to pay dividends to shareholders, they could reinvest that money back into the company and generate even more earnings. Of course, shareholders wouldn't be seeing any of those increased earnings, at least not right away. But the reasoning was that if the company's earnings were growing, more people would want to own the stock—presumably in the hope of one day receiving a share of those higher earnings when the company matured and eventually started paying dividends. Somehow investors bought into this theory even though it meant not getting an immediate return on their investment.

The reason investors bought into the no-dividend theory was that their stock was becoming more valuable in the open market. In fact, it was considered the mark of a good company *not* to pay dividends because it meant the company was plowing its earnings back into the corporation and building value for the future—even if shareholders wouldn't immediately get to pocket any portion of those earnings for themselves. There was always the presumption that eventually the company would pay dividends (otherwise why would anyone invest?). In the meantime, investors were happy buying low and selling high and seeing a return on their investment that way. So earnings, not dividends, soon became the primary criterion for investing in stocks, and the faster those earnings were growing, the higher the stock was valued in the marketplace.

By the way, some investors have always considered asset value an important criterion for investing in stocks. Going back to the fundamental right of common stockholders—to receive a share of the company's assets in the event of liquidation—these investors want their holdings backed by hard assets, not quarterly earnings, which they're not likely to ever see a penny of anyway because most growth companies aren't paying dividends. Investors who buy stocks based on their asset values are said to have a *value style* of investing. Those who buy stocks based on growing earnings are said to follow a *growth style* of investing. We'll be talking more about this in Chapters 3 and 4.

But the story doesn't end there. If it became okay for a company not to pay dividends in order to plow all of its earnings back into the company, why couldn't it be okay for a company not to show earnings in order to plow all of its revenues back into the company? After all, if a company aspires to be, say, earth's biggest online retailer, wouldn't it make sense for the company to take every penny of revenue and spend it on advertising and marketing programs so it could grow even faster than it otherwise would? And wouldn't it make sense for the company to borrow as much as possible in order to generate more revenues which could then be invested in more advertising and marketing programs and whatever else the company might need to spend money on in order to grow as fast as possible? The company's earnings might be negative, and its balance sheet might be negative, but all this negativity would be for a good cause.

And does it follow from there that a company with no revenues might even be a good investment? After all, if the company has a great idea and a well thought out business plan, it has the potential to generate revenues, which may eventually lead to earnings, which may in the far distant future lead to dividends. The question is, how far will investors carry this logic? How far away from the original premise of investing in stocks will the reasoning go? Have people become so anticipatory in their stock buying, so accustomed to buying stocks in the hope of selling them at a higher price that it doesn't even matter anymore what a company does? Or has the Internet ushered in such profound change in the way companies operate that those on the cutting edge, who are rapidly building their infrastructure and investing every penny they can, are destined to generate such extraordinary earnings in the future that investors who buy a stock for that now-quaint concept of a quarterly dividend will be more richly rewarded than they ever thought possible?

People have different ideas about what constitutes value.   The problem with investors pinning all of their hopes on what another market participant may decide to pay for their stock in the future is that there is absolutely no way to predict what that payment may turn out to be. With dividends, at least you had a company's commitment to a certain dollar amount every quarter. Without dividends, your entire investment return comes from what some other investor decides your stock is worth when you go to sell; and the whole time you own the stock you're receiving no return on your investment at all—just paper profits (or losses) that aren't good for much of anything, except maybe collateral for a loan.

And with ideas about valuation levels changing all the time, you can't even assume that the criteria that led you to choose this stock in the first place will still be in force when you sell. For example, you may buy a stock when earnings growth is considered an important criterion for investing in stocks. Then over the course of your holding period the market changes its mind about earnings growth and decides that companies without earnings are really better investments because they are the companies of the future. The company you own, which has reported excellent earnings and performed exactly the way you wanted it to, now languishes in the marketplace because those earnings are no longer valued by investors.

When the stock of a company with no earnings can command $400 per share in the marketplace, longtime market watchers shake their heads and call it a speculative bubble. Experienced investors, who are accustomed to pinning stock prices to earnings or asset values, can only explain people's willingness to pay higher prices for a company with no earnings by what they call the greater fool theory: as long as there is at least one more fool willing to pay a higher price for the stock, an investor can make money. Once the last fool is in, the stock has no-where to go but down.

At least that's the way manias and speculative bubbles have worked in the past. But never before have so many people been able to buy and sell stocks with the click of a mouse. Compared to today, the brokers under the buttonwood tree had it easy. They knew each other personally and together developed certain criteria for valuing securities. These un-written rules made for an orderly market in which buyers and sellers knew what to expect from one another whenever they entered the mar-ketplace. Throughout much of the twentieth century, the markets have largely been controlled by institutional investors and professional money managers who also had similar standards for valuing securities—with some variations, of course, because the variations are what make the markets and create buyers and sellers for the same security. Still, the band of variation was relatively narrow because everyone was trained in the same school of thought.

Individual investors, for the most part, have had little influence on the markets throughout the twentieth century. Even as more individuals and families have acquired enough assets to invest in stocks over the past couple of decades, most have done their investing through mutual funds run by professional money managers. Individual investors buying individual stocks have been in the small minority, and most of these in-vested through full-service brokers who were trained in the same school as the professionals. As gatekeepers to the markets, brokers and finan-cial planners educated their clients about P/E ratios and other such val-uation methods, and often discouraged their clients from buying what they considered to be overvalued securities.

Today we have traditional investors trained in the old school at-tempting to apply standard valuation methods to a marketplace that is increasingly being influenced by newer investors who know (or care) nothing of such methods. Needless to say, this is making for some very interesting markets.

And then there's the "new economy." To confuse the valuation issue even more, the Internet is completely redefining the way companies make their money. Even before the Internet, forecasters talked about a "new economy" that would transform our nation from an asset-based, industrial economy to a knowledge-based, high-tech economy. They told us that now that our nation's physical infrastructure was virtually complete—roads built, dams made, buildings constructed—that we as a nation could concentrate on the more ethereal aspects of life such as thoughts, knowledge, and ideas. They said that electrons would become more valuable than bricks and mortar. Companies would make "soft" wares, having no physical presence but promising value to customers nonetheless.

And then the Internet happened and the futurists' predictions came true in spades. Companies started selling invisible products from invisible locations identifiable only by a string of letters positioned between *www.* and *.com.* And in the strangest twist of all, some companies found that they could thrive by actually giving away their products and then finding a different source of revenue that could far exceed any revenues they might generate through product sales alone. The topsy-turvy economics that the Internet has ushered in has left analysts and investors scratching their heads in search of appropriate methods to value companies with assets you can't see and products you can't buy. In Chapter 4, we'll be looking at some of the standard valuation methods as they are being applied to today's leading edge companies, and also discuss some new ones that have been proposed as being more reflective of the current economy.

Yes, investing is different today. More people have access to the markets. Ideas are changing about the way securities are valued and the way companies operate in the new economy. Yet to really understand what moves the markets, you have to look inside the minds of investors. The burgeoning new field of behavioral finance attempts to explain market activity by examining investor psychology—and why people do the things they do, especially when they can have their finger on the trigger of the buy/sell mechanism 24 hours a day, 7 days a week.

2 Investor Psychology Moves Markets

Remember when keeping up with the Joneses meant a bigger house, a newer car, a more exotic vacation? Well, thanks to the media, our financial role models no longer live down the street in houses only slightly bigger than ours. Now they live in multimillion-dollar mansions with indoor lap pools and four-car garages housing a collection of $100,000 cars. As a culture, we've always been fascinated by wealth and what it can buy. Who hasn't seen at least one episode of the long-running *Lifestyles of the Rich and Famous* and felt a twinge of envy over the extravagant homes and jet-set lifestyles portrayed in beautifully photographed videos with the impeccable Robin Leach voiceover? Fantasy at its best in late twentieth-century America. And totally unattainable to those of us not born into wealth or connected to the right people.

Then along comes a guy named Bill Gates, an ordinary-looking dude who dropped out of Harvard to start a company called Microsoft. While we were busy watching the Joneses down the street and *Lifestyles* on TV, Bill was building his company. Then one day, lo and behold, he becomes a billionaire and his picture and story are all over the media. Now we see a guy who, granted, is pretty smart but for the most part is just like us (not born into royalty or anything), and he's really, really rich. Richer than those people on TV, and way richer than the Joneses down the street. And he did it all himself, in one generation and without inheriting any money from his parents.

"I could have done that," we say. Well, maybe we couldn't have founded Microsoft and built it into what it is today, but we could have gone to work there when the company was young and negotiated a few stock options as part of the deal. We could at least have bought the stock before it split a zillion times and went on to become one of the biggest companies in America in total capitalization. If we had, we'd be millionaires today, just like those lucky but also rather ordinary people who had the foresight to jump on the Microsoft bandwagon early.

And it's not just Microsoft. Lots of companies have created millionaires out of ordinary people who were smart (or lucky?) enough to take stock options in lieu of cash when the companies were barely viable. A hot company in a hot industry going public in a hot market creates, well, instant millionaires. We read about them everywhere. And we can't helping thinking, "That could have been me."

Everybody's Getting Rich

Newsweek's July 5, 1999 cover story showed an anxiety-ridden cartoon figure saying, "Everyone's getting rich but me" in a bubble caption headed by the words "The Whine of '99." Inside were stories that told of a few recent millionaires:

- Todd Krizelman, 25, and Stephan Paternot, 25, made $35 million when a company they conceived in their dorm room, theglobe. com, went public.
- Don Roberts, 29, made over $1 million day trading stocks.
- Jonathan Peters, 27, a $40,000-a-year employee, made $2.5 million when his company, broadcast.com, went public.

In April 1999, *The Wall Street Journal* published an article about a secretary who became a millionaire when she followed her boss to a start-up company called Mosaic Communications—later changed to Netscape Communications—and made over 20 years' pay on the day the company went public (Netscape was later bought by America Online). In May 1999, Alan Abelson wrote in *Barron's* about modern-day investor tycoons, including "New York City cab drivers, my cleaning lady (who just bought a new BMW), and all the 25-year-old brokers that now live in million-dollar homes in Scarsdale." In an example closer to home, I recently sat down with a young engineer who'd been with Broadcom—a company located near my office—for only six months. He was already a multi-millionaire as a result of receiving stock options just before the firm went public. In the time it has taken to write this book, several of my clients who work for Broadcom and also Qualcomm (in San Diego) have made more money than most people make in a lifetime.

The most telling thing about all these stories is that these are people just like us. The idea that there could be a fortune out there with our name on it is changing the way many of us think about money and what it takes to make us happy. A steady job with a respectable salary? Boring. Our expectations are getting higher all the time in a kind of extreme envy, which, like so many other aspects of our culture today, has to be bigger, louder, and more extreme to produce even a ripple. We don't want just a little more than the Joneses. We want a lot more. And not only do we think we deserve it, we have no doubt that it's utterly and completely within our power to attain—as long as we hurry up and grab it before the chance passes us by. And, of course, the online brokerage firms are feeding the envy frenzy with ads of ordinary people showing off extraordinary wealth acquired with point-and-click ease. This was epitomized by an ad featuring a former truck driver showing off his own private island.

This combination of wanting more than we ever did before and believing we'd better get on the bandwagon now is causing some strange behavior among investors. Like the lottery and (less popular now, thankfully) litigation, the stock market is now seen by many as the quickest route to riches. Spurred on by media reports like the ones already mentioned and countless others reported in local newspapers every day, more people are seeing that stock trading can be fun and very profitable. What they don't read about, of course, are all the companies whose stock options didn't pan out or all the day traders who lost money. That's not the kind of news we want to hear, so the media doesn't give it to us. And so we remain blissfully unaware of the downside to all these attempts to strike it rich.

New Breed of Risk Takers

It's been so long since we've seen a real bear market that lots of people have the idea that stocks can go only one way. But ask anyone who lived through the 1973–74 bear market what it's like to see your net worth go down day after day after day and you'll hear some very sad stories. A client I'll call Walter has told me many times about how his pension plan assets declined so badly during those years that he couldn't bear to look at his statements. He felt he had made the biggest mistake of his life entrusting his hard-earned dollars to the stock market. He finally sold out in total despair and frustration and moved his money into bonds. Not only was the 1973–74 bear market a grueling ten months that saw stock prices decline by 43 percent, but it took years—until 1982—for the market to finally take off and start going up. Walter eventually got back into the market, but not until 1992, when the bull market had already been underway for a decade. Fortunately he's having a better experience this time, but he'll never forget those dismal years in the 1970s when he thought his entire life savings was going down the drain.

The point I want to make is this: Anyone whose stock market experience is post-1982 has no idea what a bear market can do to one's portfolio and psyche. The periodic one-day crashes we've seen don't count. The market always seems to come roaring back, so people no longer take them seriously. Maybe that's a good thing. But I worry when people with limited stock market experience jump in with both feet without understanding how treacherous the waters can be. I recently received a letter from an 82-year-old client saying, "my portfolio's been too conservative . . . I want more in stocks. And please pick those that will go up for me." This concerns me greatly because she really doesn't understand how much she could lose in a market decline—nor does she have realistic expectations about what I can and can't do.

Generation $

People are learning about investing at ever-younger ages. While it certainly can't hurt for high school students to learn about money and finance, some kids these days are bringing a video-game mentality to the investing process. While I was pleased to hear about the nationally distributed Stock Market Game, sponsored by the securities industry's Foundation for Economic Education, I think it may be a double-edged sword when it comes to teaching kids about investing. On the one hand, it helps students learn math, economics, even social studies and geography using a real-world platform that's both fun and meaningful to students. On the other hand, it encourages students to take a short-term, competitive approach to investing. The goal is to beat the other players in one semester's time, not to save for retirement or put children through college. So what are students learning here? That investing means nailing down quick profits with volatile securities? Whatever happened to steady saving using a sensible buy-and-hold strategy that lowers taxes and trading commissions? Admittedly, that wouldn't be a very fun game.

The real world isn't much better at inducing realistic expectations about investing. *Money* magazine in January 1999 reported that if you'd been wise or daring enough to purchase 100 shares each of AOL, Yahoo!, and Amazon.com at the beginning of 1998—at a cost, then, of roughly $21,500—by the end of November the stake would have mushroomed to $111,800. That's a gain of 419 percent, or some 400 percent more than the S&P 500 Index, in less than a year. In the face of reports like this, who's going to listen when financial advisors preach long-term saving and reasonable expectations of, say, only 10 percent or 12 percent a year? (The 50-year average return for stocks is about 12 percent.) As one financial planner put it, it's really tough to convince a 26-year-old Microsoft engineer that he should put part of his portfolio into conservative investments when all the action is in high tech. So I have to ask, who's missing the boat here? Is the 26-year-old being too brash for his own good, or is the financial planner stuck in a time warp?

Probably a little of both. In Internet time, the 1973–74 bear market is ancient history. To the dot-com generation, worrying about an extended bear market happening again is like worrying about another Great Depression or the fall of Mesopotamia. We're in a different world now. The bigger risk is missing out on the opportunities at hand.

Online Traders

No one embodies the quest to capitalize on the opportunities at hand better than the amateur online day trader. A relatively recent phenomenon, ushered in by the Internet of course, online traders are people who buy and sell stocks all day long and then close out their positions at the end of the day in order to start fresh tomorrow. They may buy and sell the same security several times in one day, capturing a point (or fraction of a point) here and there. The idea is to trade often enough and capture enough points on the upside (and give up few enough on the downside) to cover trading commissions and have a decent profit left over. Some people, lured by seminars touting easy wealth, have quit their day jobs to become full-time traders. Now they spend their days hunched over a computer terminal watching numbers flash before their eyes and making split-second decisions about what to buy or sell and when, all the while knowing there are hundreds or thousands of dollars riding on each decision. This doesn't sound like my idea of a good time. In fact, these amateur traders often give it up when they realize that it's not nearly as fun, exciting, or profitable as they thought it would be.

The best thing that can be said about the online trading phenomenon is that it creates liquidity in the markets and forces the securities industry to truly serve the individual investor, offering services like after-hours trading and access to IPOs. Competition for active traders—the bread and butter of online brokerage firms—has led the industry as a whole to improve its service offerings and support free and open trading, which benefits all investors. That they also encourage hyperactive trading is another story, which brings us to the downside of online trading, or three reasons why it's dangerous.

The first affects the fewest people but causes the most devastation among the people it does affect. It's when people become addicted to trading. *Investment News* ran a story in July 1999 in which Ed Looney, the executive director of the Council on Compulsive Gambling of New Jersey, was quoted as saying "In the last three months, I've talked with a 60-year-old retired stockbroker who invested his $5 million pension in sexy Internet stocks and has just $100,000 left. I've talked to a housewife who lost her children's college tuition. I've counseled a 27-year-old who worked in the brokerage field and wiped out $40,000 that he and his wife had saved. They have a seven-month-old; he was ready to kill himself." Mr. Looney went on to say that online trading is the crack cocaine of gambling—the most addictive form of all. Needless to say, it has ruined lives, most notably that of Mark O. Barton, who in July of 1999 opened fire in a day-trading firm in Atlanta before turning the gun on himself.

The second downside is that most people simply do not make a lot of money at it. Terrance Odean, finance professor at the University of California–Davis, recently studied the behavior of 1,607 investors who switched to online trading between 1991 and 1996. Before going online, they produced superior returns, beating the market averages by more than two percentage points annually. After going online they started trading more actively and tended to speculate more. The result? Their returns started lagging the market by an average of three percentage points a year. Mr. Odean explains it simply: the more decisions an investor makes the more opportunities there are to be wrong. His research shows that an investor can improve his or her chances for higher returns simply by trading less often. Higher trading costs also figure into the equation. Because trading costs are not reflected on the screen, online traders are often unaware how much they're spending on trades until they get a statement summarizing portfolio activity. And although taxes were not taken into consideration in this study, short-term capital gains taxes can consume as much as 40 percent of an investor's profits. Between trading costs and taxes, these traders have a big hurdle to overcome before they see significant profits.

The third problem with online trading is, in my opinion, the most serious. Once the gambling addicts have sought help and the rest of the online traders give up out of exhaustion or the futility of it all, we'll still be left with the speed with which investment decisions are made today. The whole investment cycle has shortened. I've observed that many people today are not taking the time to properly evaluate any stock before buying. They buy a name or a story, letting emotions guide their decisions and ignoring such classic characteristics as P/E ratios and earnings growth rates. Then once they've made the investment, they don't give it sufficient time to perform. They want to see immediate results or they become discouraged and kick the offending stock out of the portfolio. One trader quoted in *Forbes* said, "My philosophy is to buy high and sell higher and not be afraid to take risks. I use no research tools or software. I just surf the message boards and look for volume." This kind of flighty approach to the markets contributes to volatility and unpredictable returns, as we'll see in Chapter 3.

This shortened investing cycle is also affecting the quality of companies going public today. In the past, a company had to show several years of profits before an investment banking firm would even consider taking it public. Now, any company with a shot at future profits—as long as it's got a sexy, high-tech story—can be brought to market. Investment bankers admit that they are bringing companies public much sooner today and not imposing the rigorous performance standards of the past. They justify it by saying they are meeting the insatiable demand for IPOs and that investors know they're taking a big risk when they buy stock in a newly pubic company. Maybe so, but some of the companies going public today are barely formed entities.

Deep-Seated Attitudes about Money

All this fast trading and intense focus on wealth are relatively recent phenomena, spawned by the Internet and magnified by the media. But deep-seated attitudes from childhood also play a big part in the way people invest today. In my book *Couples & Money,* I talked about *hidden investments.* These are core beliefs, both useful and harmful, that are accumulated throughout life in the natural course of learning.

Parents and Money

Parents instill the deepest attitudes about money, both by what they say and what they do. And those messages are not always the same. A parent who preaches the value of saving for a rainy day and then blows the rent money on a trip to Disneyland is giving serious mixed messages. How you interpret those messages as a child will determine what you do later in life. Does the fear of running out of money make you a serious saver—even to the point of pathological hoarding? Or do you just figure that money will take care of itself and the important thing in life is to have a good time?

Children generally believe and deeply internalize messages they get from their parents about money—whether those messages are right or wrong. Some girls grew up believing no man would ever marry them if they made too much money. Some boys saw that providing for the family is the most important goal in life, even if it means depriving the children of their time. Some people, even as successful adults, can't bring themselves to spend money on luxuries because of parental messages playing in the back of their minds admonishing them about being too extravagant. Other families never talked about money at all, and that carries its own set of messages.

Some of the beliefs instilled in us by our parents serve us well in adulthood; others inhibit our ability to achieve certain goals. Each of us could probably benefit by spending some time on the analyst's couch, figuratively speaking if not in actuality, exploring deep-seated values about money that we acquired as a child.

Peers and Money

After parents come peers. These are the people you chose to hang out with when you were growing up. Much to the dismay of a lot of parents, peers can sometimes undo many of the healthy attitudes about money that parents work so hard to instill in the home. By accepting or shunning kids depending on what they wear or where they live, peer groups often magnify money's importance while ignoring personal characteristics like kindness or a sense of humor that one normally looks for in a friend. What influence did your circle of friends have on your attitudes about money? Did you feel more confident and more accepted when you wore the latest designer clothes? Did you feel rejected because you couldn't afford them? Or did you hang out with kids who didn't place a great deal of importance on the trappings of material wealth?

Although most of us think of peer influence as a high school phenomenon, it often carries over into adulthood, sometimes in a very big way. This is what keeping up with the Joneses is all about. Some people spend a fortune on exotic vacations, not for the experience itself, but so they can come back and tell their friends where they went and what they did. For people still living under the influence of peer pressure, fancier vacations, bigger houses, more expensive cars, and designer clothes all say the same things they did in high school: I am worthy of your admiration and acceptance; please like and respect me.

Generations and Money

After parents and peers comes the influence of society, religion, and the media. We happen to be in a wealth culture right now, thanks to a strong economy and a booming stock market. It wasn't always so. During the Great Depression, people roamed the streets looking for jobs and food. Those who had a roof over their heads and food in the cupboard considered themselves lucky. They didn't dare wish for more because they knew how much worse things could be. During this period of extreme poverty and deprivation, people were grateful for anything they had. The prevailing attitude was preservation and conservation: do everything you can to keep what you have because it can all be taken away. This explains why people who are over 65 today have always been conservative in their investments—even when they were younger. One would expect them to be more conservative later in life, of course, because no one wants to be taking big risks when there are fewer years left to make it back. But this generation has always been conservative, preferring bank certificates of deposit, money market funds, and bonds over stocks and mutual funds. My father was a great example of the depression mentality. His advice to me was, "Pay off your mortgage, keep a lot in savings, and be sure you have some gold bullion." The Great Depression left indelible scars on the people who lived through it, and many of those scars were transferred to their children, who saw sad pictures and heard moving stories about hard times when they were growing up. Many of them likewise adopted conservative attitudes about money.

But those scars are fading as society moves on. Ironically, the generation that lived through the Great Depression is now one of the wealthiest in America. Thanks to booming real estate values, their homes are worth a fortune. And after a lifetime of saving and frugal spending, they've accumulated substantial nest eggs. After spending most of their lives in fear of losing it, they are only now getting used to the idea of having money. Finally, they are starting to enjoy it. Though they know they're entitled, they still feel a few pangs of guilt when they tool down the road in the RV with the bumper sticker that boasts: We're spending our children's inheritance.

With the baby boom generation, the scars of the Great Depression all but disappeared. Born during the post–World War II economic boom, baby boomers have always felt entitled to creature comforts such as plenty of food, clothing, and shelter, as well as luxuries like TV sets and a new family car every few years. Although they heard stories of the Great Depression from their parents and grandparents, they couldn't really relate. Times are good now, so why worry? One of the reasons times were so good for baby boomers growing up was that their parents overcompensated for the miseries they experienced, swearing they would never let their children go through what they had to endure. As adults, boomers have carried with them that feeling of entitlement, often running up large credit card bills to pay for things they felt entitled to but couldn't afford. Indeed, baby boomer spending has contributed significantly to our healthy economy over the past couple of decades. Harry Dent, author of *The Roaring 2000s,* bases his whole economic thesis on the idea that boomers moving into their peak spending years will continue to keep the economy robust and the stock market moving higher in the years ahead.

Generation X hates to be classified by generation, but nevertheless has shared experiences that can't help but impact them as a group. Although they've never really seen a troubled economy, many would say they are worse off than their parents. Higher college costs have forced many of them to start adult life mired in debt. High real estate values have priced some them out of the housing market. Still, they enjoy a standard of living higher than that of any generation before them, if you consider all the labor-saving devices and technological wizardry available now. Generation X investors have never seen a bear market and don't understand why they need to worry about risk. Recently I sat down with a 23-year-old who was well on his way to being *double comma* (for the hopelessly uncool, that's geekspeak for being a millionaire), thanks to a fistful of stock options with a hot little tech company. As we talked about investments in general, he shared with me that he could not fathom why bonds even existed or why anyone would have a portfolio less than 100 percent in stocks. Clearly a bear market was not part of his experience.

This generation has the best handle on technology and is fully exploiting it in their investing endeavors. John Leisure, the 16-year-old son of one of my partners, started a stock investment club at his school, runs his own portfolio (dad does the execution and acts as a sounding board to John's stock picks), and has even developed a Web site on which he discusses such things as P/E ratios and selection criteria. He does his own research and has come up with some real winners. John is one of many kids nationwide who have gained an interest in the market and become very smart about it at an early age. These kids have never experienced a world without the Internet. They're naturals at using technology in their everyday lives and are now using it to do the kind of research only professionals could do just a few years ago. A few years ago, Generation X was famous for grousing about how boomers had taken the best jobs and would probably occupy the higher rungs of the corporate ladder for many years to come. But a tight labor market and high demand for technological prowess has changed all that and opened up tremendous opportunities for the generation that is beginning to drop the *X* and adopt the moniker *dot-com generation.*

Gender and Money

As you can see, there are many factors influencing beliefs about money. The family you are born into shapes one set of values, while the peer group you grow up with shapes another. Cultural attitudes affecting you and your generation form another set of beliefs. So what's left? Your gender. Now granted, all these other things play a part, too. Cultural attitudes about gender and money have changed dramatically over the years, so depending on when you were born, your gender influences will be different. For example, a 45-year-old woman who grew up with a stay-at-home mom will have a very different relationship with money than a 25-year-old woman whose mother worked full time and made more money than her father. Generally, I would say that as the world has become more egalitarian with respect to the genders, there are fewer hang-ups about money and the sexes. You may not agree with this if you're going out on a date tonight and wondering who should pay, but that's exactly my point. Men and women are much freer today to adopt new approaches to money. No longer must they cling to old conventions that clearly don't work for them.

Still, you are a product of your gender. And though you may wish to believe you have risen above any gender-related issues that might influence your attitudes about money, it's worth taking a look at some of the more common stereotypes to see if: (1) yep, that's you, or (2) nope, that's not you. Please keep in mind that these are indeed stereotypes. While I do not wish to perpetuate them, I point them out as a way of examining your own personal attitudes about money. Reject any or all of them if you wish.

Women tend to be more uncertain or fearful about money. Regardless of age, women don't seem to have the same confidence in their ability to make money as men do. Some women experience the "bag lady syndrome," or the fear of being poor, even when they hold good jobs. Diedre has been a client for a number of years and is CFO of a small but very successful manufacturing firm. I've always been impressed by her take-charge attitude and head for numbers. Yet from time to time she shares concerns about ending up poor. She admits it's an irrational fear, but that doesn't make it go away. Men are more confident in their ability to make money and don't worry as much about becoming destitute. They do, however, worry that hard times may force them to lower their standard of living and cause them to lose face. Men seem to suffer from the burden that society puts on them that they should understand investments and always make the right decisions. Mark, another client, said it rather poignantly when I asked him what his biggest fear was about investing. It wasn't the potential loss of money that scared him. "I'm afraid I'll look stupid if I make a bad investment. After all, as a man, I should know this stuff."

Women tend to take fewer risks. As a natural consequence of their fear of losing money, women tend to avoid situations in which that fear might play itself out. Sometimes it's a matter of understanding the risks and choosing not to accept them. Other times it's a matter of not understanding the investment and reading more risk into it than is there. Men are much more cavalier about risk, assuming that if they lose money they can always make it back. As expected, most of the trigger-happy online traders mentioned earlier in this chapter are men.

Women base their decisions on a combination of reasoning and intuition while men rely mostly on facts. A female-oriented approach to evaluating a stock would be to consider the company's image, the quality of its products, and management practices such as diversity in hiring and family-friendly policies. A male-oriented approach would be to look at the numbers and compare them to other companies' numbers. Interestingly, men are more likely to rely on tips from friends, whereas women will take another person's advice and invest only if it feels right.

Men trade more. In a study of the trading habits of 35,000 households, Brad Barber and Terrance Odean of the University of California at Davis found that men traded 45 percent more than women but earned annual risk-adjusted net returns of 1.4 percent less than women. The results were even worse for single men versus single women: single men traded 67 percent more than single women and earned 2.3 percent less.

Why People Invest the Way They Do

The field of behavioral finance has been around for 30 years, but only recently has it gone mainstream. It seems academicians have been quietly studying the impact of investor psychology on the markets while Wall Street has largely ignored this field of study. I find it interesting that Wall Street has an indicator for practically everything, including how the market acts in years of presidential elections and which way it goes depending on who wins the Super Bowl, but they've all but ignored the influence of investor psychology. Perhaps it's too touchy-feely and not factual enough for them.

But behavioral finance is gaining respectability, especially among those who have done serious studies linking attitudes and investor behavior. The difficulty researchers have had in testing their theories against real-world experience is that the major brokerage houses have carefully guarded their client records. So many of the conclusions that have been drawn about how and why people invest have been based on anecdotal evidence or small academic studies and have therefore been easy to dismiss. I personally have taken a great interest in the field of behavioral finance because it combines my early background—my parents were active in the stock market and the subject was common dinner table conversation—with cognitive psychology, the field in which I earned my doctorate degree. I have always been fascinated by how people manage their money, and I've found that it has little to do with numbers and everything to do with expectations and messages from the past.

Overconfidence

One fallout from the ongoing bull market is that people are becoming overconfident. They think they know more about investing than they actually do. And when investors think they're hot, they tend to be less careful. They make quicker decisions based on less information and this is a key dynamic affecting our markets today. Overconfidence leads to active trading, and active trading leads to lower investment returns. This is partly because of trading costs, but also because the more decisions a person makes, the more chances there are to be wrong. New investors are especially susceptible to overconfidence: they get lucky on one or two trades and figure they've got what it takes to lick the market.

Professionals have also been accused of succumbing to overconfidence. As one behavioral finance expert put it, "Because [professionals] have the ability to build fairly sophisticated mathematical models, they believe their mathematical models will actually be right." My firm tries very hard not to fall into this trap.

Loss Aversion

People will do anything to avoid a loss. Is this bad? Well, it can be. Loss aversion makes people hang onto losers far longer than they should. As long as the loss is on paper, the thinking goes, it doesn't count. After all, the stock could turn around and go back up again, proving that you're not so stupid after all. But if you sell the stock and realize the loss, then you're forced to admit you made a mistake. Meanwhile, that dumb stock just sits there (or keeps going down), tying up funds that could be put to better use elsewhere. Loss aversion also makes people sell their winners too soon, forcing them to pay taxes and trading costs and missing out on future appreciation. I've seen many cases where investors' stocks kept going up after they sold them. This often gives rise to seller's remorse, that nagging suspicion that you've just shot yourself in your foot.

One client, Jim, likes to micromanage his portfolio even though he is paying us to provide professional management services. When the Dow reached 11,000 in mid-1999, Jim called and instructed us to sell everything in his portfolio. After much discussion about long-term goals, we finally conceded and followed his wishes. A few weeks later the Dow retreated to 10,000 and Jim wanted back in. Unfortunately, the stocks he had owned and wanted to buy back had risen in price (despite the Dow's decline), so he was forced to buy them back at higher prices. Several stocks had moved up beyond our buy price range; according to firm policy we could not buy them for this one client when we were not buying them for other clients unless Jim specifically gave us permission to do so. He didn't feel comfortable doing that which turned out to be the ultimate bad move. He missed out on Qualcomm's major year-end move and also missed a significant portion of appreciation in other stocks like Cisco and Oracle as a result of being out of the market at a critical time. Jim's portfolio was up 43 percent for the year, while his wife Vicki, who did not sell out, was up 172 percent. Paradoxically, Jim's aversion to loss caused his performance to suffer.

Another problem with loss aversion affects older, more conservative investors (the ones who lived through the Great Depression) who refuse to take any risks at all with their portfolio. They avoid any investments that fluctuate in value, fearing they could lose it all. When loss aversion is this extreme, the portfolio fails to keep up with inflation. The irony here is that in 1999, people who tried to avoid risk actually fared worse than those who took risks. With the exception of 1994, 1999 was the worst year for bonds in 30 years. As a money manager I find it particularly difficult to explain how performance can be so dismal for something that should be so safe.

Illusion of Control

One of the reasons some people shun a buy-and-hold strategy in favor of active trading is that it makes them feel more in control. When you're sitting at the computer, mouse in hand, you're doing something, not just standing by helplessly waiting for your stocks to go up. It's human nature to want to do something when you're in a hurry for a particular result. That's why people push elevator buttons over and over again or honk their horns in traffic. Rationally, they know such actions are futile, but it still gives them the illusion of control. To make matters worse, the online brokerage firms cater to this bias: "Invest online, you're in control." The next time you're tempted to enter an order simply because your stocks aren't moving fast enough, remember that active trading means more transaction costs, possibly more taxes, and often lower investment returns.

Hindsight

When you engage in hindsight, you honestly believe that you could have predicted the thing that ultimately turned out to be true. Hindsight makes you think you could have known in the 1980s that Microsoft would turn out to be such a good investment in the 1990s. After all, it's so obvious! Microsoft had popular products, good marketing strategies, and an ambitious CEO. But the truth is that in the 1980s Microsoft was one of many software companies, most of which eventually were acquired or went out of business. By the time it became clear that Microsoft was the winner in the software wars, its lead was well established and the stock was already on its way to the moon. If you doubt this theory, try picking the next decade's big winner. Will it be Amazon.com?

America Online? Or some new company that nobody's even heard of yet?

Meir Statman, finance professor at Santa Clara University says, "Hindsight bias makes it easy to believe not only that the future is pre-ordained, but that anybody with half a brain could have seen it." It's often used by investors to blame financial advisors who should have known, "to invest the entire portfolio in Japanese stocks from 1987 to 1988, switch to U.S. stocks from 1989 to 1992, back to Japanese stocks from 1993 to 1994 and to U.S. stocks again from 1995 to 1997." According to Dr. Statman, hindsight bias lets people shirk responsibility and save face: "I'm not stupid, my financial planner is stupid." As a financial advisor I have to deal with this all the time. Clients just assume that I can see into the future. When they hear about an event that has already happened—good news or bad news about a certain stock—they wonder why I didn't let them know about it ahead of time. In hindsight it always looks so obvious. I only wish it were.

The danger of hindsight is that it can lead to overconfidence and rash investment decisions. If you're so smart about Microsoft, you may be tempted to put your entire retirement fund into the next big opportunity. Just remember, there is a difference between what *worked* on Wall Street and what *will work* on Wall Street.

Anchoring

Anchoring is letting a particular reference point keep you from objectively reacting to new information. You buy a stock at $20. It goes down to $15 on a bad earnings report. You decide you don't like the stock anymore and as soon as it gets back to $20 you'll sell it. But what if it never gets back to $20? Then you're in the same boat as the loss aversion folks, hanging onto a stock you don't like and tying up assets when they could do better elsewhere, all because you're anchored to that $20 purchase price. To see if anchoring is causing you to hold onto a stock you should have sold, I suggest you ask yourself, "If I didn't own this stock, would I buy it today?" If the answer is no, dump it.

Anchoring is what causes longtime market watchers to stand back in horror as they watch stock prices go higher and higher and higher. They remember when the S&P 500 had an average P/E ratio of 20. When it gets over 30, they assume the market will have to come crashing down in order for the P/E ratio to get back to 20. New investors, who are not anchored to any particular reference point, don't have the same perspective. Why not a P/E ratio of 40 or even 100?

Fallacy of Small Numbers

One common psychological error is to read too much into a small observation. You base your assumptions on what the market has been doing since you've been watching it, ignoring previous time periods because they're not part of your personal experience. Or you use Microsoft, Amazon.com, and America Online as your indicators for how all stocks perform. Everyone who follows the Dow Jones Industrial Average—which includes most of us—falls into this trap. The Dow comprises just 30 stocks, yet we use it to gauge the behavior of all stocks. The next time you're tempted to draw far-reaching conclusions based on (1) last week's market performance, (2) last night's news report, or (3) your last successful trade, keep in mind that it's a pretty small sample you're using.

Jane has had a portfolio with us for a short time. When I recently ran her performance, the numbers showed that the tech section—comprising just three stocks—had dramatically outperformed her mutual funds. Naturally, she wanted more of the same and assumed I could pick another three or four stocks that would allow her portfolio to grow by 247 percent in 2000 as it did in 1999. The fact is, this kind of performance is highly unusual and not likely to be replicated again. The fallacy of small numbers is causing Jane to have unrealistic expectations about future portfolio performance.

Mental Accounting

When we do mental accounting, we treat money differently depending on where we got it, where we keep it, or how we spend it. People tend to treat a windfall, such as a gift or tax refund, more frivolously than they treat other money. Mental accounting may cause you to treat investment profits differently from the money you started out with. For example, you invest $10,000 and it goes up to $15,000, so you take out your original $10,000 and put it in the bank and start playing with the "house money." Like all of the psychological issues listed here, mental accounting—though perfectly normal and practiced by nearly everybody at one time or another—keeps you from being completely rational in the way you handle money.

Thought Contagion

Thought contagion is an old concept with a new name. You may know it as the *madness of crowds* or the *herd mentality* or even *tulipmania*. *Thought Contagion* is the title of a book by Aaron Lynch, in which he explains how an epidemic of delusion can spread, even when it has no basis in fact. Once an idea or a piece of (mis)information gets broad TV coverage or makes the rounds in Internet chat rooms, it takes on a life of its own. More people buy into it simply because everybody else is. Logic tells you it's crazy, but because it's so pervasive and widely touted you begin to question your basis for reasoning. If it's so popular, maybe you're the one who's crazy. Eventually, you abandon your old beliefs and jump on board.

It is exactly this dilemma that is making market watchers so nervous today. They've studied their history and know how tulipmania played out—eventually people in seventeenth-century Holland came to their senses and realized that a tulip bulb wasn't worth a small castle after all, causing tulip prices to come crashing down. But that's hindsight. Today, when you see the market driving up prices on the stocks of companies with no earnings, are you being smart for staying out or stupid for not getting in? Is anchoring inhibiting your ability to objectively process new information, or is the run-up in these stocks a product of thought contagion, in which case you're wise to stay away? I don't have a clear answer to this—nobody does—which is why I wrote this book: to suggest strategies that will enable you to cope with these dichotomies and invest successfully even when you don't have all the answers. For now, just understand that there are many complex forces ruling the markets and your own individual investment decisions. My goal is not to confuse you, but to expand your awareness of how complex investing can be so you won't make poor decisions because you thought it was all so simple.

3

A Stock Market
or a Market of Stocks?

Quick, what did the market do yesterday? If you're a longtime market watcher, you know exactly what is meant by this question. To answer, you would check this morning's newspaper or remember yesterday's news after the close and then report how many points the Dow Jones Industrial Average was up or was down for the day. Simple question, simple answer.

But when you think about it, the market is much more than the 30 stocks that comprise the Dow Jones Industrial Average. It's really all publicly traded stocks—and bonds, for that matter—plus warrants, rights, convertible securities, and even futures and options. However, if we were to include all those securities in our definition of the market, it would be impossible to describe how the market did on any given day. You'd have to answer with something like, "Well, some stocks were up while some were down, some bonds were up and some were down, and I don't know what futures and options did because I don't follow those markets." Complicated question, long drawn-out answer that doesn't say much of anything.

So this simple convention that we've all adopted, thanks to *The Wall Street Journal* which established the Dow Jones Industrial Average over 100 years ago, makes it easy for investors everywhere to get a sense of what kind of day it was for stocks. If you own stocks or mutual funds—never mind which ones—you cheer if the Dow is up and jeer if it's down. It's only after you've checked the Dow that you look at your own portfolio. If the Dow is up and your stocks are down, you may feel a twinge of regret, thinking you must be in the wrong stocks. If the Dow is down and your stocks are up, you may feel a little smug, satisfied that on this day at least you've managed to beat the market. So the Dow, in addition to providing a quick snapshot of the market, also serves as a powerful psychological reference point by which we tend to judge our own investment success.

A Stock Market or a Market of Stocks?

The big problem with using a single index—and a narrow one at that—to evaluate stock market performance is that it's easy to base your investment decisions on the wrong information. Remember, the Dow Jones Industrial Average was created as a convenience to journalists. Although *The Wall Street Journal* does publish daily closing prices of most of the stocks traded on major exchanges, it still needed a way to give readers a quick summarization of market activity. That doesn't mean you should necessarily use the Dow, or any other information package handed down by the financial press, as the primary basis for your investment strategy. Placing too much importance on the indexes can be misleading because it masks the underlying activity of the market and says nothing at all about risk. I'd like to challenge some of the conventional ways of looking at the market and suggest that we treat the day's Dow report as an interesting part of the news, much like the weather or sports, but nothing that relates directly to our own portfolio or individual investment objectives.

Here's a simple example of what I mean. In the first three months of 1999, the Russell 2000 small-stock index was down 1.7 percent. This might cause one to believe that small stocks went virtually nowhere during that three-month time period. Yet the 26 Internet stocks in the index were up an average of 99 percent. If you had looked at the index alone, you never would have seen the spectacular performance of this small group of Internet stocks. You might have assumed that all small stocks were relatively flat for the quarter, when really they were all over the place. There had to have been lots of losers for the index to remain flat while the Internet group performed that well. Another thing you wouldn't have known by focusing on the performance of the index is that many of those Internet stocks reported no earnings. To those of us trained in the earnings school of stock evaluation, that spells big risk. In fact, this is a big problem for money managers who are expected to beat or exceed the indexes but whose legal responsibility as a fiduciary prohibits them from buying companies with no profits. The point here is that the 1.7 percent performance figure for the index can be very misleading because it doesn't begin to tell the whole story.

Still, as misleading as indexes can be, I do recognize their value in helping us make sense of this gigantic thing called *the market*. The human brain, when faced with more bits of information than it can process at once, tends to classify the bits into groups. This is a natural phenomenon and can be very helpful in understanding the market. However, I would like to suggest that there are many ways to classify stocks. Each method of classification offers its own perspective on the market, illuminating certain areas and masking others. Depending on which method of classification you use, you'll get a remarkably different sense of the market.

Note: No discussion of market activity would be complete without actual performance figures, despite the drawbacks of using historical data to understand the future, as noted later in this chapter. Although the use of 1999 calendar-year performance figures may appear to date this book, especially if you're reading it in 2000 or 2001, 1999 was when the Internet phenomenon really took off and essentially separated the haves (technology stocks) from the have-nots (everything else).

Classifying by Index

I'll start with the indexes, because I've already talked about the Dow and the Russell 2000. Besides, indexing is the most popular method of examining the market today, in no small part due to the fact that sponsors of indexes get lots of publicity. It certainly doesn't hurt Dow Jones & Company that its name is uttered by market watchers several times a day and published in hundreds of newspapers across the country in addition to its own *The Wall Street Journal*. Standard & Poor's and the Frank B. Russell Company also get publicity every time their indexes are mentioned.

Dow Jones Industrial Average

The Dow Jones Industrial Average is composed of 30 stocks selected for total market value and broad public ownership. It's a subjective determination, not based on preset criteria, and periodically certain stocks are replaced by others to make the index more reflective of the current economy. The October 1999 move to replace Chevron, Goodyear, Sears, and Union Carbide with Home Depot, Intel, Microsoft, and SBC Communications was notable for the index's somewhat tardy recognition of technology companies in today's economy. The value of the Dow is the sum of the closing share prices of the 30 stocks, divided by a divisor, which changes whenever there's a stock split or company replacement. The purpose of the divisor is to make the Dow useful for time-series comparisons. In fact, this is why the Dow has endured for so long despite its narrow focus: it's a great comparison tool. Many of us remember when the Dow was under 1,000. Now it's over 11,000. This tells us how far stocks have come (30 of them, anyway). Because the index is based on the sum of closing prices, higher-priced stocks tend to affect the index more than lower-priced stocks. In 1999, the Dow Jones Industrial Average was up 25.2 percent. Components of the Dow Jones Industrial Average as of December 31, 1999 were:

AT&T	Intel
Alcoa	International Business Machines
American Express	International Paper
Boeing	Johnson & Johnson
Caterpillar	McDonald's
Citigroup	Merck
Coca-Cola	Microsoft
DuPont	Minnesota Mining & Manufacturing
Eastman Kodak	J.P. Morgan
ExxonMobil	Philip Morris
General Electric	Procter & Gamble
General Motors	SBC Communications
Hewlett-Packard	United Technologies
Home Depot	Wal-Mart
Honeywell	Walt Disney Co.

Standard & Poor's 500

The Standard & Poor's 500 index consists of 500 companies chosen to reflect the relative contributions of the industries that comprise the U.S. economy. The list changes over time as companies merge or fail, and replacements are added as needed. The main difference between the S&P 500 and the Dow (in addition to the number of stocks) is that the S&P 500 is weighted by market value. This means companies with large capitalizations (share price multiplied by number of shares outstanding) influence the index more than companies with smaller capitalizations. The S&P 500 is by far the most common benchmark for index funds. In 1999, the S&P 500 provided a total return (capital appreciation plus dividends) of 21.0 percent. But about half of that gain came from just eight high-flying technology stocks. Indeed, 230 of the stocks in the S&P 500—almost half—are trading below their level of two years ago.

Nasdaq Composite

The Nasdaq Composite consists of the more than 5,000 stocks that trade on the Nasdaq Stock Market. Until it broke 3,000 on November 3, 1999, the Nasdaq Composite had received very little attention from investors. Then, when it went on to produce a whopping 85.6 percent return in 1999—with more than half of that return occurring after the November 3 crossing of 3,000—the index became one of the most widely watched of all. More than any other index, the Nasdaq Composite masks underlying market activity due to the wide range of stocks represented by it, from Microsoft on down to the tiniest of companies. In 1999, more than 800 stocks, or about one in six, doubled in value; a remarkable 37 stocks gained over 1,000 percent. Despite posting a one-year rise exceeding that of any market index in history, nearly half of all Nasdaq stocks actually declined in value.

Russell 2000 Index

The Russell 2000 Index is the most widely watched index of small stocks. Actually, the index is composed of the smallest 2,000 of the largest 3,000 stocks. To create the index, all stocks are ranked in total market capitalization. The top 3,000 stocks make up the Russell 3000 index. Then the top 1,000 stocks are sliced off for the Russell 1000 and the rest make up the Russell 2000 index. In 1999, the Russell 2000 was up 19.6 percent.

Wilshire 5000 Total Market Index

The Wilshire 5000 Total Market Index attempts to gauge the entire U.S. stock market and now comprises more than 7,000 stocks. It gives a better snapshot of the market, but obviously says nothing about which sectors or stocks did better than others. In 1999, the Wilshire 5000 Total Market Index was up 23.6 percent.

As you can see by the varying performance figures for each of these indexes, *the market* can mean many different things depending on how you slice it. Anyone who compares his own portfolio's performance against the Dow, the S&P 500, or any other index, is making an arbitrary comparison against a benchmark that may or may not be appropriate. In order to do a valid comparison you have to look at other characteristics, namely risk. A suitable analogy here may be the benchmarks one uses for personal fitness. A 25-year-old and a 55-year-old would naturally have different training goals; for both to try to hit the same benchmarks for running or weight lifting would not serve either one very well. So what should you compare your portfolio's performance to? As I'll be discussing later in this book, you should compare it to your own personal investment objectives.

Note: This argument against using the indexes as benchmarks for your own investment performance has nothing to do with the use of index funds as an investment vehicle. Index funds can indeed be suitable investments, as you'll see in Chapter 10. In the meantime, let's look at some other ways to classify stocks that will come in handy when we talk about specific strategies.

Classifying by Industry Sector

Another popular way to group stocks is by industry. Several of the indexes do this to some degree. In addition to the 30 stocks in its well-known industrial average, Dow Jones also has a transportation average (20 stocks) and a utilities average (15 stocks). The S&P 500 is classified into 11 broad industries: basic materials, capital goods, communication services, consumer cyclicals, consumer staples, energy, financial, health care, technology, transportation, and utilities. By going to <www. spglobal.com>, you can see what percentage of the S&P 500 each sector represents and how each sector performed apart from the others. To save you a trip to the site, here's how each sector performed in 1999:

Basic Materials	24.0%
Capital Goods	27.2%
Communication Services	17.4%
Consumer Cyclicals	20.9%
Consumer Staples	–7.5%
Energy	16.2%
Financial	2.2%
Health Care	–9.3%
Technology	74.8%
Transportation	–10.7%
Utilities	–12.5%

Hindsight would tell us that technology stocks were definitely the place to be in 1999. If we had put our entire portfolio into this one sector we would have far outperformed the S&P 500. In fact, because it is so clear here that sector concentration yields the best results, one might argue that diversification dilutes returns and is therefore a bad idea. Having any money at all in utility stocks would have dragged down returns. So why would anybody want to do that? The obvious reason is that at the beginning of 1999 nobody knew that the technology sector would outperform utilities. The reason we diversify is to protect ourselves in case the sector we think will perform the best doesn't.

The S&P 500 further breaks down each sector into several subsectors. Technology, for example, includes the following subsectors (with 1999 returns shown):

Communication Equipment	119.1%
Computers (hardware)	43.7%
Computers (networking)	127.9%
Computers (peripherals)	133.9%
Computers (software & services)	84.9%
Electronics (component distributors)	14.9%
Electronics (defense)	–50.1%

Electronics (instrumentation)	122.6%
Electronics (semiconductors)	56.6%
Equipment (semiconductor)	196.1%
Photography/Imaging	−40.9%
Services (computer systems)	33.1%
Services (data processing)	25.2%

Now you can really get a sense of which industries were leading and lagging the market in 1999. Anyone who thinks all stocks move in tandem would get a vastly different picture of the market by looking at this sector breakdown. Furthermore, these performance figures suggest that sector selection can greatly influence investment returns. The reason for this is has a lot to do with the economy, most notably our continuing transition to a knowledge-based economy. It also has to do with investors' expectations and which sectors are deemed *hot* at any given time. Although we need diversification to keep from putting all our money into the wrong sector, it certainly can't hurt to be somewhat discerning about the sectors we do choose, perhaps avoiding those old economy sectors and concentrating on the ones with particularly bright futures. More on this in Chapter 10.

It's also worth noting here that stocks within a particular sector may move either together or separately in reaction to specific news events. For example, if a key company within the semiconductor industry reports a negative earnings outlook, all semiconductor stocks may decline on the news. On the other hand, sometimes the market interprets the news as specific to that company only, in which case the sector would not move in tandem. This is one of those phenomena that leaves investors scratching their heads because it's impossible to predict in advance how far the spillover will extend whenever there is news affecting just one company.

Classifying by Growth or Value

The money management industry likes to put stocks into one of two categories based on (1) their earnings growth, or (2) their price relative to the company's intrinsic value. Companies with growing earnings are considered growth stocks, while companies selling at low prices are considered value stocks. One of the reasons for making this classification is that the two groups are considered negatively corre-lated, which means they generally move opposite to one another. When growth stocks are in favor, value stocks are usually out of favor and vice versa. Some managers use this classification method to be sure they include some of each in an individual's or fund's portfolio and therefore ensure broad diversification; others choose one or the other—pursuing what's called a *growth style* or a *value style*—in an attempt to beat the averages.

Note: *Style drift* is becoming common today because value fund managers have underperformed the benchmarks due to the extended popularity of growth stocks. While you can't blame them for wanting to improve performance, style drift can be misleading for investors specifically looking for a value style of management.

The growth versus value debate has reached a feverish pitch as technology stocks have surged ahead of so-called old economy stocks and reached unprecedented values. Growth stock proponents say the future is all that matters. Yes, the stocks may be expensive in relation to their earnings and highly leveraged balance sheets, but with revenues growing so rapidly these stocks are sure to grow into their price. If you wait to buy them, you'll end up paying much more. Value stock propo-nents say the future is too uncertain and the present is all we can count on. You can never go wrong with a stock that is reasonably priced in re-lation to its earnings and assets. Even if investors don't find it attractive now, eventually they'll see it as a bargain and increased demand will drive up its price.

Value stocks have been out of favor for several years now, aside from brief flurries of activity that had value proponents prematurely be-lieving their time had come. But more and more, market watchers are questioning whether value stocks will ever come back into favor. In fact, this relates to the fundamental question I asked at the beginning of this book. Is the economy so different now that value stocks have fal-len into the category of railroads and buggy whips? Or are they sim-ply laying low until the Internet bubble pops, at which time they will come roaring back as investors recognize the value of value, so to speak? I'll be dealing with this crucial issue later in this book and will offer strategies that attempt to get around a question that is, at this point, unanswerable.

Classifying by Capitalization

Another popular way to group stocks is by capitalization. This is determined by multiplying a company's stock price by the number of shares outstanding. Large-cap stocks generally have market capitalizations above $2 billion, while small-cap stocks are under $500 million. Anything in the middle is considered a mid-cap stock. While there are far fewer large-cap stocks, they represent the vast majority of the market's total capitalization. There can be variations from company to company, but large-cap stocks tend to be more stable and better established and small-cap stocks tend to be newer and less certain. Volatility varies, but small-cap stocks are generally considered riskier than large-cap stocks.

Note that this is a different way of classifying stocks than by sector. This means you can combine the two methods of classification to achieve varying objectives. For example, within the technology sector you'll find companies of all sizes. If you want to minimize risk yet still take advantage of the opportunities available within the technology sector, you can concentrate on the larger, more established companies like Cisco and Lucent. More on this in Chapter 10.

Classifying by Domestic or International Location

Another traditional way of classifying stocks is by their location: in the United States or elsewhere in the world. Despite the us-versus-them sound of this method of classification, it does have its merits. The various regional economies around the world go through cycles just as ours does (or used to). By focusing on certain countries' stocks you can take advantage of favorable cycles or even favorable currency exchange rates. Alternatively, by diversifying among several world economies you can hedge your bets and protect against being in the wrong country at the wrong time. The reason Americans have been so egocentric lately is that our economy truly has been the strongest in the world. Why go outside our borders, some people ask, when the best investments in the world are right here? Besides, many of our largest companies are already doing business around the globe, so by investing in a U.S.-based multinational company you automatically achieve global diversification. Still, U.S. dominance may not continue forever.

Classifying companies by country provides yet another way of looking at stocks and allows you to concentrate or diversify, depending on your objectives and outlook for the markets.

Classifications for the Internet Age

As technology continues to dominate our world, it's becoming clear that we need new ways of classifying stocks so we can keep track of those companies which are leading us into the next economy. Hence we have not one, but many Internet indexes, all of which purport to include the primary Internet stocks. The race to become the Dow Jones of Internet indexes is intense because everyone knows how much publicity, not to mention licensing fees, you can get when your index is widely followed.

Dow Jones knows this, of course, so it has developed its own Internet index. For this index, companies are divided into two groups. The Internet commerce group represents companies that sell goods or services over the Web, while the Internet services group provides Internet access or offers other types of Internet enabling services. Although the index is still in its infancy and will necessarily undergo many changes as it attempts to meet its goal of including 80 percent of the universe of Internet companies, at this writing the Internet commerce group consisted of 15 stocks and the Internet services group consisted of 25 stocks. (See <indexes.dowjones.com> for current information on this index.)

Dow Jones Internet Index as of December 31, 1999

Commerce Index	*Internet Services Index*
Amazon.com	America Online
Ameritrade Holding	AXENT Technologies
Beyond.com	BroadVision
CNET	Check Point Software Technologies
eBay	CheckFree Holdings
Etoys	CMGI
E*Trade Group	Covad Communications
Go2net	Cybercash
Healtheon	Doubleclick
Lycos	Earthlink Network

MP3.com	Excite@Home
NetB@nk	Exodus Communications
Priceline	HighSpeed Access
Ticketmaster Online Citysearch	IDT
Yahoo!	Infospace.com
	Inktomi
	MindSpring Enterprises
	Network Solutions
	Open Market
	PSI Net
	RealNetworks
	Sterling Commerce
	USWeb
	Verio
	Verisign

TheStreet.com also has its Internet index, but includes just 20 companies which are believed to represent a cross-sampling of the industry. As of December 31, 1999 these included:

Amazon.com	Inktomi
America Online	Lycos
BroadVision	Macromedia
Check Point Software Technologies	MindSpring Enterprises
CMGI	Network Associates
eBay	Open Market
Egghead.com	RealNetworks
E*Trade	RSA Security
Excite@Home	USWeb
Go.com	Yahoo!

Past Performance: Predictor of the Future or Irrelevant Data?

Throughout this chapter I've been referring to the performance of the various indexes and sectors as a way to illustrate how different your perception of the market can be depending on which slice of it you look at. Now I'd like to make the same point with historical performance. If you take indexing to its extreme, you might assume that all stocks match the performance of the S&P 500. If you take historical perform- ance to the extreme, you might assume that because the S&P 500 was up 21 percent last year, it will do the same this year. Don't laugh. A lot of people really believe this. But even smart, sophisticated investors use past performance as a way to justify or refute certain theories. Why? Because it's the only thing we have to go on. Past performance repre- sents real-world results, as opposed to unsubstantiated theories. If you believe that stocks tend to go up in years of presidential elections, you can look at historical data to see if that's indeed the case. If it turns out to be true, you may conclude that in the future, stocks are more likely to go up than down in years of presidential elections. Now, you can as- cribe all kinds of theories to explain why: investors are optimistic about the new administration; people buy more stocks because they're paying more attention to the news and are therefore more aware of economic events; people feel more patriotic when they vote and this love of coun- try extends to ownership in American corporations. It doesn't matter how wild the rationale is, the theory is presumed to be valid because the data says it's true.

Choosing a Time Period

So if historical performance can be useful information, the next question is which time period do you use? Maybe we're smart enough to know that just because the S&P 500 was up 21 percent last year doesn't mean it will do it again this year. But might it be safe to assume that if it averaged 28 percent over the past five years that it will aver- age about the same over the next five years? No? Still too short a time period? How about 10 years? (S&P averaged 18 percent.) 20 years? We could gain the greatest historical perspective by going back 40 or 50 years (S&P averaged 12 percent and 13 percent respectively). But do we really need to go back to a time when airplane travel was a rarity, tele- phones didn't have area codes, and personal computers didn't exist to get that time-honored, long-term perspective everyone raves about? How relevant can stock market data from the 1950s be when we're in the midst of a technological revolution that is boosting productivity in ways no one ever could have imagined? And if something as unpredictable as the Internet can have such a profound influence on our lives, what's next on the horizon that we can't even begin to contemplate? As we pon-der these profound questions, let's look at some of the practical ways past performance can be used in the development of investment strategy.

Using Past Performance to Measure Volatility

One of the best uses of historical data is to measure a stock's vola-tility. This enables you to evaluate risk before investing. Remember, in-vesting is all about balancing risk and return so you can refrain from taking on more risk than is necessary to achieve the potential returns for which you're looking. This is not to say that you should never assume some risk. But your risk tolerance and return expectations must bear some relationship to each other. One of my clients recently said to me, "I don't want to lose money, but I'd like to get returns in the range of 15 percent." I explained to her that it would be impossible to achieve 15 per-cent returns in investments that had no risk of declining in value. She could choose one objective or the other but not both. The important thing is to know the type and degree of risk you're assuming so you can decide if the expected return will compensate you for taking on that risk. Otherwise, you might as well forget all this stock business and buy Treasury bills.

Risk can be measured in many ways. One way to measure it is in terms of volatility, or how much a stock moves up and down in the course of trading. The measurement that's used to describe a stock's volatility in relation to the overall market is called its *beta coefficient.* A stock with a beta of 1.0 has the same amount of fluctuation as the market as a whole. A beta higher than 1.0 means that when the market goes up, this stock is likely to go up more, and if the market declines, this stock may experience a greater loss. A beta lower than 1.0 means the stock fluctuates less than the market. Because it's impossible to know how volatile a stock will be in the future, the beta is always de-termined using historical information. This means, of course, that it could change. Still, it's a useful tool for gauging risk as measured by the degree of "upness" or "downness" a stock may experience. One other caveat to keep in mind: beta measures a stock's volatility in rela-tion to the general market. This means that if the market is undergoing extreme volatility, even a stock with a low beta may carry more risk than you feel comfortable with.

How can you use beta information in your investing strategy? For one thing, you can vary your portfolio depending on how optimistic or pessimistic you are about the market. If you're optimistic, you can maximize potential returns by leaning toward high-beta stocks—making hay while the sun shines, so to speak. If you're pessimistic but don't want to pull out of the market entirely, you can shift into low-beta stocks and lay low until the outlook is more positive. This will allow you to participate in some—but not all—of the upside while limiting your losses on the downside. You can also include a mix of high-beta stocks and low-beta stocks to give yourself the opportunity to earn high returns without subjecting your entire portfolio to extreme volatility. Another way to use beta is in relation to your own investment time horizon. If you're investing for retirement in 20 years, you may not care how volatile a stock is on a daily basis because you won't be selling it for a long while. As you move closer to needing the money, whether for retirement or to purchase property or start a business, you can shift into low-beta stocks to reduce the risk that your stocks will be down in value when you need to sell them.

As you might expect, Internet stocks tend to be more volatile than the average. Here are the respective betas of the stocks making up TheStreet. com's Internet Index as of December 31, 1999:

Stock	Beta
RealNetworks	3.62
E*Trade	3.56
Yahoo!	3.13
MindSpring	3.09
Open Market	3.04
Lycos	3.03
CMGI	3.00
Amazon.com	2.98
Excite@Home	2.74
America Online	2.47
RSA Security	2.40
Macromedia	2.13
BroadVision	2.07
Check Point Software	1.83
Network Associates	1.35

Inktomi	N/A
Egghead.com	N/A
USWeb/CKS	N/A
eBay	N/A
Go.com	N/A

RealNetworks' beta of 3.62 means that when the market is up, we can expect RealNetworks' rise to be more than three times that of the market. That's why people love Internet stocks. But when the market declines, RealNetworks' drop could be more than three times that of the market—and that hurts. This can easily cause short-term traders and novice investors to panic and sell, increasing volatility all the more. That's why so many professionals are worried about individuals entering the market en masse without a disciplined method of investing. Panic selling could create tremendous volatility and lead to extreme market dislocations.

Contrast the relatively high betas of these Internet stocks with the stocks making up the Dow Jones Industrial Average:

Stock	Beta
Citigroup	1.51
United Technologies	1.38
American Express	1.38
Microsoft	1.30
Intel	1.26
Hewlett-Packard	1.24
J.P. Morgan	1.21
Coca-Cola	1.18
AlliedSignal	1.17
General Motors	1.15
General Electric	1.10
International Business Machines	1.09
Merck	1.09
International Paper	1.02
Johnson & Johnson	1.01
Boeing	0.99
Walt Disney Co.	0.99
Alcoa	0.97

Wal-Mart	0.97
Home Depot	0.90
AT&T	0.86
Caterpillar	0.85
McDonald's	0.85
Procter & Gamble	0.83
SBC Communications	0.82
DuPont	0.76
Minnesota Mining & Manufacturing	0.62
Philip Morris	0.55
Eastman Kodak	0.23
ExxonMobile Corp.	N/A

And now look at the low betas of the stocks in the Dow Jones Utility Average. No wonder utility stocks are so popular with risk-averse retirees.

Stock	Beta
Enron Corp.	0.90
Williams Cos.	0.85
Consolidated Natural Gas Co.	0.75
Columbia Energy Group	0.56
Edison International	0.31
PG&E Corp.	0.27
Reliant Energy	0.24
Public Service Enterprise Group	0.20
PECO Energy	0.19
Consolidated Edison	0.18
Unicom Corp.	0.10
Southern Co.	0.09
Texas Utilities Co.	0.05
Duke Energy	0.04
American Electric Power	0.02

Using Past Performance to Identify Trends

Another useful purpose of historical data is to identify the price trends of individual stocks. This gets into the field of technical analysis, which uses stock charts to understand trading activity. Although there are some theories of technical analysis that border on voodooism, one aspect of it that has actually been embraced by academia is the validity of the moving average line. On a stock chart, this is the rather smooth line that lies on top of the daily price movements to show whether the price is trending up or down. The obvious assumption is that the trend which is currently in force will continue unless something happens to change it.

Short-term traders use the moving average line to identify price breakouts; if a stock moves through its moving average line on the upside or the downside, it can indicate a reversal of the trend. Long-term investors, on the other hand, look more to the direction the trend line is pointing in an attempt to buy (or sell) a security at a favorable price. If you find a stock you like, take a look at its chart. If the 200-day moving average line shows that the price is trending downward, you may want to wait awhile before buying to see if the trend reverses itself. A favorable time to buy is when a downtrend has bottomed out and is just starting to turn up.

Figure 3.1 illustrates the smooth 200-day moving average line compared to the lines for daily trading and the 30-day moving average.

Keeping Market Information in Perspective

Anyone can manipulate market statistics to make a point. Virtually any theory about investing can be substantiated by historical performance, depending on which segment of the market you're looking at and which time period you use for reporting purposes. One of the main points I'm trying to make in this chapter is that all stocks do not move in tandem and that reliance on the indexes for performance information can be misleading because it doesn't tell you which sectors or which stocks are outperforming the averages. Understanding this fragmentation of the stock market is essential for investing in the Internet age because the market seems to be approaching a duality between the haves (technology) and the have-nots (basic industry). This is a recent phenomenon, not backed by decades of historical performance, but that's exactly the point. It *is* a recent phenomenon. To insist upon many years of historical pricing information to validate a theory can keep you from changing with the times. It borders on the old "but we've always done

FIGURE 3.1 200-Day Moving Average

Dow Jones Industrial Average

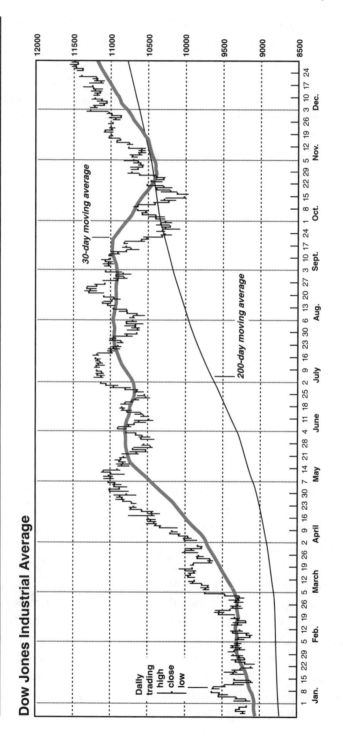

it this way" argument that has been the death knell for companies that have refused to acknowledge the new management directives emerging from today's highly competitive marketplace.

I believe much of Wall Street is still clinging to the old ways of doing things. This is causing individual investors who are frustrated by mediocre performance to repudiate much of the conventional wisdom and apply their own trigger-happy approach to buying the latest hot stocks. But investing without discipline can spell disaster when you find yourself in over your head and don't know where to go next. That's when it can be helpful to take a look at some of the tried-and-true investment theories. While it's true that some of them are no longer appropriate for today's world, understanding these theories can lead to insights about which ones to toss out, which ones to keep, and which ones to adapt for investing in an age where many—but certainly not all—of the rules have changed.

PART TWO

How Investing Used to Be

4

Do Traditional Valuations Apply in a Nontraditional Market?

If we're in a new economy that calls for a new approach to investing, why in the world would we want to look backward and rehash some of the old ways of picking stocks? One simple reason. Many of these tried-and-true investment methods still work. And although the Internet appears to be filled with possibilities for investors who jump on the bandwagon early, the jury is still out on whether or not this is a bubble. The high valuations being assigned to Internet-related stocks could turn out to be fully justified once these young companies are given a chance to perform. Or they could fizzle out fast if investors return to traditional methods of valuation. We won't know which scenario will turn out to be true until after it has played itself out. In the meantime, we need an investing approach that does not require a crystal ball, one that will allow us to capitalize on the opportunities at hand without subjecting ourselves to a high degree of risk. So in this chapter, I'll be reviewing some of the tried-and-true investment approaches that, depending on your knowledge and experience, may seem either old hat or interesting from an old-is-now-new perspective. The idea here is to develop discipline and structure in your investing program in order to minimize emotional involvement and provide stability for the rough times ahead (and you can be sure there'll be some).

There have been many theories about the best way to invest. You'll be glad to know I'm not going to cover all of them here. And although some numbers will be necessary, I will spare you the complex mathematical formulas that stock market theorists like to use to support their ideas. At the risk of oversimplifying (but in the interest of keeping you awake), I'll be describing the theories in brief. My goal is not to convince you of their validity, but to acquaint you with them so that when I incorporate some of them into the strategies discussed later in this book, you'll have a basic understanding of where they came from. Chapter 6 tells where to find the financial information you need to do your own stock research.

Nearly all investment theories boil down to two themes:

1. Buy undervalued stocks (and sell them when they're no longer undervalued)
2. Diversify

Within these two themes there are practically as many ideas as there are investors. It seems everyone has an idea about what constitutes an undervalued stock. Indeed, that's what makes a market. If everyone agreed at the same time that, say, IBM was an undervalued stock, nobody would want to sell it. So the many ideas about what constitutes value in a stock, while frustrating to anyone looking for full consensus, actually create an active, liquid market with plenty of buyers and sellers. And the fact that people's ideas are always changing contributes to the dynamic nature of the market. What appears undervalued today may not seem so tomorrow when a better opportunity presents itself. So let's look at the first theme: what it means to buy an undervalued stock.

The Theory of Intrinsic Value

The idea of intrinsic value was first proposed by Benjamin Graham and David Dodd in their book *Security Analysis,* written in 1934. The simple idea here was to distinguish a stock's price, or what a security trades for on the open market, from the company's underlying worth as measured by the actual assets owned by the company. Although stocks may move up and down as investors buy and sell, the price will always be anchored in some way to the company's intrinsic value. Note that this theory is quite the opposite from the approach used by momentum investors, who look only at trading activity and care nothing about what a company does, much less what it owns. For investors who subscribe to the theory of intrinsic value—and who believe that without it stocks are nothing more than gambling vehicles—the perennial challenge is figuring out what a stock's intrinsic value actually is. The first part, identifying a company's assets, is easy. All you have to do is look at a company's balance sheet, which all publicly traded companies are required to make public. The tricky part is deciding which assets to consider and assigning a valuation to those assets. That's where opinions differ.

Asset-Based Valuation Theories

Net Working Capital

Graham originally based his theory on nothing more than cash versus total indebtedness. He would add up all the cash and near-cash assets of a company (including liquid investments, accounts receivable, and inventories), and subtract all short-term and long-term debt. Then he would divide by the number of shares outstanding to arrive at the *price-to-net ratio,* the *net* here referring to net working capital.

Price-to-net ratio = Price per share ÷ Net working capital per share

If he could buy a company trading at or below its price-to-net ratio, he knew he had a bargain because theoretically the company could shut down and liquidate all its assets, and shareholders would end up with more than their original investment. You would be hard-pressed today to find a company whose share price is anywhere near its price-to-net ratio. But in Graham's day, before people started examining financial statements and bidding up stocks, it was not unusual for a company to trade below its price-to-net ratio simply because people hadn't caught on to the fact that it represented something very close to free money. Today, if you were to find a stock trading near its price-to-net ratio you would have reason to be very skeptical. The fact that investors have not priced the stock higher means the company is probably in trouble. The price-to-net ratio is a good example of an investment theory that was once quite meaningful but has outlived its usefulness as newer theories have been developed to justify higher stock prices. Still, it can serve as a good reminder of what it means to buy stock in a company: as a shareholder you become part owner of that company's assets, and when it comes right down to it, the only assets you can really count on are those that are readily convertible into cash.

Book Value

Another asset-based valuation theory looks at a company's book value. This expands the definition of assets to include all of a company's assets, not just cash or near-cash. To arrive at a company's book value per share, you (actually, the accountants) add up all of the company's assets, subtract all liabilities, and divide by the number of shares outstanding. This is also called *shareholder's equity.*

Book value = Assets − Liabilities ÷ Number of shares outstanding

Price-to-book-value ratio = Price per share ÷ Book value

To find out if the stock is undervalued or overvalued, you would compare the stock's current trading price to its book value. If the stock is trading within some reasonable range of its book value (and this is where differences of opinion come in), you could consider it undervalued. Proponents of the value style of investing pay a lot of attention to book value because it represents real, tangible assets, not some wild idea about what the company may be worth in the future. However, the drawback to both the price-to-net ratio and the price-to-book-value ratio is that neither method considers a company's earnings or how the company is deploying its assets to make money. A stock can be greatly undervalued and not represent a bargain at all, if it has a flawed business model or inept management. Also, some people see book value as an outmoded concept, subject to accounting manipulations, and not very representative of the kinds of assets that will count in the next economy. What good are land and buildings when the real money being made today is with human intellect and creativity?

Earnings-Based Valuation Theories

Because of the limitations of asset-based valuation theories, even value investors now look at a company's earnings, or how much money the company makes each year after expenses are subtracted from revenues. A company's earnings per share, or total earnings divided by the number of shares outstanding, is the most closely watched number today. Analysts go to great lengths to try to predict a company's earnings, and their compensation often depends on how accurate they are. At the same time, companies work very hard to manage investors' expectations because they know that the market's reaction to earnings news has more to do with expectations than the actual number itself. Even a negative earnings report can cause a stock to go up, if the news turns out not to be as bad as investors were expecting. Conversely, a positive earnings announcement can cause a stock to go down if street expectations were higher.

Price-to-earnings Ratio

Value investors pay particular attention to the price of the stock in relation to its earnings—called the *price-to-earnings ratio*—to determine if the stock is undervalued or overvalued. Earnings may be just as important as assets, value investors say, but they still do not want to pay too much for them. Here again you'll find widely varying ideas about what constitutes a reasonable price-to-earnings, or P/E, ratio. And although it may seem that the calculation of the P/E ratio is fairly cut and dried—simply divide the stock price by the earnings per share—there's even some difference of opinion on that.

Price-to-earnings ratio = Price per share ÷ Earnings per share

Do you use trailing 12 months' earnings, which are verifiable but say nothing about the future? Or do you use the next 12 months' earnings, which are more reflective of where the company is going, but are subject to erroneous estimates? The P/E ratio you see in the newspaper is based on trailing 12 months earnings. Since 1945, the average P/E ratio for the S&P 500 has been about 14. Today it's nearly 30. This has value investors in a conundrum as their list of undervalued stocks dwindles by the minute. With fewer items left on the bargain table, value investors are faced with the equally distasteful options of either staying out of the market until stocks fall to meet their valuation criteria (which may never happen), or changing their ideas about what constitutes reasonable value (which is anathema to contrarians who refuse to follow the herd).

Cash Flow

Cash flow is what a company has left after it has taken in revenues and paid out expenses. For most companies, it's similar to earnings. But because earnings factor in depreciation—even on assets that are rising in value—they sometimes understate the amount of cash a company has to reinvest in the business. So some investors use a price-to-cash-flow method of valuation, which is the current stock price divided by annual cash flow (earnings plus depreciation and amortization).

Price-to-cash-flow ratio = Price per share ÷ Cash flow
(Earnings + Depreciation & Amortization)

Some value investors, like Warren Buffett, consider cash flow to be one of the most important criteria. The idea here is that a share of stock is considered ownership in a stream of cash. To calculate the value of that stream, he projects how much money a business could generate over a given period of time and then translates or discounts that amount into current dollars. This is not something you should try at home. Some of the ratios mentioned in this chapter require complex calculations and information not easily accessible to investors. I call them out mainly to illustrate some of the ways investors have traditionally determined whether or not a stock is a good buy.

Dividend Yield

Although it seems most investors today are focused on the buy-low-sell-high method of stock investing, some people still consider dividends important. A dividend is a portion of the earnings that a company distributes to shareholders. It may represent 50 percent of earnings or 80 percent or even 100 percent. The dividend yield is calculated by dividing the dollar amount of the annual dividend into the stock price.

Dividend yield = Dividend per share ÷ Price per share

With the average dividend yield of the S&P 500 now around 1.2 percent it hardly seems worth bothering with dividends when they seem to represent such a small portion of total return. But there are a few reasons why some people consider dividends important. First, over the past 50 years dividends have represented about half of an investor's total return in stocks. Yes, we're talking historical returns again, but it puts that 1.2 percent in perspective and suggests that just possibly, over time, dividends may play a more important role than it first appears. Second—and this is the reason why dividends may be more important than you think—strong, established, growing companies usually raise their dividends over the years. So what appears to be a pittance now could actually be worth something later on. And third, the mere presence of a dividend suggests that a company is confident about its earnings. Companies that pay dividends to shareholders do not do so lightly; they tend to work very hard to maintain or increase the dividend and will strive for consistent earnings in order to fulfill their commitment to shareholders. Dividend-based stock valuation theories usually focus on three things: (1) the current dividend yield (which tells how expensive the stock is in relation to its dividend); (2) the dividend payout ratio (the percentage of earnings paid out in dividends—low number is better); and (3) the company's history of raising dividends (how many consecutive years the dividend has been raised and the average annual increase).

Earnings Growth

The problem with a dividend-oriented valuation philosophy is that you miss out on all those great stocks that don't pay any dividends at all. And the problem with relying too much on the P/E ratio to identify undervalued stocks is that it fails to consider the growth potential of a company. One year's worth of earnings—whether trailing or based on the next 12-month estimates—is a static number. But companies are living, breathing organisms that are constantly moving forward (or should be), creating new products, developing new markets, and expanding their earnings capabilities. Should a company whose earnings are growing by 50 percent a year be valued the same as a company growing at 15 percent a year? Growth-oriented investors don't think so. That's why they consider the *trend* in earnings to be equally—if not more—important than the latest earnings number. Still, there must be some way to value earnings growth in order to avoid overpaying for a stock. So a new ratio has been developed. It's called *growth at a reasonable price,* or GARP, and it pegs a company's P/E ratio to its growth rate. Under this theory, a company growing by 50 percent a year may warrant a P/E ratio of up to 50; a company growing at 40 percent a year may have a P/E ratio of 40, and so on. When searching for undervalued stocks you would look for P/E ratios which are lower than growth rates. Another measure of price-to-earnings growth is called the PEG ratio. This is the P/E ratio divided by the earnings growth rate.

$$\text{PEG ratio} = \text{P/E ratio} \div \text{Earnings growth rate}$$

For example, a stock with a P/E ratio of 100 and a growth rate of 50 percent would have a PEG ratio of 2. In today's market, a PEG ratio below 1.5 suggests good value; a ratio above 2 can be a sign of an overheated stock.

Sales

A company that is working hard and fast to establish dominance in a new industry doesn't have the luxury of enjoying current earnings, much less paying out dividends to shareholders. Instead, it plows every available dollar back into the business so it can gain market share and build an infrastructure to support future earnings. For these companies—mostly Internet-related companies scrambling to become market leaders—the key number is sales. Expenses are expected to be high. A company that holds back may lose its position in the race for dominance, so it sells, spends, sells, spends, sells, spends. Absent current profits, the amount of sales is therefore an important indicator of a company's growth. But some investors like to consider sales, or revenues, even when a company has positive earnings. Their reasoning here is that earnings can easily be manipulated to achieve certain corporate goals. For example, a company may accelerate expenses this year in an effort to report lower earnings so it can show a greater earnings improvement next year. Because sales precede earnings and revenue numbers are not easily manipulated, they tend to be a purer gauge of the company's activity. The way to value a stock based on its sales is to divide the share price by annual sales per share.

Return on Equity

Corporate finance people consider return on equity a key indicator of how the company is doing. Corporations are less concerned than investors about a company's current stock price (except when they enter the capital markets for additional financing), so the P/E ratio is not as important as return on equity, or the amount of profits generated from corporate assets. Return on equity is calculated by dividing net income by book value. A high and rising number is good.

$$\text{Return on equity} = \text{Net income} \div \text{Book value}$$

The Limitations of Valuation Ratios

You'll notice that with the exception of return on equity, all the preceding measures of value relate some financial attribute of the company, such as assets or earnings, to the stock's current price. This is how studious investors determine if a stock is expensive or not. It's amazing how some people will do rigorous comparison shopping before buying a car or a stereo, and yet plunk down any amount of money on a stock that has a good story. Somehow, if a stock seems cheap enough (i.e., the share price is not too high) it must be fairly valued. But to state the obvious here, you can't tell if a stock is fairly valued purely by its price. A $30 stock could be far more overvalued than a $100 stock. It all depends on what the company owns, how much it earns, and how many shares are outstanding.

However, there is one problem with using any of these ratios to determine if a stock is overvalued or undervalued: the market's standards of value are changing. A P/E ratio of 30 used to be considered too high. Now it's the market average. Does this mean stocks are doomed to fall back to their 50-year average P/E of 14? Or should we get used to high P/Es now that we're in this new, highly productive, technology-driven economy? Clearly, many value investors have missed out on tremendous opportunities because they've refused to pay what they consider to be outrageous prices for stocks with mediocre fundamentals, while investors paying little or no attention to traditional measures of value have done very well over the past few years. They've essentially been rewarded for ignoring the many truisms that have guided investors for years. Does this mean we should throw out all these valuation methods and buy whatever looks good? I don't think so. Without some idea of what constitutes reasonable value, investing is nothing more than a gigantic pyramid scheme. You'd be buying high with the hope of selling higher, but there would be no fundamental basis for that expectation other than momentum, which can reverse itself at any time.

How to Use Valuation Ratios in a Bull Market

There's no question that the bull market has played havoc with historical measures of value. Anyone looking for a stock with a P/E ratio of less than 14 will find slim pickings these days. If a stock is priced that low, there's probably a reason. High growth companies have high P/Es for the same reason well-made cars have high sticker prices. But that doesn't mean you have to stay out of the market. When automobile prices jumped from four figures to five figures in the 1980s, did you stop buying cars? No, you just became a more astute comparison shopper. You weighed one car against another, compared features and costs, and chose the one that represented the best value. I'd like to suggest that you take the same approach with stocks. It is possible to let go of certain outmoded historical valuation standards without ignoring the fundamental financial considerations that tell you whether or not a company is a good investment. All you have to do is forget about what stocks used to cost in relation to their assets or earnings and use traditional valuation methods to compare one stock to another. For example, let's say you want to invest in an Internet company and you're trying to decide between two network companies, Cicso Systems and Novell. You can go to <finance.yahoo.com> and get the following information:

	Cisco Systems	Novell
Price/book ratio	25	8
Price/earnings ratio	182	73
Price/sales ratio	27	11
Price/earnings growth (PEG) ratio	3.33	1.74

Keep in mind that with valuation ratios, lower numbers are better. They mean the stock is priced at a more reasonable level based on earnings or whatever metric you're looking at, and therefore represent a better value. Based on these four ratios, Novell is clearly the more undervalued stock compared to Cisco Systems. Does this mean Novell is sure to outperform Cisco Systems in the years ahead? Not necessarily. The theory of intrinsic value is just one way to evaluate stocks. It focuses on current price in relation to the company's fundamentals as a way to avoid paying sky-high prices for today's hottest stocks. If the Internet bubble does pop someday, stocks that are reasonably priced to begin with have less far to fall. You can therefore reduce your risk by sticking with the more reasonably priced stocks. In Chapter 9, I'll discuss some of the current thinking about how to value technology and Internet stocks.

When using ratios to comparison-shop stocks, make sure your comparisons are appropriate. You wouldn't expect a Volkswagen and a Mercedes to be priced the same, so don't compare the P/E ratios and growth rates of an oil stock and a semiconductor stock. If you hear of an interesting stock, look at other stocks in the same industry and make the relevant comparisons. For example, the PEG ratio is appropriate for fast-growing technology stocks, but not for utility stocks, for which the dividend ratio is more important. This is the danger in lumping all stocks into one gigantic basket called *the market* as discussed in Chapter 3, and it's also why traditional value investors are having a hard time getting used to today's valuations. Ten years ago, the S&P 500 was dominated by autos, oil, and other cyclical stocks. Today, fast-growing, high-tech stocks make up nearly 30 percent of the index. The average P/E has risen because a different kind of company is having a bigger influence on the average.

Modern Portfolio Theory

It seems the word *modern* paradoxically labels an item out of date, conjuring up notions of poodle skirts and turquoise vinyl. And indeed, modern portfolio theory developed by Harry Markowitz in the 1950s was very modern at the time. But unlike poodle skirts and vinyl which fell out of favor once the '50s were over (except for retro appeal), modern portfolio theory has endured through the decades, with periodic tweaking here and there. The essence of modern portfolio theory is that instead of looking at securities in isolation, you consider the risk/reward characteristics of the whole portfolio. Gold bullion, for example, is generally considered a risky investment on its own. But it can be a complementary addition to a portfolio of stocks and bonds because it protects against inflation: when inflation is rising, stocks and bonds usually fall in value while gold rises. Used in this way, gold bullion actually reduces overall risk. Modern portfolio theory suggests that you can diversify away some of the risks of owning a particular security by adding another security that is negatively correlated with the first. Without getting into the dry, statistical rationale that will have you turning this page faster than you can blink, let's just say that the idea behind modern portfolio theory is not just diversification, but the right kind of diversification. It's putting together a portfolio of securities that will act differently depending on what happens in the world. With respect to

inflation, stocks and bonds would be considered to have a positive correlation because they move in tandem, while stocks and gold would be
considered to have a negative correlation because they move opposite
to each other. (Please note that by using this example I am not recommending gold as an investment; as I'll be discussing in Chapter 11, high
inflation is something investors need not be concerned about in the age
of Alan Greenspan.)

For many years now, the conventional wisdom has been to diversify portfolios by methods corresponding to several of the classifica-
tions noted in Chapter 3. So a money manager may first divide the
portfolio between stocks and bonds and maybe some real estate as an
inflation hedge. Then the stock portion of the portfolio would be divided
between growth stocks and value stocks, then between large-cap stocks
and small-cap stocks, and then between domestic and international
stocks. The result would be a well-rounded, broadly diversified portfolio that contains several negative correlations—in other words, it would
cover all the bases and reduce portfolio risk.

But with the recent fragmentation of the market and the soaring
popularity of technology stocks, these nice, well-rounded portfolios
seem to be missing something—namely, high investment returns. For
several years now, value stocks have been a drag on the growth portion
of the portfolio, many small-cap stocks have lagged large-cap stocks,
and international stocks have diluted the returns of domestic companies. People whose advisors have suggested this traditional approach
have been patiently watching their portfolios attain mediocre performance. They scratch their heads when the manager explains things like
risk-indifferent curves and capital asset pricing models. They can't help
wondering if they could do a better job themselves by selling everything and buying some of those high-tech stocks that they read about in
the newspaper. So let's consider why diversification is still a good idea.

First, it's important to note that when Harry Markowitz first developed his modern portfolio theory, risk was defined as standard deviation, or the amount of fluctuation an investment experiences, similar to
beta described in Chapter 3. Think of it as zigzags on a chart—up,
down, up, down—hopefully with an overall upward bias. And so your
whole portfolio won't be zigging and zagging in tandem, you combine
assets with negative correlations so that when some are zagging others
are zigging. Now, this seems like a good idea and it's great for people

who watch their portfolio every day, but if you're investing with a long time horizon, you may not be too concerned about the daily zigs and zags. You just want to earn a nice return on your money and have it be there when you're ready for it. So with all due respect to Dr. Markowitz, I'd like to throw out the idea of standard deviation and bring the discussion of modern portfolio theory a little closer to home. Let's say you have $30,000 to invest. As you go about constructing your investment portfolio you're considering the following options:

- Portfolio 1: Invest it all in stock A
- Portfolio 2: Divide it evenly among stocks A, B, C, D and E
- Portfolio 3: Invest $10,000 in bonds and divide $20,000 evenly among stocks A, B, C, D and E

Now let's consider the following scenarios over a five-year period. Scenario 1: Stocks earn the following average annual returns:

Stock A: +20%
Stock B: +15%
Stock C: +10%
Stock D: −5%
Stock E: −20%
Bonds: 8%

Under this scenario our hypothetical portfolios would be worth the following amounts after five years:

- Portfolio 1: $74,649
- Portfolio 2: $42,869
- Portfolio 3: $43,538

Clearly, Portfolio 1 outperformed the rest because all of it was invested in the best-performing security. You might say we got lucky on that one. Now, let's see what would happen under a different scenario. Scenario 2: Stocks earn the following average annual returns:

Stock A: −20%
Stock B: −5%
Stock C: +10%
Stock D: +15%
Stock E: +20%
Bonds: 8%

Under this scenario our hypothetical portfolios would be worth the following after five years:

- Portfolio 1: $9,830
- Portfolio 2: $42,869
- Portfolio 3: $43,538

Obviously, the two diversified portfolios do better when compared to a portfolio that is 100 percent invested in the worst-performing security. Oh, you say you'd never hang onto a stock for five years if it was doing so poorly? Well, what if it were to drop 70 percent in one fell swoop a week after you'd bought it? Then it wouldn't take five years for your portfolio to go from $30,000 to $9,830. It would take just one week. And you'd have only $9,830 to reinvest in something else. Assuming you're not totally shell-shocked by now and racing for your nice, safe, savings account, you'd want to invest in something that will give you a chance to get up to the $42,000 or $43,000 you would have by diversifying as shown in Portfolios 2 and 3. And guess what rate of return you'd have to earn on your $9,830 to reach $43,000? Over a five-year period you'd have to achieve a compounded average annual return of 34 percent to match what you would have had by spreading your money among several investments. And as you know, any investment with the potential to return 34 percent per year, compounded, over five years would involve a heck of a lot of risk.

Now granted, this is a hypothetical situation. But it's not unrealistic. Some stocks have dropped 70 percent in one week. And it's not because anyone expected them to. Any number of things can happen to cause the bottom to fall out of a stock, and it's impossible to know in advance when something like that will happen. That's why we diversify.

By the way, I purposely did not use historical market data for this illustration because I believe one of the flaws with the current use of modern portfolio theory is its overreliance on historical data to determine which asset classes to invest in. Many financial advisors use sophisticated portfolio optimization software to help clients position their portfolios among the different asset classes. By entering the client's expected rate of return (i.e., what will be needed in earnings to achieve desired goals), along with the number of years the money will be invested, the software figures out where the assets should be positioned. And all of this is based on historical returns of about 12 percent for stocks and 8 percent for bonds, as well as more finely tuned assumptions for small-cap stocks, large-cap stocks, and so on. So if the client is late getting started and needs to invest somewhat aggressively in order to achieve desired goals, the software may suggest that a higher percentage of the assets be invested in small-cap stocks. This is because small-cap stocks have historically outperformed large-cap stocks—until the last five years, that is, when large-cap stocks outperformed smaller ones.

I believe portfolio optimization software can give people a false sense of security because of the black-and-white nature of it (actually, the pie charts show up in beautiful color). The computerized results look so official that they lead people to think that the 12 percent return for stocks is cast in stone. Now, it so happens we've been enjoying a robust stock market (as of this writing, anyway), so people are actually questioning the 12 percent assumption as being too conservative and not in touch with the real world. But all it will take is a flat or down year to bring people to their senses and convince them that stock market returns are never predictable in advance.

One other flaw with the current use of modern portfolio theory, which I alluded to earlier in this book, is the choice of asset classes that have become standard in the industry. By dividing portfolios among growth and value stocks, large-cap and small-cap stocks, domestic and international, and so on, advisors think they have all the bases covered. But many of these portfolios, though broadly diversified, are still positively correlated. That is, all or most of the securities move in tandem in response to economic events. Once again, no one is complaining too loudly because the economy and the markets have been strong, and it seems perfectly OK for securities to move in tandem if they're all going up. But what we have here is the worst of both worlds. The broad sector diversification is diluting investment returns without really protecting against possible economic catastrophe. In Chapter 10, I'll be talking about a new approach to modern portfolio theory, incorporating the brilliant concept as Markowitz first conceived it and updating it for today's new economy. In the meantime, let's look at what some of Wall Street's greatest legends have done over the years and see if some of their wisdom can be applied to portfolio construction in the twenty-first century.

5 Wall Street Legends and What We Can Learn from Them

It's not easy to become a legend on Wall Street. First, you have to have a disciplined, repeatable investment methodology that you can explain to other people in a way that makes sense. It should be something unique—not commonly in use—yet at its core it should be very, very simple, almost obvious in its commonsense approach. Second, you have to stick to your methodology, even when the market is going against you. This means you must be a true believer in what you're doing, despite criticisms from other people and the fear that creeps in when your stocks are down yet another day in a row. Third, in the end your theories must be proven sound by the ultimate judge in such matters: the market.

There's a big difference between a legend and a guru. A legend is venerated and respected. A guru is followed for his or her latest ideas. Legends are forgiven if they go through a slump; it's all part of the investing process. Gurus are dropped like a hot potato if an idea turns out to be wrong. Legends stick around for a long time, growing in respectability. Gurus are only as popular as their latest idea and are often here today, gone tomorrow (unless they prove themselves and go on to become a legend). Legends go quietly about their work, with fame being a byproduct of their expertise. Gurus constantly seek the limelight and crave attention by avid followers.

There's room for both legends and gurus in this world. What we followers must understand is the difference between the two. We must understand that the ideas of legends generally work over time and that we can't always expect immediate results. And although a guru may have turned out a string of uncanny predictions, the next one could be the one that leads to his or her demise. The bottom line is that we can learn from these experienced investors, but we must keep their theories in perspective and not follow them blindly. The legends profiled in this chapter are widely recognized for their investment methodologies and long-term success. Each one takes a different approach, so if you're looking for consensus here, you won't find it. You may even find some contradictions. But I remind you once again that differences of opinion are what make a market. I am not suggesting that you should pick the one you like and do everything he says. Indeed, these are twentieth-century legends. Some of their ideas already seem dated and it remains to be seen if their legendary status will carry into the twenty-first century. But in the interest of instilling discipline and balance into your investing process, I believe these famous investors can teach us a lot about developing—and sticking to—a sensible investment program with carefully laid-out guidelines.

Benjamin Graham: The Father of Value

In the 1920s, when Benjamin Graham was in his 20s, he was a partner in an investment firm earning an annual salary of over $600,000. In 1929, he lost everything in the stock market crash. It seems the man who literally wrote the book on value investing had a deep, personal reason to eschew an emotional approach to the stock market. The book he wrote with David Dodd in 1934, when the country was recovering from the worst depression in history, was desperately needed by a nation that had experienced the highs and lows of speculation and had lost all sense of what stocks were worth. Their college textbook, *Security Analysis,* introduced the concept of intrinsic value and essentially separated the notion of investment from speculation. Graham later repackaged the information for lay investors in a book called *The Intelligent Investor* which he updated in 1973.

Graham is widely credited with being the first proponent of a value style of investing. He said that without some idea of intrinsic value, the "tides of pessimism and euphoria which sweep the market" could mislead investors into overvaluing or undervaluing a stock. He suggested that most investors are unlikely to beat the averages because it's too easy to misjudge a company's future prospects. Investors should instead focus on reducing risk by finding companies whose stocks are trading at or near their intrinsic value. This approach would provide some protection against adversity.

Although Graham never really explained how to determine intrinsic value, he said that a company's tangible assets were an important component. He also looked at earnings, dividends, financial strength, and stability. Most important, he said, was to determine a security's value independent of its stock price. He was generally very cynical of Wall Street and believed that stock prices reflected either the pessimism or euphoria of the times. By removing oneself from the emotionalism of the markets and doing one's own calculation of what a company is truly worth, an investor could make an intelligent, independent assessment of a company's true value.

Graham eschewed subjective thinking, believing it could too easily mislead investors. He therefore did not study economic or industry trends in an attempt to determine a company's future performance—no chats with CEOs or guesses about next year's earnings. His approach was almost entirely quantitative and focused on the here-and-now (or some would say the there-and-then due to its reliance on numbers reflecting the past). He set forth the following criteria for stock selection:

- *Adequate size.* A company should have at least $100 million in annual sales. (Keep in mind that these criteria were developed in 1973; assuming a 5 percent annual growth rate, this would translate to $355 million today.)
- *Strong financial condition.* Current assets (cash, accounts receivable, and inventory) should be at least twice current liabilities.
- *Earnings stability.* The company should have positive earnings for at least the past five years.
- *Strong dividend record.* A minimum 20-year history of uninterrupted dividends.
- *Earnings growth.* A minimum 2.9 percent annual average growth rate over ten years.
- *Moderate price-to-earnings ratio.* The current price should be no more than 15 times average earnings for the past three years.
- *Moderate price-to-book ratio.* The current price should be no more than 1.5 times the last reported book value.

Anyone accustomed to evaluating today's growth stocks would find these criteria to be somewhere out in left field. But Graham believed that growth stocks were too risky because it was impossible to predict their future. And because growth stocks were subject to the euphoria of overly optimistic investors, their prices were generally too high. So Graham recommended buying large, unpopular companies and holding them until investors recognized their true worth. (He felt small, unpopular companies may lack the stability necessary to sustain themselves during adversity.) As soon as a stock rises above its intrinsic value, it should be sold and replaced with another undervalued stock.

I entered Graham's criteria into Quicken's stock screener on the Web (except for the 20-year history of uninterrupted dividends, which Quicken's screener didn't offer; I used a minimum dividend yield of 1 percent instead). The screener came up with 63 stocks, some of which are even household names. These companies may not set your heart racing, especially compared to the ones getting media attention today, but if today's high flyers ever drop like a lead balloon, these stodgy old companies may look pretty attractive. Here's a sampling:

Stock	P/E Ratio	Price/Book	Dividend Yield	Price
General Cable	5	1.43	2.8%	7.12
Ampco-Pittsburgh	7	0.64	3.9	10.12
Coachmen Industries	8	1.25	1.2	16.31
Cooper Tire & Rubber	10	1.47	2.3	17.81
Farmer Brothers	10	1.11	1.8	159.00

Graham did relax some of the criteria for what he termed *enterprising investors* (as opposed to defensive investors who lack the time to devote a large amount of intelligent effort to the investing process). But he didn't relax them much. He certainly would not approve of all the speculation going on today. In an interview shortly before his death in 1976 he said, "I have no confidence whatever in the future behavior of the Wall Street people. I think this business of greed—the excessive hopes and fears and so on—will be with us as long as there will be people. . . . I am very cynical about Wall Street." Clearly, Graham's attitude would have prevented him from enjoying the explosive growth of the stock market over the past few years had he been alive to see it. This points out the failings of relying too much on past experience and being so reluctant to change with the times. But when dealing with the stock market, a certain amount of skepticism is always healthy, and we can thank Graham for reminding us of that.

Warren Buffett: The World's Most Famous Investor

When Warren Buffett was a senior at the University of Nebraska, he read Benjamin Graham's book, *The Intelligent Investor.* He was so influenced by the book that upon graduation he left his hometown of Omaha and traveled to New York to study with Graham at the Columbia Graduate Business School. After receiving his master's degree he worked in Graham's investment firm and became totally immersed in his mentor's investment approach. When the firm disbanded and Graham retired in 1961, Buffett returned to Omaha and put together a limited partnership of seven investors who together contributed $105,000. Over the next 13 years, Buffett compounded the partnership's money at an annual rate of 29.5 percent.

Buffett promised his investors that he would choose investments "on the basis of value, not popularity." His most notable investment, at least in retrospect, was an ailing textile company called Berkshire Hathaway. Textiles were phased out in 1980s and Buffett used the cash from insurance operations, which had been purchased earlier, to invest in other businesses. Since then, Berkshire Hathaway has become famous as Warren Buffett's investment portfolio. Today the company has investments in insurance, a newspaper, a candy company, a furniture store, a jewelry store, a fast food company, and dozens of other businesses. The portfolio has earned an average annual gain of 30 percent since 1965. If you had put $10,000 into Berkshire Hathaway in 1965, it would be worth over $50 million today, versus around $500,000 if the money were invested in the S&P 500 index.

Buffett's investment philosophy can be summed up in this paragraph from a recent annual report:

> Whenever Charlie [Munger, his partner] and I buy common stocks . . . we approach the transaction as if we were buying into a private business. We look at the economic prospects of the business, the people in charge of running it, and the price we must pay. We do

not have in mind any time or price for sale. Indeed, we are willing to hold a stock indefinitely so long as we expect the business to increase in intrinsic value at a satisfactory rate. When investing, we view ourselves as business analysts—not as market analysts, not as macro-economic analysts, and not even as security analysts.

Like Graham, Buffett talks a lot about intrinsic value. But he defines it somewhat differently. Buffett's definition of intrinsic value is the discounted cash that can be taken out of a business during its remaining life. So he goes to great lengths to estimate the future earnings of a company. And because many companies are in businesses whose earnings are impossible to predict (think Internet), he concentrates his investments in a few key areas, primarily consumer goods and services like Coca-Cola, Gillette, McDonald's, and See's Candy. Diversification, by the way, is not Buffett's thing. He says it's too demanding to find investments of superior value, so he would rather focus on a few companies that he understands. Although Bill Gates is one of his friends, Buffett doesn't own Microsoft or any other technology company because he says their future earnings are too hard to understand.

Although Buffett is very communicative in his annual report, he talks more about how the companies are doing rather than outlining his criteria for investing in stocks. However, his former daughter-in-law, Mary Buffett, wrote a book with David Clark, family friend and portfolio manager, called *Buffettology: The Previously Unexplained Techniques That Have Made Warren Buffett the World's Most Famous Investor.* The book explains Buffett's approach. He believes that when he buys a stock he is investing in an underlying business. Any business delivers its greatest value to the owner when it generates earnings at an increasing rate each year. The price is a consideration, of course, but not as much as it was for Graham. In fact, he believes that if a business is mediocre, the stock will do poorly even if purchased cheaply because it will rise no higher than its intrinsic value—and maybe not even that high—whereas a company with growing earnings can keep going up forever because its intrinsic value keeps rising. Consequently, he targets successful businesses with expanding intrinsic values.

There are certain kinds of businesses Buffett won't invest in. Technology, as already mentioned, is too difficult to understand from the perspective of future earnings prospects. Commodity-based companies like manufacturers are low-margin, highly competitive, and must work hard just to survive. His favorite type of company is a consumer monopoly. This is one that has a unique product or service which is difficult to reproduce by competitors, either because of brand-name loyalty, a narrow market niche, or a proprietary asset like a patent. He tends to prefer low-tech products like soda, hamburgers, and candy—not because he's a fast-food junkie (or maybe he is)—but because he likes businesses that make products that wear out or are used up quickly. That's because the brand is reinforced each time consumers go back to the store to buy more of the same product.

Like Graham, Buffett looks for capable management. But whereas Graham let the numbers do all the talking, Buffett is noted for his excellent judge of character and ability to size up a person in a single brief meeting. Still, he looks for certain key numbers:

- *A strong upward trend in earnings.* He pays particular attention to year-by-year earnings increases.
- *Conservative financing.* He doesn't object to long-term debt as long as it's used to produce good results. Consumer monopolies tend to have strong cash flows with little need for long-term debt.
- *High return on shareholder's equity.* He looks for an ROE of 15 percent or higher.
- *High level of retained earnings.* He believes the real growth in stock value comes from reinvesting earnings to expand operations or purchase new ventures. He therefore prefers companies that pay little or no dividends.

Once Buffett has identified a company he wants to own, he then determines whether the purchase price makes economic sense. One approach he uses is to project earnings over the next ten years (based on the previous earnings growth rate) and divide by the current share price to see if he is likely to earn a rate of return of at least 15 percent. General Re and Executive Jet are two of his recent purchases. He uses several other methods to evaluate the current share price, some of which are quite complicated. In fact, Buffett has been lauded for his deep understanding of financial statements and the fact that he can look at an income statement or balance sheet and see things nobody else can see. When people ask him about financial details at Berkshire Hathaway's annual shareholder meetings, he's been known to refer them to the financial statements so they can see for themselves. To him, the numbers are obvious and pretty much tell the story.

Despite Buffett's gratitude to his mentor, Graham, and his continued belief in the notion of intrinsic value, it has become clear that Buffett has moved away from Graham's strict adherence to asset values and past earnings and dividends as the primary determinants of value. In fact, he once said that the last time it was easy to profit from Graham's methodology was the period from 1973 to 1974. More recently we've seen the influence of another Buffett mentor, one not so famous as Graham but who balanced the value father's quantitative methods with a more qualitative approach.

Philip Fisher was in the investment business about the same time as Graham but on the opposite coast. Fisher had an investment counseling firm in San Francisco that didn't have a whole lot to do in the depression-era 1930s but talk to business managers about their companies. It was these talks that led him to believe that superior profits could be made by aligning oneself with the most capable management. Capable managers, he said, will develop new products and services designed to spur sales growth long after current products or services are largely exploited. This meant subordinating (not sacrificing) immediate profits for greater long-range gains. He looked for things Graham never would have found on a financial statement, like honesty and integrity. He evaluated management's motives: were they interested in creating value for shareholders or for themselves? One way to tell was how management communicated with its shareholders, particularly during adverse times. He observed how managers treated their employees, believing that a good company was one where employees feel privileged to work.

Fisher argued that financial reports did not tell enough about a company; the essential step in prudent investing was to uncover as much about a company as possible from the individuals who were closely connected with it, including customers and suppliers as well as management and employees. As early as 1969, Buffett was studying Fisher's writings. But it was Charlie Munger, Buffett's longtime friend and now vice chairman of Berkshire Hathaway, who embraced Fisher's qualitative theories and persuaded Buffett to incorporate them into his Graham-style value methodology.

Today, we see equal parts Graham and Fisher, quantitative and qualitative, in the unique and highly individualized investing style of Warren

Buffett. Although Buffett doesn't apply his methodologies to technology stocks, that doesn't mean we can't. At the very least, we can be reminded that investing in a stock means investing in a business, and our return on investment will depend on how well that business does in the years ahead.

Peter Lynch: Originator of the Buy-What-You-Know Investing Philosophy

If you had invested $1,000 in the Fidelity Magellan Fund on the first day Peter Lynch started managing it in 1977, your investment would have been worth $28,142 when he retired 13 years later. Despite the bull run that picked up most of its steam *after* Lynch left the fund in 1990, his record is pretty much unparalleled. But Peter Lynch is more than a successful fund manager. He is largely responsible for showing individual investors that they, too, can pick good stocks, as long as they stick with what they know and do their homework. Lynch's most famous example is Hanes. In his book *One Up on Wall Street,* he describes how his wife discovered L'eggs pantyhose in a rack at the grocery store, bought them, tried them on, and liked them. Lynch reasoned that if women could buy quality pantyhose at the grocery store (a relatively new concept at the time), they could save a trip to the department store and also cut their pantyhose budgets. He did his customary research and discovered that the Hanes story was even better than he thought. Hanes turned out to be a sixbagger (increased six-fold) before the company was acquired by Sara Lee; Lynch thinks it would have been a 50-bagger if the company hadn't been bought out. This story has been an inspiration to investors everywhere who have taken to examining the products and services they use everyday in an attempt to find stock ideas right under their noses.

Since leaving Magellan to spend more time with his family, Lynch has reentered the investment arena as consultant and spokesman for Fidelity Investments. He is on a mission to educate investors about the realities of investing in stocks. As such, he is walking a fine line between encouraging individual investors to believe in their own stock-picking ability while cautioning them about the dangers of an overpriced stock market. He is clearly disturbed by the unrealistic expectations he is seeing today, noting that many people think of annual returns of 15 percent to 30 percent as normal and that a return of only 5 percent to 7 percent would constitute a bad year. From his pulpit, he reminds investors that since 1926, stocks have earned an average return of less than 12 percent, and in a bad year stocks have lost as much as 35 percent. In a July 1998 interview, when the Dow was around 9,000 and the average P/E ratio for the S&P 500 was 25, he cautioned that stocks were getting ahead of themselves because prices had outstripped corporate earnings. He said in an interview, "I never thought I'd root for the market *not* to go up, but if it went sideways for a couple of years, took a breather while the earnings caught up to the prices, that would be a happy outcome."

Lynch is also dismayed by the lack of research that precedes many people's stock selections. Although he is a proponent of "story" stocks—find a good story like Hanes because it can tell you about the future prospects of the company—it seems people are getting so hung up on the story that they are failing to examine a company's underlying fundamentals. Paradoxically, people are interpreting the buy-what-you-know theory to mean that they know a company just because they use its products everyday. But there's a lot more to stock selection than the usefulness of a company's products. According to Lynch, you want to thoroughly understand the company, its prospects, its competitive environment, and whether the stock can be purchased at a reasonable price. To do this, you must look at a number of fundamentals.

Lynch doesn't start with a list of screening criteria as Graham did. Instead, he believes stock ideas must be picked up one-by-one, discovered through a variety of means similar to the way he found Hanes. The next step is to thoroughly familiarize yourself with the company and its future prospects. He doesn't believe you can predict actual growth rates but says you can get a feel for a company's future by examining its plans. There are five ways a company can increase earnings: (1) reduce costs, (2) raise prices, (3) expand into new markets, (4) sell more in old markets, and (5) revitalize, close, or sell a losing operation. He pays a lot of attention to P/E ratios to avoid overpaying for a stock. He says that the P/E ratio basically tells you how many years of corporate earnings it will take to get your investment back. So a company with earnings of $3.50 and a share price of $35 would take ten years to return a shareholder's original investment. However, this assumes earnings remain static, which they rarely do. Fast-growing companies deserve higher P/E ratios than slow-growing companies, but investors still should not get carried away. In general, a P/E ratio that's half the growth rate is very positive, and one that's twice the growth rate is very negative. So a company growing by 30 percent a year could have a P/E ratio of 15 to 30, but if it gets to 60 the stock is overpriced. He also suggests comparing the company's current P/E ratio to its historical trend; if it has creeped up too far, the stock may be overpriced and due for a fall.

Here are some other numbers he looks at:

- *Percent of sales.* What percentage of overall sales does the product you like represent? One product may not have much impact on a company with a large product portfolio.
- *Year-by-year earnings.* Look for stability, consistency, and an upward trend; the pattern of earnings growth will help reveal the stability and strength of the company.
- *Earnings growth.* The earnings growth rate should be appropriate for the firm's story. Extremely high earnings growth is not sustainable, but continued high growth may justify a higher stock price.
- *Debt-to-equity ratio.* The company's balance sheet should be strong; more than anything else, it's debt that determines which companies will survive and which will go bankrupt in a crisis. He's especially wary of bank debt.
- *Dividends.* The key issue is how the dividend (or lack of it) affects the value of a company and the price of its stock over time. One strong argument in favor of dividends is that historically, companies have a tendency to fritter away extra cash in unproductive operations—Lynch calls them "diworseifications." Also, the dividend can keep the stock price from falling as far as it would if there were no dividend. Still, he leans toward growth companies which typically do not pay dividends.
- *Book value.* Lynch does not put a lot of stock in book value because it can be a misleading number. He notes that when Warren Buffett decided to close down Berkshire Hathaway's textile operations, looms that were purchased for $5,000 just a few years earlier sold at public auction for just $26 each. The company's book value had been listed at $866,000, but once everything was sold off it brought just $163,000 actual cash. On the other hand,

sometimes book value can understate a company's true worth, such as when land or timber has been depreciated over the years and is carried on the books at a fraction of its true value.

When it comes to the question of diversification, Lynch hedges on his answer. He simply says that it's best to own as many stocks as there are situations in which: (1) you've got an edge; and (2) you've uncovered an exciting prospect that passes all the tests of research. Maybe that's a single stock, or maybe it's a dozen stocks. He says there's no use diversifying into unknown companies just for the sake of diversity, and he's famous for the quote: "A foolish diversity is the hobgoblin of small investors."

Here are some of Peter Lynch's pointers:

- Understand the nature of the companies you own and the specific reasons for holding the stock ("It is really going up!" doesn't count).
- Look for small companies that are already profitable and have proven that their concept can be replicated.
- Be suspicious of companies with growth rates of 50 percent to 100 percent a year.
- Moderately fast growers (20 percent to 25 percent) in nongrowth industries are ideal investments.
- Avoid hot stocks in hot industries.
- It's better to miss the first move in a stock and wait to see if a company's plans are working out.
- Separate all stock tips from the tipper, even if the tipper is very smart, very rich, and his or her last tip went up.
- Invest in simple companies that appear dull, mundane, out of favor, and haven't caught the fancy of Wall Street.
- Carefully consider the P/E ratio. If the stock is grossly overpriced, even if everything else goes right, you won't make any money.
- Look for companies that constantly buy back their own shares.
- Look for companies with little or no institutional ownership.
- All else being equal, favor companies in which management has a significant personal investment over companies run by people that benefit only from their salaries.

Lynch devotes a whole chapter of his book to stocks that should be avoided. Although he wrote *One Up on Wall Street* over ten years ago, these caveats seem even more relevant today:

- *Beware the next something.* He cautioned against buying the next IBM or the next McDonald's (today we would say the next Microsoft or AOL) because the next of something never is.
- *Beware the whisper stock.* Whisper companies are touted as being on the brink of solving the latest national problem. The stories have highly emotional appeal—but no substance.
- *Beware the stock with the exciting name.* In 1989, the flashy names had *advanced, leading,* and *micro* in their names. Today, of course, it's *dot-com.*

Lynch does not have a specific sell discipline but he does advocate rechecking the story every few months to see if the earnings are holding up as expected. Rather than simply selling a stock, he suggests rotation, or selling the stock and replacing it with another one that has a similar story but better prospects. The main thing is to know why you bought a stock in the first place. That will automatically tell you when to get rid of it.

Like Warren Buffett, Peter Lynch eschews technology stocks because he doesn't understand them. "I thought Yahoo! was a chocolate drink until last week," he said in a recent interview. That doesn't mean other people shouldn't buy them, however. Always preaching the buy-what-you-know gospel, he says working for a company can provide some of the best insights of all. Does this mean we should all go to work for Internet companies in order to better understand this new growth sector? Probably not, but we can certainly benefit from Lynch's teachings, particularly when it comes to learning all we can about the companies we invest in and making sure the prices we pay are reasonable.

Sir John Templeton: Steward of God's Wealth

Well into his 80s, Sir John Templeton meets the classic definition of a legend. He avoids the limelight, except when he is giving away the annual Templeton Prize for distinguished achievement in the field of religion, and he has always gone against the crowd, believing deeply in his investment methodology and refusing to be swayed by contrary opinions. After a long and successful career managing the Templeton Funds, which have been acquired by Franklin Resources and with which Sir John Templeton is no longer involved, he has turned his attention to religion. He still manages his own investment portfolio and that of his charitable foundations, but his mission is to spread the cause of spiritual wealth, which is "the most fundamental need that humanity ever had."

Templeton is best known for buying stocks that nobody else wants. He has always looked for stocks that were at their "point of maximum pessimism"—when no one else would touch them. Then he would simply wait for the world to discover their value. In 1939, at the age of 27, Templeton had the idea that World War II would revitalize the U.S. economy. He borrowed $10,000 ($117,000 in today's dollars) and invested $100 in each of 104 companies, 37 of which were in bankruptcy. When he liquidated his holdings five years later, he had made roughly five times his money. Throughout most of his investing career, Templeton has searched beyond U.S. borders, taking a truly global approach to investing. In the 1950s, when Japan's economy was at a low point and stocks were selling at P/E ratios of 3, he saw bargains where others saw lousy companies that made cheap knock-offs of American goods. By 1980, the Japanese economy was flying high and investors were clamoring to get into Japanese stocks. It was about this time that Templeton liquidated his holdings after quintupling his money. He has always had an amazing ability to be emotionally unaffected by the pessimism and euphoria that has ravaged Wall Street throughout its history.

Here are some of Templeton's maxims:

- There is only one long-term investment objective: maximum total after-tax return.
- In order to outperform the majority of investors you have to do what they are not doing.
- Buy when pessimism is at its maximum, sell when optimism is at its maximum.
- Popularity is temporary. When a sector goes out of fashion, it stays out for many years.
- Focus on value because most investors focus on outlooks and trends.
- Invest worldwide.

- Sell when you find a better bargain to replace what you are selling.
- When your method becomes popular, switch to an unpopular method.
- If you begin with prayer, you will think more clearly and make fewer mistakes.

James O'Shaughnessy: Blending Value and Growth

In 1997, James O'Shaughnessy wrote a book called *What Works on Wall Street*. The book became a bestseller and has been highly praised for its detailed examination of stock market performance going back to 1951. Although O'Shaughnessy himself is too young to be a legend, his "track record" is based on 45 years of stock market data and his book appears to be on its way to becoming a classic. I am including him in this chapter because his findings represent the next step in the evolution of value-based theories started by Graham and refined by Buffett and Templeton, and also incorporate ideas about growth for which Peter Lynch was famous. O'Shaughnessy found that both value and growth strategies can work, but on different kinds of stocks. A value strategy works best for large-capitalization stocks, while a growth strategy works best for smaller stocks. Value offers less volatility, while growth offers greater potential for capital appreciation.

O'Shaughnessy's approach is strictly quantitative. If a stock meets the criteria, it's bought. If not, it's not. No personal, emotional judgments ever enter the process, and in fact he believes that the reason most money managers fail to beat the market averages is that they follow a hit-and-miss approach to investing and end up being very inconsistent. He says, "While we may understand what we should do, we usually are overwhelmed by our nature, allowing the intensely emotional present to overpower our better judgment." Why do we do this? Because statistical models are boring. "We make the simple complex, follow the crowd, fall in love with the story about some stock, let our emotions dictate decisions, buy and sell on tips and hunches, and approach each investment decision on a case-by-case basis, with no underlying consistency or strategy."

So O'Shaughnessy has provided reams of data which show, beyond the shadow of doubt or human emotion, which stock selection criteria lead to superior market returns. Before summarizing his two sets of criteria for investing in value and growth stocks, I'd like to highlight two of his findings. One relates to the price-to-sales ratio, which he calls the king of the value factors. Although everyone focuses on price-to-earnings ratios, O'Shaughnessy's research found that it was low price-to-sales ratios that beat the market more than any other value ratio and did so more consistently throughout the decades. This supports the idea mentioned in Chapter 4 that earnings are not always the most reliable indicator of a company's performance because the numbers can be manipulated. The second relates to relative strength, or price momentum. Although most fundamental investors disdain the use of past prices to predict future price movements, O'Shaughnessy's research showed that stocks with the highest relative strength (the highest price changes over the prior year) produced the highest returns the following year. He found this to be true for stocks of all sizes, although he warns that it is a very volatile approach that can severely test investor discipline. By way of explanation, he says that a momentum indicator like this simply shows the market putting its money where its mouth is.

He recommends combining both value and growth approaches, adjusting the mix to conform to your risk tolerance. Risk-averse investors should focus more on value strategies, which include:

- *Large market capitalizations.* These firms are less volatile and have long operating histories; they are more likely to survive adverse conditions.
- *High number of shares outstanding.* This offers the best liquidity.
- *Higher-than-average cash flows.* Companies with high cash flows are less likely to cut their dividend.
- *Sales that are 1.5 times the average.* The goal is to identify market-leading companies.

Growth strategies are appropriate for people who can tolerate more risk in pursuit of higher returns. These strategies include the following:

- Market capitalization of $150 million or greater
- Earnings gains five years in a row
- Price-to-sales ratio of 1.5 or below
- Ranking among the highest in one-year price increase for all stocks

In order to get adequate diversification, the portfolio should consist of at least 16 stocks. For both value and growth strategies, portfolios should be rebalanced once a year, with stocks no longer meeting the criteria being replaced by those that do.

John Bogle: Champion of Index Funds

If Graham, Buffett, Lynch, and Templeton all believed smart stock-picking could increase investment returns, John Bogle is the ultimate contrarian. This founder and longtime chairman of the Vanguard Group believes investors are better off buying index funds and not even trying to beat the market. He says that in this increasingly complex world, simplicity is the key to financial success, and that the ultimate in simplicity comes with the additional virtue of low cost. For the simplest of all approaches, he says to invest in a single market index fund—just one fund. Such a fund offers a broadly diversified middle-of-the-road investment program for a typical conservative investor, allocating about 65 percent of assets to large growth and value stocks and 35 percent to high-grade bonds.

He makes his point by comparing the cumulative returns of mutual funds which are actively managed with index funds having the same mix of securities (65 percent large stocks and 35 percent bonds). [Index funds are stable portfolios designed to mimic the market index on which they are based; in this case it was 65 percent S&P 500, and 35 percent Lehman Brothers Bond Index.] Over a 15-year period, from 1983 to 1998, the managed funds provided an average annual return of 13.0 percent, versus 15.1 percent for the index funds. Stated another way, a $10,000 investment in the actively managed fund grew to $62,700, while the same investment in the index fund grew to $81,900—a difference of $19,200. Bogle further explains that the superiority of the index fund is accounted for not by magic, but by costs. It was the heavy costs of the managed funds that were primarily responsible for their shortfall. The average managed fund incurred annual costs of 1.7 percent, compared to 0.2 percent for the index fund. This 1.5 percent difference in costs made up the lion's share of the 2.1 percent difference in annual return.

Bogle does concede, however, that it's human nature to want to try to beat the market. He notes that about one in five mutual funds has managed to outperform the indexes. While these are heavy odds, they are not insurmountable, so he offers a few basic rules for choosing mutual funds. (Bogle clearly has a mutual fund orientation; implicit in his advice is the belief that if professional portfolio managers can't beat the market, how can individual investors expect to do so?)

Here is Bogle's advice for choosing mutual funds:

- *Rule 1: Select low-cost funds.* The average equity fund now carries total annual expenses of 2 percent or more. Such a levy is likely to cut returns by 20 percent or more over time. Look at both the expense ratio and portfolio turnover. High turnover results in high transaction costs and, if you're investing in a taxable account, higher taxes.
- *Rule 2: Consider carefully the added costs of advice.* It is the essence of simplicity for the self-reliant, intelligent, informed investor to purchase shares without an intermediary salesman or financial advisor. However, if you do go through a broker or advisor, select one with care and evaluate their services against the higher costs. No one can pick the top-performing managers in advance, so avoid any advisor who makes extravagant claims of future performance.
- *Rule 3: Do not overrate past fund performance.* Top-performing funds inevitably lose their edge due to a financial principle called regression to the mean, or what Bogle calls the law of gravity in the financial markets. Yet fund sponsors persist in promoting their most successful (past) performers. This brings in lots of new money and new fees to the advisor, but such promotions lead investors in precisely the wrong direction. Ignore them.
- *Rule 4: Study performance to determine consistency and risk.* Look at year-by-year performance to check for consistency, comparing funds with similar policies and objectives. Also check to see how much risk the fund typically assumes relative to its peer group.
- *Rule 5: Beware of portfolio manager "stars."* The Peter Lynches of the world are few and far between. And the precious few managers who can truly be called superstars are rarely, if ever, identified in advance of their accomplishments. The average portfolio manager lasts five years at the helm of a fund, and when the new

manager takes over, the result is high portfolio turnover, which is costly and tax-inefficient. Fund stars are like comets: they brighten the firmament for a moment in time, only to burn out and vanish into the dark universe.

- *Rule 6: Beware of asset size.* Funds can get too big for their britches. This is especially true for funds investing in smaller stocks. There's no easy way to determine if a fund is too big, but basically beware of large fund organizations that have no history of closing funds to new investors. When funds get too large, they eventually become closet index funds, with most of their assets in index companies, but with lower performance due to higher costs.
- *Rule 7: Don't own too many funds.* A study by Morningstar revealed that owning more than three funds did not reduce risk appreciably. A single large-blend or all-market index fund could actually be less risky (if risk is measured by standard deviation) than multiple fund portfolios.

George Soros: Mystery Man of Wealth

George Soros has been called the world's greatest investor, the man who broke the Bank of England, and the man who moves markets. A world-famous financier, Soros makes his money in the sophisticated realm of currencies and interest rate futures as well as stocks and bonds. His phenomenal record was established with the Quantum Fund, an off-shore fund launched in 1969 designed for wealthy investors willing to take high risks in the hope of earning extraordinary returns. His fund sold short, used complex financial instruments, and borrowed large amounts of money—strategies not available to the average mutual fund. But his approach paid off. If you had invested $100,000 in Soros' fund in 1969, it would have been worth $130 million by the spring of 1994— a compound growth rate of 35 percent.

In his book *The Alchemy of Finance,* Soros presents a new take on the concept of value. He says that stock prices often depart from real value because of gaps between perception and reality. When these gaps become wide enough they create boom-bust cycles that offer the opportunity to make a lot of money. Further, he said in the preface to the paperback edition of the book published in 1994, market participants' value judgments are always biased and these biases actually become one of the fundamentals which shape the evolution of prices. In other words, changes in market prices lead to changes in market prices.

Soros departs from our definition of a legend in that he does not offer a clearly articulated investing methodology. In fact, his methods are often termed secretive by people who are looking for the elusive Soros formula. However, it appears that Soros's secret is simply an uncanny instinct about the forces that influence securities prices. "Basically," said Soros, "the way I operate is I have a thesis and I test it in the market. When I'm short and the market acts a certain way, I get very nervous. I get a backache and then I cover my short and suddenly the backache goes away. I feel better. There's where the instinct comes in."

Soros defies the conventional wisdom that says you should investigate before you invest. Instead, he invests first and investigates later, essentially formulating theses and testing them in the marketplace. He doesn't believe the market can be predicted in advance. So the only thing you can do is formulate an idea about what you think will happen and then see if the idea pans out. He's often wrong and isn't afraid to admit it. But what sets him apart is his willingness to take extraordinary risks—even when he's unsure of the outcome. He says, "It's not whether you're right or wrong but how much money you make when you're right and how much you lose when you're wrong." Soros has never been interested in showing other people how to invest. Rather, in writing his book *The Alchemy of Finance,* he was more interested in explaining how his financial theories were part of a wider set of general theories about how the world functioned. The book was not a hit on Wall Street because it did not clarify what his financial theories were all about. On his book tour, he was disappointed when interviewers seemed uninterested in discussing his philosophical theories and instead wanted to know what stocks he was buying. Even on *Wall Street Week,* which is famous for asking guests about their favorite stocks, Soros refused to cooperate by saying, "I'm not going to tell you."

What is there for us to learn from this mystery man who's had phenomenal success as an investor but doesn't seem very willing to tell us how he does it? Perhaps we can pay heed to some of these quotes which are sprinkled throughout his unauthorized biography, *Soros: The Life, Times and Trading Secrets of the World Greatest Investor* by Robert Slater.

- "Once you know what the market is thinking, jump the other way, bet on the unexpected."
- "Flawed perceptions cause markets to feed on themselves. Markets that feed on their own frenzy always overreact."
- "Detect self-reinforcing moves in the stock market and you will reap great profits."
- "Develop a thesis and test it in the market."
- "Look for a sudden change in the stock market, a change not yet identified by anyone else."
- "The stock market is always wrong, so that if you copy everybody else on Wall Street, you're doomed to do poorly."
- "To be in the game, you have to be willing to endure the pain."
- "If your investment is going well, follow your instincts and go with all you've got."
- "Short-term volatility is greatest at turning points and diminishes as a trend becomes established."
- "Attain superior long-term returns through preservation of capital and home runs."

Maybe what Soros is really telling us by his refusal to articulate an established investment methodology is that the market is always changing and in order to be successful you have to change with it. For an investor willing to accept a high degree of risk, it's all about seizing opportunities. And opportunities never appear in the same form twice.

The ideas and investing methods of these highly respected Wall Street legends can teach us a lot about investing in the twenty-first century, even if it's just to recognize that different methodologies go in and out of favor over the years. Regardless of whether or not you think their investment approaches are relevant today, keep in mind some of the fundamental truths embodied in these men. Benjamin Graham stood for value: he reminds us that we should not overpay for a stock, no matter how much we like it. Warren Buffett is a businessman: he reminds us that every stock we buy represents an investment in a going concern, and the more cash that business generates, the more our investment will be worth. Peter Lynch gives us confidence: as long as we do our research, we can pick stocks as well as the experts. Sir John Templeton stands for patience and independence: buy what nobody else wants and wait for the world to discover its value. James O'Shaughnessy is the voice of reason: let the numbers do the talking and keep emotion out of the investing process. John Bogle teaches simplicity: buy index funds and save on the high costs and aggravation normally associated with investing. George Soros may hold the key to investing in the Internet age, if that key depends on abandoning set methods and being nimble in the marketplace. Let's keep these philosophies in mind as we explore the current investing environment.

PART THREE

Where to Go for Information and Advice

6 Information Is Everywhere

Financial journalism is one of the hottest growth industries today. Now that the Internet has empowered people to do their own investing, the appetite for knowledge is insatiable. And content providers who have figured out a way to profit from this appetite—and even some who haven't—are filling the airwaves and cyberspace with information in all its many forms. Individual investors have more information at their disposal today than professionals did just a few years ago. Does that make people better investors? Sometimes, sometimes not. But it certainly helps level the playing field and gives more people a shot at improving their investment returns. And though you may still turn to a financial advisor for help and advice, the widespread availability of information enables you to be a better client, even if it's just to ask the right questions and better understand the answers.

The biggest difficulty with all this information, of course, is just getting through it. If it takes a minute to read a page, and if there are three million pages out there, it would take over five years of around-the-clock reading to absorb it all. Clearly, we need to figure out a way to organize the information available to us so we can get what we need and still have a life. This means determining what we don't need as well as what we do, and using a discerning mind to separate the good from the bad.

Categories of Information

In an attempt to break down and make sense of this mammoth thing called financial information, we can slice it up several different ways. The first is the format it appears in. Most information comes in print (books, magazines, newspapers, and newsletters), over the airwaves (television and radio), or via the Internet. One way of judging the quality of information might be the effort the publisher has to go to in order to bring it to us. An established newspaper with a staff of researchers and reporters has a bigger investment in the process than does a lone person who posts his musings on a home-grown Web site. Does that mean the newspaper will always be of more value to you? Not necessarily. If the guy posting musings on the Web site happens to be an expert in an area of the stock market you're interested in, you may get more in-depth information from the site. Still, you can usually depend on traditional journalism for quality and accuracy, whereas the Web can be dicey simply because it's so easy to post information there.

This brings us to the next way to slice up the information: according to its value to you. If you are a buy-and-hold kind of investor, you don't need real-time quotes and up-to-the-minute trading data. In fact, this kind of information can be counterproductive because it distracts you from your long-term view. A lot of retirees fall into the trap of checking their stocks and watching CNBC all day long, figuring they can now tend to their portfolio full time. All this does is make them nervous and cause them to question their long-term strategy, perhaps even make inappropriate buy-sell decisions. Information will be of more or less value to you depending on your style of investing and the type of information you're looking for. If you are a novice investor seeking basic education, your information needs will differ from those of an experienced investor looking for sophisticated stock research. If you invest exclusively in mutual funds, you have little need for information on individual companies. So an important step in sorting through the data is to decide what type of information you need so you can ignore the rest.

Another thing to look at is cost. With so much free information available on the Web, you might be wondering if it's worth paying for information at all. The answer is yes, if it's useful to you and if you feel the cost is worth it. The old you-get-what-you-pay-for argument doesn't exactly apply here because some financial Web sites give away great information in the hope that you'll become a customer (or read their ads), while certain research services charge an arm and a leg for reports that may not be useful to you at all. By the way, consider any money you spend on financial information as part of your investing costs. By factoring these expenses into your investment returns, you'll be less likely to go overboard on expensive newsletters and research services, knowing the costs will be cutting into your profits. At the same time, don't skimp if you feel a particular information resource will give you an edge in increasing your investment returns. Also note that some investment expenses are tax-deductible.

As I pointed out earlier in this book, it worries me when people base their investment decisions on a story or a hunch rather than solid research. It's ironic that in this information age, where it's possible to find virtually any piece of data you could ever want, people are buying stocks based on opinions picked up in chat rooms. Part of the problem, of course, is that there's just too much information out there. Rather than sift through it, people either ignore it all or focus on the wrong kind of information. The other problem is that many people are new to investing and haven't learned what kind of information they should consider before making an investment decision. Rather than read a book or take a class to understand the basics of stock market analysis, they jump right in and start trading.

So let's consider the five broad categories of information that can help you become a better investor.

1. Research
2. News
3. Tools
4. Discussion groups
5. Basic education

Warning: The sections below contain explicit references to information sources available at the time of this writing. If they are no longer available, or if newer, better sources have come along since this book was published, it's because the field is changing by the minute. Also, please understand that there are far more information sources than could possibly be listed here. While the ones I've selected are known to be good, there may be many other good ones not listed here. Consider this a sampling.

Getting Started

Information management is an art in itself. By getting a handle on the many sources of information out there and evaluating which ones are useful to you, you can compile your list of preferred magazines, newspapers, newsletters, books, Web sites, and TV programs. These should be the ones you like to read/watch on a regular basis and that you have time for. By investing some time in the beginning to explore the various information sources, you can pick out your favorites and tune out the rest. This will allow you to stay on top of new developments without becoming overwhelmed. In the sections that follow, I have suggested a few good information sources in the areas of research, news, tools, discussion groups, and basic education. But first I'd like to recommend some general sources of financial information that do not fit neatly into one of the five categories. They fall into the category of general business news and information, which every investor should stay on top of to some degree. I also include tips on how to find your own sources of information so you can expand on these lists. Given the limited amount of time you have each week, the emphasis here is on quality, not quantity.

Newspapers

- *The Wall Street Journal* (daily). The definitive newspaper for business and finance. Excellent research, great writing.
- *Investor's Business Daily* (daily). Very user-friendly with many "quick read" and to-the-point sections. Stock and mutual fund tables give information not found elsewhere.
- *Barron's* (weekly). For active investors. Good reporting and analysis of the markets and the economy.

Magazines

- *Business Week* (weekly). The definitive magazine for business and finance. Great table of contents. Even if you don't make it through the rest of the magazine, a quick scan of the contents will keep you abreast of what's going on.

- *Money* (monthly). A popular magazine for personal finance and investing. Good research, wonderful selection of articles. Very reader-friendly.
- *Fortune* (bimonthly). Lots of corporate news, especially good if you invest in individual stocks.
- *Worth* (monthly). Well-written articles on a broad variety of topics; covers strategies and concepts. Has an index of individual stocks and funds covered in the issue. Has an annual listing of the best 250 financial advisers in the country.
- *Smart Money* (monthly). The Wall Street Journal Magazine of Personal Business. Wide range of financial planning and investment topics. Good columns such as "Ten Things ___ Won't Tell You."
- *Kiplingers Personal Finance* (monthly). The first magazine to offer advice on personal finance, starting in 1947.

Books

- *The Wall Street Journal Guide to Understanding Money and Investing,* by Kenneth M. Morris and Alan M. Siegel (Simon and Shuster, 1994). Very good, basic information. Also covers sophisticated investments like futures and options. Makes arcane world of finance very easy to grasp; superb graphics help convey the information.
- *The Only Investment Guide You'll Ever Need,* by Andrew Tobias (Harcourt Brace, 1998). Funny and smart.
- *One Up on Wall Street: How to Use What You Already Know to Make Money in the Market,* by Peter Lynch with John Rothchild (Penguin, 1990). This book started the invest-in-what-you-know trend of the 1990s. A little dated in the Internet age but worth reading.
- *The Intelligent Investor: A Book of Practical Counsel,* by Benjamin Graham (HarperCollins, 1985). First written in 1949, the definitive book on fundamental investing. Latest edition includes an introduction by Warren Buffett, one of Graham's best-known disciples.
- *How to Retire Rich* by James O'Shaughnessy (Broadway Books, 1997). Uses decades of stock market data to present a logical, consistent approach to investing.

- *Charles Schwab's Guide to Financial Independence: Simple Solutions for Busy People* (Three Rivers Press, 1999). Excellent book for beginners. Presents fundamentals of stock market investing, from goal setting to designing an investment plan.

Internet Portals

There are several financial portals where you'll find news, quotes, research, portfolio tracking tools, message boards, and general articles on personal finance. Picking a portal is strictly a matter of preference; all the ones listed are good. I recommend that you find one or two portals that you like and make them your first stop of the day. Then go on to other sites that specialize in the areas you're interested in, either following links found on the portal or bookmarks you've developed from the sources listed in this chapter or that you've discovered on your own.

- Yahoo! Finance <finance.yahoo.com>
- Smart Money <www.smartmoney.com>
- Money Central <www.moneycentral.com>
- Quicken <www.quicken.com>
- Bloomberg <www.bloomberg.com>
- Kiplinger <www.kiplinger.com>
- Quote.com <www.quote.com>
- America Online Personal Finance (available to AOL members)

Tips for Discovering Good Information Sources

There are two simple rules for uncovering your own information sources. One is to let your curiosity be your guide and read what you're interested in. The other is to follow your nose, so to speak, by pursuing links to related sources. This is obvious on the Web, but books, magazines, and newspapers also refer to other resources, either embedded in the article you're reading or as a separate bibliography. If something piques your interest and you don't have time to follow up on it, either clip the article or jot down the name of the book or Web site on a piece of paper and throw it into a folder labeled Information Resources. That way you won't forget about it and can follow up on it when you have the time.

In addition to being on the lookout for recommendations, periodically you may want to do a broad survey of books and magazines just to see what's out there. Set aside a few hours, go to several different bookstores and start browsing. Don't forget about the newsstand section of the bookstore. If you can't get to a big bookstore, visit <www.amazon.com> or <www.barnesandnoble.com> and check the summaries and reviews of the various business books. Again, let your curiosity be your guide. And don't forget about your local library. The selection may be limited and dated, but the price is right.

When it comes to surveying Web sites, you must do it in a methodical manner or you'll find yourself all over the place. You can't just type *stocks* into a search engine subject field because it will return a list of about 3 million sites, including sites dealing with rifles and flowers. Fortunately, there are many financial directories on the Web which feature links grouped by categories, such as news, quotes, or research. If your goal is to check out all the quotes links so you can find the one you like best, find a good directory (see the list on the next page), put it in your browser's page holder and then go down the list of links. (If your browser doesn't have a page holder just click "back" to get back to the directory after checking each link.) Remember that your goal is to find your favorite site in each category so you can hone your list to a manageable number. That means sticking to the task during this exercise and resisting the temptation to follow links and get caught up in content. Make a note to go back later if you find something interesting.

Here's how to do a survey of financial Web sites starting at the top. First go to <www.searchenginewatch.com> for a list of all the search engines. (Once again, be aware that sites change, consolidate, and disappear, so any site mentioned in this book may not be there when you get to it.) In addition to providing a list of all the search engines, Search Engine Watch also ranks them so you can see who's good at what. Starting with the best ones and eventually trying all of them, go to each search engine's home page. Click on Business or Finance or Investing or whatever terminology they use. Keep clicking until the word *directory* appears. Then check each directory by following the links one at a time as described above. Sometimes what they call a directory really isn't. A real directory has little content of its own, but consists almost exclusively of links to other sites, sometimes with brief descriptions of the sites. What you'll be looking for are comprehensive directories with lots of links.

When you find a good directory, you may not be able to follow all the links in one sitting. To avoid having to do another directory search, bookmark the directory in your browser or consider printing out the list of links so you can make notations as you check out each site. Bookmark only the best sites and try to keep your bookmarks organized, perhaps filing them into folders to correspond to the directory's groupings. Here is a list of directories I've found to be very good:

- InvestorGuide <www.investorguide.com/Investing>. Very comprehensive list of links; some descriptions.
- InvestorMap <www.investormap.com>. Manageable list of links; well categorized.
- Investors.Org <www.investors.org/iea/relatedsites.htm>. Manageable list; good descriptions.
- Investorama <www.investorama.com>. Probably the most comprehensive directory on the Web, with over 11,000 links at last count.
- Open Directory Project <www.dmoz.org>. This directory utilizes volunteer editors for human review; includes brief descriptions.
- JustQuoteMe <www.justquoteme.com>. Focuses on news sites, announcement calendars, and technology stocks.
- The Web Investor <www.thewebinvestor.com/sitemap.html>. Focuses on sites featuring news and market activity.
- Ohio State University <www.cob.ohio-state.edu/cept/fin/cern>. Interesting sites, some with descriptions; the list is not categorized but has sites you won't find in other directories.
- Daily Stocks <www.dailystocks.com>. Features sites leading to market numbers, market commentary, and technology information.
- Corporate Information <www.corporateinformation.com>. Focuses on sites featuring information on public companies.

Now let's look at each of the five specific areas of information that relate to investing.

Research

Research is all the information you take into account when making an investment decision. Your purpose in gathering all this information is to develop some idea of the risk/return potential of the investments you're considering. Some research is *descriptive,* consisting of facts on the past behavior of the economy, the market, the industry, the company, or the given investment vehicle (such as stocks or bonds). Other research is *analytical,* which means it includes projections or opinions about what the data mean for the future of an investment. Descriptive research is pretty easy to come by if you know where to look, and most of it is free. Analytical research can be very expensive depending on who's doing the analyzing—or it can be free if you know where to look on the Web and if you include Internet columnists, chat room participants, your next-door neighbor, or anyone else with an opinion about the market.

Descriptive Research

Descriptive research is all the dry stuff that most people skip in the face of a sizzling story about the next big thing. Granted, descriptive research deals with events that have already happened, whereas most of us care only about the future when making an investment. But facts put future possibilities into context and suggest how likely those opportunities are to be realized. They form the basis for analysis. For example, when evaluating an Internet start-up company, you may want to know more about the people behind it and how much experience they've had running other successful companies. Once you know the facts about their education and career experience, along with the financial details of the other companies they've been involved with, you can analyze how successful their next venture is likely to be. This is far preferable to going on blind faith.

The trick to gathering factual data is to focus on the right kind of information and to know what you're going to do with it. Otherwise you end up drowning in facts and numbers with no clue as to what they all mean. That's when you throw up your hands and run to the nearest message board to see what other people are buying. Incidentally, no one says you have to gather factual information on investments. You can skip this step and focus only on analytical research if you'd rather let someone else do your data gathering and analysis for you (just be discerning about whose analysis you rely on). But if you'd rather uncover your own gems, and if you have your own ideas about what constitutes a good investment, consider the following sources of information.

Corporate Information

You can get corporate information directly from the company or from sources that gather and package corporate information in a consistent, reader-friendly format. Many analysts start with the company's 10-K. This is the document every public company must file annually with the Securities and Exchange Commission (SEC). If you're used to reading slick annual reports that get you to focus on the company's bright future, the 10-K can be a sobering experience. It focuses more on the risk factors, as required by the SEC, and the numbers. It does, however, give a very complete description of the company's business—probably more comprehensive than you'll find anywhere else—and you won't be distracted by any pretty pictures. You can download any public company's latest 10-K off the Internet for free by visiting <www.sec.gov> and clicking on the EDGAR database. Or call or write to the Securities and Exchange Commission, 450 5th Street NW, Washington, DC, 20549, telephone 202-942-7050. Alternatively, go to EDGAR Online <www.edgar-online.com> or <www.freedgar.com>, each of which also offers free downloads as well as premium services for serious readers of 10-Ks and other SEC filings.

Companies can update you on their latest doings by providing annual reports, recent press releases, and even product brochures. You can visit a company's corporate Web site or call its main headquarters and ask for a packet from the investor relations department. You can order annual reports from:

- Yahoo! Finance <finance.yahoo.com>. A directory of public companies with direct links to corporate Web sites.
- Online Annual Report Service <www.annualreportservice.com>. Choice of hard copy or online reports, also has links to EDGAR Online and the NYSE Web site.

Hoover's is probably the biggest compiler of corporate information. Some of it is free; most you have to pay for. However, it is very comprehensive, displayed in a concise format, and delivered either electronically or online. Visit <www.hoovers.com> or call 800-456-8666 and ask for a catalog. Other Web sites featuring corporate information include:

- Zacks Research <www.zacks.com>. More numbers than you'll ever know what to do with.
- Yahoo! Finance <finance.yahoo.com>. Very comprehensive compilation of data.

Economic Information

Economic information deals with the bigger picture, or the setting within which an investment is made. It includes key economic data and also considers the political climate and social trends, both domestic and international. Many professional portfolio managers start with this before they ever get into specific company research. They want to know how fast the economy is growing, whether or not inflation is a problem, and where interest rates are headed, among other things, before they narrow their search by industry and company. They evaluate these trends through major reports such as the gross domestic product (GDP) and the consumer price index (CPI), as well as other statistics which are considered leading indicators of these trends, such as consumer spending and the unemployment rate. *Business Week* (800-635-1200 and <www. businessweek.com>) is an excellent source of economic data, as is *The Wall Street Journal* (800-568-7625 and <www.wsj.com>). You can also get raw statistical data from the government at:

- Bureau of Economic Analysis <www.bea.doc.gov>
- Bureau of Labor Statistics <www.bls.gov>
- Census Bureau <www.census.gov>

Market Information

Sometimes knowing how a stock has traded in the past can be helpful in assessing where it may go in the future. The field of technical analysis is devoted to the study of chart patterns and trading activity as a way to identify trends in pricing. While the old disclaimer "past performance is no guarantee of future results" is certainly true here, previous market activity can reveal certain insights depending on how you interpret it. For historical pricing information visit:

- Big Charts <www.bigcharts.com>
- Prophet Finance <www.prophetfinance.com>

Analytical Research

Analytical research bundles factual data with a person's judgment as to what the information means for the future of the investment. This is very big business. And it's really what investing is all about. It's one thing to determine that a stock has earnings per share of $1.50 and a

P/E ratio of 30. But the information does you no good unless you put it into context and exercise some judgment as to whether that means the stock is a buy, hold, or sell. Stock analysts generally focus their work on estimating future earnings and then assigning some reasonable value to those earnings as a way of estimating future stock prices. So the last sentence of an analyst's report might read: "We believe XYZ Co. will earn $2.10 per share next year and carry a price/earnings ratio of 25, suggesting a potential market price of $52.50." Of course, the analyst may be wrong about the earnings and wrong about the P/E, but at least the estimation was gained in a methodical manner. Contrast this with a chat room participant who says, "XYZ's got a great story; I think the stock will double in six months."

Some analytical research is very expensive. Some is free. And some can't be obtained at any price unless you have an account with the brokerage firm that publishes it. But regardless of how you obtain it or how much you pay for it, it's worth questioning its validity and deciding for yourself if it's useful to you. There are two ways to evaluate analytical research. One is to put your faith in the person doing it based on his or her track record and proven skill as an analyst. This seems to be Wall Street's favorite method, given all the star analysts and investment gurus that have come in and out of favor over the years. The other way is to read the report with a critical eye, noting which factual data were used in the analysis, and deciding if you agree with the interpretation. In other words, does it make sense to you? Here are some sources of analytical data.

Research Reports

- Multex Investor <www.multexinvestor.com>. This source offers 300,000 research reports from over 250 top brokerage firms. Free, but requires registration.
- Earnings Whispers <www.earningswhispers.com>. All the gossip, rumors, and speculation about upcoming earnings reports. At least one study has shown that these unofficial earnings estimates are more accurate than the analysts' official ones.

Economic and Market Commentary

- TheStreet.com <www.thestreet.com>. Lots of columnists; very timely market information. Definitely geared for the active investor.

- Ibbotson Associates <www.ibbotson.com>. Click on Research for lots of good research articles.
- Investools <www.investools.com>. Very comprehensive site. Specializes in "actionable investing advice from 35 proven portfolio managers." For an extensive list of newsletters and trial subscription information, click on Stock Advisors.

Mutual Funds

- Morningstar <www.morningstar.com>. The definitive source for mutual fund data and analysis. This site also has tools, news and market reports, and educational information, and could therefore be considered a portal. The site offers a lot of free information, but the more advanced analyses will cost you.
- Brill <www.brill.com>. Features a panel of experts that write articles on different topics. Profiles section highlights fund managers and what they're buying.
- Fund Alarm <www.fundalarm.com>. Watches out for funds that underperform their benchmarks, stray from their objective, or otherwise might provide a reason to sell.
- IndexFunds.com <www.indexfunds.com>. All about index funds, including great articles and commentary.

News

News makes the market move, there's no question about it. The question is, what type of news matters to the market and what impact does it have in the short-run and long-run? Or to be more precise, what news should *you* be watching for—and what can you safely ignore? From the investor's standpoint, news falls into three main categories: (1) general economic news, (2) industry news, and (3) company-specific news. In general, most economic news is fairly short-lived. The market will react to the labor report for a day or two and then go on to something else. Unless you're an active trader, you can watch the economic news with mild disinterest or ignore it altogether. In most cases the same can be said about industry and company news. Unless a company makes a major announcement that changes your opinion of its merit as a long-term investment, you can take company news with a grain of salt. If you are an active trader, on the other hand, you'll want to pay close attention to all business news because there can be lots of spillover. For example, an announcement by IBM after today's close can affect the way all tech stocks trade tomorrow; however, in the long run such an announcement will likely have little effect on the broader market and may not even matter much to the future of IBM.

News comes in a variety of ways. You can choose by format (TV, radio, print, or Internet), schedule (morning, evening, or at your convenience), and selection (type of news you're interested in, such as market activity or general business news). The important thing is to exercise judgment in how and when you absorb your news so you're neither missing what's important nor wasting time on news you don't need. Five minutes a day may be enough—give *The Wall Street Journal* a quick scan in the morning and catch the business news headlines on the way home from work. Of course, that means you won't be taking advantage of the many wonderful news sources available to investors today, but it will leave you more time to play with your kids.

If you read the magazines and newspapers listed earlier in this chapter, especially *The Wall Street Journal* and *Business Week,* you can keep up on the news without ever turning on your television or computer. If you prefer to get your news by TV or radio, check your local listings. However, note that with TV business news you're forced to sit through reports on companies you may not be interested in (as well as those inane commercials), whereas with the written word, whether newspaper, magazine, or Web site, you can quickly skip over news that doesn't pertain to your portfolio.

Here are some good Web sites for business and financial news.

- Dow Jones <www.dowjones.com>. Very extensive business news by the publishers of *The Wall Street Journal.* You can call up news by industry.
- CBS Marketwatch <www.cbsmarketwatch.com>. Very comprehensive list of news stories; easy to scan through the titles, then click on what you want to read.
- CNN Financial News <www.cnnfn.com>. Extensive financial news, very timely, categorized for easy perusal.
- CNBC <www.cnbc.com>. TV—and more of it—on the Web. A favorite of many investors.

- Briefing.com <www.briefing.com>. Very detailed market information.
- Wall Street City <www.wallstreetcity.com>. For people who miss the old brokerage environment. Site has a ticker tape running across the top; click on a symbol and a chart appears.
- Free Real Time Quotes <www.freerealtime.com>. Just what is says: free real-time quotes. Registration required.
- CNET News <www.news.com>. Business and market news with a high-tech focus.
- Financial Times <www.ft.com>. Financial news with a global orientation.

Tools

Tools are interactive devices that give you detailed information relevant to your own situation. For example, a retirement calculator lets you enter your current age, the amount you plan to invest each month, your expected annual return, and the age at which you plan to retire. It will then tell you how much money you can expect to have at retirement age. If you also enter your life expectancy and withdrawal rate, it will tell you how long your money will last. Financial software programs like Intuit's Quicken and Microsoft Money have financial calculators as well as some of the other tools listed below. Financenter <www.financenter.com> has a very comprehensive collection of calculators that can help you answer such questions as "What is my return if I sell now?" and "How much do fees affect my return?"

Stock screening tools allow you to enter specific criteria and receive a list of stocks meeting those criteria. You might use a stock screening tool to find all stocks having P/E ratios under 30 and paying dividends of at least 1 percent. Many investors use stock screening tools as their first step in winnowing the universe of some 10,000 public companies into a manageable list warranting further investigation. Some stock screeners are good for ease of use—just click on preset radio buttons— while others let you enter a very comprehensive set of values. You might start your search with the preset screeners and refine your list with the more comprehensive ones. The following sites have very good stock screening tools:

- Zacks <www.zacks.com>. Probably the most comprehensive stock screening tools on the Web. Choose from screeners with preset values to one that offers 96 criteria. Also has predefined screens, like "stocks with low P/E ratios." Once you've run a screen you can save it for future use.
- Quicken <www.quicken.com>. Three levels of stock screeners: quick, detailed, and advanced; click on preset values or enter your own.
- Hoover's <www.hoovers.com>. Allows you to screen for various financial data, such as price/earnings ratio and revenues. Once a list of stocks comes up, you can click on a link to Hoover's capsule description or, if you're a member, a more complete profile of the company.
- Morningstar <www.morningstar.com>. Mutual fund screening tool. Screens through 6,500 funds. Basic screener calls up top performing funds for time period requested. Preset screeners call up Morningstar's favorites in various categories. Advanced screener allows you to enter more detailed criteria, but you must subscribe to get it.

Portfolio tracking software, both on CD-ROM and via the Web, lets you keep track of your holdings and analyze your portfolio in many different ways. The basic Web-based trackers update stock prices and alert you when there's news on the companies in your portfolio. The software programs do more comprehensive portfolio management; they keep a record of all your transactions, maintain your cost basis, update the value of your portfolio on a regular basis, compute investment returns, and print charts and graphs. Consider the following portfolio tracking resources:

Software

- Quicken. Visit <www.quicken.com> for information on how to order the latest version of Intuit's money management program.
- Microsoft Money. Visit <www.microsoft.com/money> for information on how to order the latest version of Microsoft's money management program.
- National Association of Investors Corporation (NAIC) offers Personal Record Keeper software for Windows. See <www.better-investing.org> for description and pricing information.

- Market Watcher.com <www.marketwatcher.com> offers a free Windows program that you can download off the Web.

Web Sites

- Excite <www.excite.com>. Lets you set up a personal portfolio and get updated quotes and news.
- Mutual Fund Investor Center <www.mfea.com>. Offers mutual fund portfolio tracking.
- Individual brokerage sites. Most brokerage firms offer portfolio tracking via the Web.

Portfolio allocation tools help you decide how much of your portfolio to put in stocks, bonds, and cash based on your risk tolerance and expected returns. You can find a portfolio allocation tool at Fidelity Mutual Funds' Web site <www.fidelity.com>, which leads you through a series of questions and then shows a pie chart with a suggested asset allocation. I must point out that Fidelity's approach is the traditional one: first allocating among stocks, bonds, and cash, and then allocating among large-cap stocks, small-cap stocks, and international. One of the reasons I wrote this book was to suggest that this traditional approach may not be appropriate in today's world, as you'll see in the later chapters. However, if you're going to use the traditional approach, Fidelity's Web site is straightforward and easy to use.

Discussion Groups

Other investors can sometimes be your best source of investment information and ideas, whether you make contact with them through cyberspace or in your living room. Investment clubs have been around for a long time. They generally meet once a month and share research and ideas over coffee or wine. Online discussion groups are newer and usually less structured. Some are real-time chat rooms, where people type at each other all times of the day or night. Others are message boards, where people post questions or comments for others to read at their convenience. Chat rooms generally have a bad reputation for inciting rumors and trashy talk, but some are fairly respectable. Finding an investment group to hang out with is like picking any group of friends: just look for people you feel comfortable with.

The National Association of Investors Corporation (NAIC) is the grandfather of investment clubs. They've been around since 1951 and have established guidelines to help investment clubs operate smoothly. They also publish workbooks and other materials to help people get started investing. If you'd like to find an investment club near you, or if you have a group of friends who would like to start an investment club, visit <www.better-investing.org> on the Web or call 877-275-6242.

On the Web you'll find many discussion groups. Some popular ones are:

- Motley Fool <www.fool.com>
- Raging Bull <www.ragingbull.com>
- Armchair Millionaire <www.armchairmillionaire.com>

Basic Education

Whether you're a brand-new investor or want to go back and fill in some of the basics that you never learned, you can benefit from some of the excellent investor education materials being produced today. Many people, in their first attempt to learn about investing, pick up the latest issues of *Barron's* and *The Wall Street Journal.* This is like walking into a calculus class in the middle of the semester. If you don't understand what they're talking about, you're likely to get discouraged and give up. So start out slowly and gather the basic building blocks. Understand how common stock is issued and how the markets work before you try to master options. Learn about asset classes and the different categories of mutual funds before you try to choose a specific fund. Also understand your preferred learning style. Do you like to sit down with a book and read as much as you can whenever you have the time, or would you rather take a class where you can have your questions answered? The world of investments is changing all the time. Everyone should periodically review the basics and see what's new. In addition to the books listed earlier in this chapter, the following Web sites offer basic investment education:

- American Association of Individual Investors <www.aaii.com>. Membership organization; Web site has some free information, but you can get more if you're a member. You can also call 800-428-2244.

- National Association of Investors Corporation <www.better-investing.org>. Publishes a variety of materials on the basics of investing.
- SEC Guide to Investing <www.sec.gov>. Very good source of investing information, much of it designed to protect unwary investors from fraud and scams. Go to the SEC's home page, click on Investor Education and Assistance, and follow the links.
- Mutual Fund Investor's Center <www.mfea.com>. Good source of basic investment education, with an emphasis on mutual funds.
- Investment Company Institute <www.ici.org>. The mutual fund industry's trade organization. In addition to industry goings-on, the site also has good educational materials.
- Vanguard Funds <www.vanguard.com>. Most of the mutual funds and brokerage firms have some basic education on their sites. "Vanguard University" is especially good, although it does have a bias toward mutual funds in general and index funds in particular.
- Brill <www.fundsinteractive.com>. Lots of articles on mutual funds.
- Efficient Frontier <www.efficientfrontier.com>. Basics of asset allocation and modern portfolio theory (Warning: this material is pretty complex and may be more than you need to know).
- Chicago Board Options Exchange <www.cboe.com/education>. Very extensive explanation of how options work.
- Young Investor <www.younginvestor.com>. Games, articles, kid-friendly library, and kid and parent message boards.

Tips for Using the Internet

To say the Internet has revolutionized investing combines cliché and understatement all in the same breath. Still, I can't emphasize enough how valuable this resource can be in making anyone a better investor—as long as you are able to navigate the Web quickly and efficiently. To make the most of this extraordinarily useful resource, assess your computer set-up and your surfing habits, and streamline the process as much as possible. One objection people have to using the Internet is that the Web is so vast it's easy to get lost—you spend time surfing irrelevant sites and never get around to the good ones. I hope that the list of selected sites in this chapter will help you zero in on some of the good sites so you can make maximum use of your time at the computer. Another objection people have is that the pages take too long to download. This is one of the criteria you'll take into consideration when developing your list of favorite sites. The better sites know you're busy and have designed their pages for speedy loading; don't waste your time on the ones that haven't. Here are some other ideas for speeding up your load rate.

Upgrade Your Hardware

First, check your modem speed and upgrade to the fastest baud rate available. If you're lucky enough to have DSL (digital subscriber line) or cable modem service in your area, get it. It's only a little more expensive than regular Internet service, but it's many times faster and well worth the cost. Next, make sure your computer has plenty of memory. If your computer freezes or crashes a lot while you're browsing, it could be due to insufficient memory. And finally, how fast is your computer? An old, kludgy computer that's good enough for word processing and balancing your checkbook may be a dinosaur lumbering around the Internet. This may be the perfect time to upgrade.

Customize Your Start Page

You can configure your own start page to feature headlines from your favorite news sources and links to other sites. Want to see what the market is doing the instant you log on? You can have your start page show the Dow, the S&P 500, the Nasdaq, as well as your favorite stocks. Some online brokerage firms let you design your own start page, as do the following:

- My Yahoo! <my.yahoo.com>
- My Excite <my.excite.com>
- The Wall Street Journal Interactive Edition <interactive.wsj.com/archive/personal.cgi>

Tips for Faster Browsing

If you're like most people, the minute you got your computer set up for the Internet you jumped right in and started browsing. But your browser has features you may not even know about that can make your Internet experience faster and more enjoyable. Here are some tips to improve browser performance.

- Take a few minutes to scan through your browser's Help file. Check out the latest features and all the things it can do to make searching and browsing more efficient.
- Go through the Preferences file and set up your browser the way you want. For example, you can specify whether you want pictures to load faster or better. Choose the font size that's easy on your eyes.
- Bookmark your favorite pages, and keep the list manageable by filing sites by category. Periodically go through the list and delete any sites you're no longer visiting regularly.
- Increase the size of your cache to browse previously viewed pages faster.
- Turn off sound, video, and pictures to display text faster. You can always download pictures on an individual basis.
- To browse now and read later, save pages to your hard disk or spool them to your printer while you continue to browse.

Keeping Information in Perspective

I can't emphasize enough how important it is to keep all this information in perspective and use it to your best advantage. Individual investors are extremely fortunate today to have so much information at their disposal. It's really narrowed the gap between professional and lay investors. You can see corporate earnings releases the same time the analysts do; you can even listen in on live analyst conference calls via the Internet. In today's information free-for-all, no longer do analysts and professional portfolio managers have a jump on the news that drives the markets. As a matter of fact, individual investors are collectively creating their own information source which is having no small effect on the markets. The ideas expressed on message boards and in discussion groups are frequently responsible for trading volume and price changes in certain stocks. Although the professionals tend to pooh-pooh the opinions expressed there, they have been known to sit in and listen so they can evaluate investor sentiment, often as a contrary indicator (i.e., if everyone is bullish, it means a bear market is overdue). One of these days, the professionals may be forced to accept the fact that individual investors do have intelligent opinions and are perfectly capable of moving the market their way.

But the sheer volume of information can have its negative effects, too. Most investors who also work for a living and have families to take care of simply don't have time to stay on top of it all. And unless you're discerning in the type and frequency of news you allow into your brain, you run the risk of letting the wrong kind of information influence your investment decisions—for example, reacting to short-term news events when you've already selected a long-term investment strategy and, worse, not understanding that there's a difference between the two. That's when you think about consulting an investment advisor.

7

Using Advice
to Your Advantage

With so much information available to investors today, it's been suggested that we financial advisors might as well pack up our briefcases and CFP certificates and find another career. Why should investors pay an advisor, the reasoning goes, when all the research, news, software, and other tools an advisor might use are also available to the investor? Why can't investors simply download what's needed from the Internet or buy the appropriate software package and move on, putting tens of thousands of financial advisors out of business?

If you believe everything you read in the financial press, you might indeed think that the Internet has made a dinosaur out of anyone who dispenses investment advice for a living. To make their point, the financial press publishes myriad how-to articles and books to show how much people don't need financial advisors. "You can do it," they say. "Save on fees," they plead. "Buy our books and magazines and we'll tell you more than any financial advisor will tell you—and then some."

Information Is Not the Same as Advice

What this argument fails to address is the difference between information and advice. Information is indeed an essential part of knowing how to invest. But due to its necessarily generic approach, it doesn't always tell you how *you* should invest. Or how your investments will affect the other parts of your financial life, like taxes. By sifting through

enough information you may be able to find the answers. But you'll encounter a lot of contradiction and confusion along the way, not to mention the amount of time it takes to sort through it all. Financial advisors
can spare you this aggravation by zeroing in on your needs and tailoring
their recommendations to fit your specific circumstances. This doesn't
mean all advisors are good, of course, or that you'll be able to work
comfortably with the first advisor you come across. But financial advisors can be an extremely valuable resource for investors who lack the
time to sift through all the information or don't have the confidence to
manage an investment portfolio on their own.

In a 1998 study called "The Value of Advice," Dalbar, a research
firm serving the financial services industry, investigated why people
pay financial professionals for services they could perform themselves.
Professionals in this case included financial planners, stockbrokers, insurance agents, accountants, bankers, and mutual fund companies—pretty
much anyone who gets paid for offering personal financial advice. The
study found that 85 percent, or some 17 million households who use
paid advisors, say their services are worthwhile. And what is really interesting is that a good part of these people's satisfaction is considered
nonfinancial—in other words, not directly related to investment performance. More important is a person's comfort index: 92 percent of
consumers who use financial professionals report comfort with their finances, compared to 76 percent who do not use an advisor.

So maybe those fuddy-duddy financial advisors who urge their
clients to diversify into the nonhot sectors of the market, even when it
results in lower investment returns, are respected by their clients after
all. But why? Are these advisors performing a major snow job on their
clients, using some twisted form of logic to convince them that it's better not to aim for the highest returns possible? Or is there something
going on here that the financial press is missing when they point to the
indexes and report that the majority of financial professionals fail to
beat the market?

Believe me, there's something going on. But it's nothing mysteri-
ous or unique. It's simply the other side of the performance equation—
the risk side. It seems the clients of financial advisors are equally
interested in protecting what they have. Many of them would gladly
give up a few percentage points of investment returns in exchange for
the ability to sleep better at night. But even more important than per-

centage returns is the shift in focus. Real people care about achieving their financial goals, not how their portfolio performed against some arbitrary index. Whoever decided the S&P 500, or any other index you want to name, is the benchmark against which every person's investment portfolio should be measured? This focus on indexes—and the fact that most portfolio managers fail to beat them—is a media thing. In the real world, all that counts is the ability to send the kids to college and retire comfortably someday. And although most people know this, the biggest challenge facing financial advisors is combating the media influence that pulls people's attention toward the hot stocks and arbitrary benchmarks. For example, when the Smiths noted that their portfolio had not matched the performance of the S&P 500, I had to explain that their long-term objectives and risk profile suggested a different mix of investments than the 100 percent U.S. large-cap stocks represented in the S&P 500. To reduce risk and achieve better diversification, I recommended that the Smiths have a portfolio of 40 percent bonds, 8 percent small cap stocks, and 12 percent international. This is not at all the composition of the S&P 500, making any direct comparison to the index meaningless.

Advisors must constantly bring our clients' attention back to what's important in life and show them what they need to do to achieve their financial goals.

Financial Planning magazine recently asked a number of financial advisors what their most important role is. The question came at a time when a few high-flying tech stocks were dominating the news and the "Everybody's getting rich but me" sentiment described in Chapter 2 was at its peak. The financial press was filled with stories about people who were having great success investing on their own, and financial advisors themselves were beginning to question their own value. But instead of apologizing for underperforming the market or suggesting that, yes, their services really aren't needed today, they presented a whole different side of the advisor-client relationship, a side the media never shows. The question *Financial Planning* posed to advisors was, "What do you think clients pay you to do?" Their answers fell into the following six areas:

1. Define goals
2. Understand risk

3. Manage expectations
4. Monitor investments
5. Coordinate financial affairs
6. Give peace of mind

Define Goals

Most people have some idea of what they want to accomplish in life financially. But simply knowing that you want to send your kids to college or retire at age 60 is a far cry from knowing what it will take to achieve these goals. Sure, you can use a retirement calculator to find out how much you need to save for retirement. But what if you have several concurrent goals? Which do you work on first, college for the kids or retirement for yourself? What if your goals are so lofty that they're completely out of the question? Conversely, what if you're depriving yourself of a good life now because you're overly worried about the future? What if you've missed something important? What if you and your spouse don't agree? What if you're not sure what you want out of life? When it comes to goal setting, financial advisors often serve as sounding boards as much as numbers crunchers. By exploring our clients' life goals in the context of financial reality, we act as both therapist and spread sheet. We integrate the concern of a caring listener with the function of an impersonal calculator to come up with a unique plan for financial success. And investment performance is only part of the equation. Mary Rowland, a prominent financial journalist, announced at an industry meeting that she once believed that people go to a financial planner to get a better return on their investments. But after years of covering the industry, she concluded that the primary role of a financial planner is to help people overcome their personal dysfunctions and lead better and more rewarding lives. Anyone who thinks financial goal setting means sitting down with a pencil and a calculator hasn't had the privilege of sitting down with a financial planner who listens to you and says, "Have you thought about this?"

Understand Risk

We financial professionals pay as much attention to risk as we do to returns. To a professional portfolio manager, risk and return go hand in hand and one is rarely mentioned without the other. What good are astronomical investment returns if the risk is equally astronomical? Risk must always be kept within reason, and the universal goal of every portfolio manager is to maximize returns while minimizing risk. Individual investors often ignore the risk side of the equation, which is why financial advisors consider it an important part of their job to educate clients about risk. Now, it's true that advisors do this because we don't want clients coming back and blaming us if their investments go down in value. "You never said this could happen," is the worst thing an advisor can hear. Still, financial advisors who balance their clients' unbridled optimism with a realistic assessment of what could happen are performing a valuable and necessary service (whether their clients want to hear it at the time or not). Often, we save clients from themselves, either talking them out of risky investments or setting up a compromise plan that allows clients to play with a portion of their portfolio while the rest stays in more conservative investments.

Manage Expectations

Many of the same investors who don't like to think about stocks going down also have unrealistic expectations for future performance. A common one today is to think that just because the S&P 500 provided a total return of 21.0 percent last year that it will happen again this year, and every year for that matter. It's up to financial advisors to help people understand the way markets work and to form realistic expectations about portfolio performance. Again, this is often out of self-interest to keep disappointed clients from coming back at us later. But it's rooted in sound planning principles because having unrealistic expectations can do more than make an advisor look bad. It can throw off your whole financial plan. If you base your saving and investing plan on, say, an expected return of 18 percent or 20 percent a year, you could fall seriously short of your goals if those returns do not materialize. So if your advisor tells you to expect annual returns of 8 percent or 10 percent, it's to help you plan for modest returns so you'll stay on course if the market goes into a slump. Remember, the 50-year average annual return for stocks is just under 12 percent. That means some 20 percent years were balanced by 4 percent years and some 30 percent years were balanced by minus 6 percent years. In the end, it certainly can't hurt to have modest expectations. If your portfolio does better than you expect, the worst thing that will happen is you'll have more money than you thought you'd have.

Monitor Investments

This is what people usually think of when they consider what financial advisors do. They watch your investments so you don't have to. Paradoxically, financial advisors sometimes watch their clients' investments less often than their clients do. That's because of the whole long-term/short-term perspective I talked about in Chapter 3. The noise of the market, which includes all the news reports and commentary about the day's market events, can easily distract you from sticking to a long-term investment strategy. It's like listening to a beautiful symphony on the radio and having it frequently interrupted by bursts of static and tinny rock and roll. At best it's irritating; at worst, you may be tempted to change the station. Financial advisors are accustomed to differentiating between market noise and the significant events that can change the long-term outlook for an investment. Even more important, we monitor your portfolio in relation to your goals and make adjustments to help you stay on track.

Coordinate Financial Affairs

I call this tying up loose ends. When I sat down with Jim and Sandi recently, I wanted to make sure that all the different parts of their financial life worked together with no conflicts and no gaps. Did their IRA beneficiary designation agree with their estate plan? Were they minimizing taxes through year-end investment strategies and contributions to retirement plans? Were they using the right savings vehicle (Education IRA, Section 529 or Uniform Gift to Minors Account, or other type of account) to fund their kids' college education? These are all the things we financial advisors deal with every day. And because it's not terribly interesting subject matter, most people aren't very motivated to learn about it. One of the reasons people feel a financial advisor's services are worthwhile is that it may take an advisor just one time to ask, "But have you thought about this?" to save the client thousands of dollars or otherwise make the client far better off financially.

Give Peace of Mind

Pooh-pooh it if you wish, but peace of mind is a very important goal to a lot of people. I try to help clients achieve peace of mind in several ways. For some clients, it's simply a matter of having a financial plan in place, with goals quantified and a savings plan outlined. For others, it's the comfort of having a trusted professional to turn to whenever a complicated financial issue comes up. I often become confidant and problem-solver, answering questions ranging from "Should I buy or lease my next car?" to "How do I make sure my learning-disabled child is provided for after I'm gone?" The peace of mind that financial advisors impart is one of those intangible qualities that's hard to put a value on. In fact, most of these activities—goal setting, managing expectations, and so forth—don't carry a price tag in the advisor's inventory of services. Instead, we charge for financial planning or investment management and throw these other services in as part of the deal because we know people would never pay for them directly.

One client who recently lost her husband is a good example of this. My job focused not only on helping her get a handle of where all financial assets were held, but in helping her know what to ask the estate attorney, the pension administrator for her husband's company, the CPA, and the life insurance professional. Clearly my work went beyond money management. Peace of mind was what she thanked me for, not financial advice.

How Financial Advisors Charge for Their Services

The subject of compensation is the most complex, talked about, and studied issue of anything financial advisors do. It's because of where the profession began, how it has evolved, and the conflicts of interest that have plagued it since its beginnings. In the old days, when a stockbroker or insurance agent sold a financial product to a customer, the customer was deemed smart enough to know whether or not the product was right for the situation, and the salesperson pocketed a commission for the work. It was a simple sales transaction and no one expected it to be anything more. But the industry soon realized that customers were not always in a position to know whether or not financial products were right for them. Some products were very complex. So customers, especially those who had formed close relationships with their salespeople, came to depend on them to tell them what to do. And the salespeople—most of them anyway—started accepting responsibility for knowing their customers and offering them suitable products. Gradually, sales-people started assuming more of an advisory role. Their attitude shifted from one of trying to sell a line of products to anyone they could get to buy them, to one of matching people with the right products, develop-ing long-term relationships, and ultimately advising clients on other matters as well. Over the years, this shift led many stockbrokers and in-surance agents to call themselves financial advisors in an attempt to shed the salesperson image. Some brokers and insurance agents took this one step further by disassociating themselves from the brokerage firms and insurance companies that imposed high production quotas. It was impossible, the advisors said, to give ethical, unbiased advice when their managers were standing over them urging them to sell.

There remains one problem, however. Many financial advisors today—whether affiliated with a big investment firm or operating on their own—are still paid as salespeople. They earn commissions on the products they "sell" to clients—whether these products are pushed upon them or recommended as part of long-term financial plan based on the client's goals and objectives. The financial press has made a big deal out of this and suggested that anyone who earns a commission cannot pos-sibly be objective. Most advisors would argue vehemently against this, saying that not only are they able to select products for clients without regard for their own compensation, they actually try to save their clients money by choosing the most favorable fee arrangement. Clearly, there are salespeople in advisors' clothing who will take advantage of cus-tomers whenever they can. The problem for you is that you never know which kind of advisor you're getting. Later in this chapter, I'll give you some guidelines for evaluating a commission-based advisor's integrity.

The outgrowth of the conflict that results when advisors are paid to sell has been some creative fee structures designed by financial advi-sors who want to (1) be paid fairly for their work, and (2) remove con-flicts of interest. One of the most popular arrangements is for the advisor to charge a flat fee for the initial planning plus a percentage of the client's assets for ongoing management. The planning fee can range from $500 to $15,000, depending on how complex the client's financial situation is, while the ongoing management fee usually averages about

1 percent of assets. Some advisors have a tiered fee structure, charging, say, 1.5 percent for the first $200,000, 1 percent from $200,000 to $1 million, and 0.75 percent on assets over $1 million.

What Financial Advisors Do

When talking to an industry publication like *Financial Planning* magazine, financial advisors will let their hair down and say their most valuable services are managing expectations and delivering peace of mind as discussed earlier. However, they know you'd never pay real money for these nebulous services (affectionately called hand-holding), so when telling you about what they do, they'll be much more concrete about the specific services they provide. Their services usually fall into two categories corresponding to the fee arrangement described above: (1) initial planning services, and (2) ongoing investment management. Although you can ask for one or the other, most advisors like to do both. The initial planning is necessary in order for the advisor to know how to manage your portfolio, and the ongoing management is necessary if the goals identified in the planning session are to be achieved. Some advisors do lean toward one or the other, however, and this is one of the considerations you'll keep in mind when choosing a financial advisor.

In my experience, new clients usually come in asking for a retirement projection or advice on a specific issue. This gives them a chance to kick the tires and see if they'd feel comfortable working with us. When they understand how complex managing investments can be, they often decide to hire us for ongoing money management in addition to the financial planning services they originally came in for.

Financial Planning

A planning-oriented advisor, called a Certified Financial Planner or CFP, specializes in identifying your goals, quantifying them, and developing a plan for saving and investing. The emphasis here is on the planning, not the execution. You may get a personalized report that states your goals and the various considerations unique to your financial situation. Planners are getting away from the 250-page reports that once carried a high perception of value but that nobody ever read. Reports today range from 3 to 20 pages and are considered a tool to facilitate the process, not an end-product in themselves. Please note that financial advisors vary considerably in the extent of planning services they offer. Some ask just enough questions to decide which investment products you need. Others go into great detail, considering taxes, estate planning, and other aspects of your financial life. The fee can provide some clue as to how detailed your plan will be, but be sure to ask what is involved in the advisor's planning services. Some advisors offer multitiered plans, recommending the level that corresponds to the complexity of your financial situation.

When I first meet with a new client, I do everything I can to make the person feel comfortable, understanding that it's not always easy to talk about intimate financial details. If you came in to see me, I'd ask lots of questions about you, your family, your career, your lifestyle, your long-term goals, and your interests, in addition to the usual queries about income, assets, debts, and other financial matters. This is not idle chatter. I'm listening for clues that will help me understand you better. All of this information—including your expensive hobbies and your dream of starting a company someday—will go into my assessment of your overall financial needs. If it seems that I'm asking questions unrelated to your reason for coming in, understand that it's part of my job. It's like a doctor who looks in your mouth when you come in with a stomachache. Not only may what's going on in your mouth help the doctor determine what to do for the stomachache, it may also reveal ailments you didn't even know about. And that's the most valuable service a financial planner can perform: discovering needs you didn't know you had. It's why you can't always rely on information alone to be sure you're doing the right thing. If you don't know that you may be subject to the alternative minimum tax this year, for example, you won't be inclined to read up on this rather uninteresting subject. But an advisor who discovers this about you during the course of an interview can bring it to your attention and offer specific suggestions for dealing with it (and spare you from midnight readings of the tax code).

Investment Management

Most advisors agree that planning is just the first step in the process. What really matters is the action you take to achieve your goals.

This is why most financial planners also work with investments, even if they don't manage them directly but instead recommend mutual funds or professional portfolio managers. With over 10,000 mutual funds out there and thousands of professional portfolio managers, it's no easy task to sift through them all and identify (1) the good ones, and (2) the ones that are right for you. Advisors who specialize in matching clients with mutual funds or money managers take a far more in-depth approach to this process than some of the financial magazines do with their top-performing lists. These advisors stay on top of developments in the field and are often privy to information not available to the general public, such as which portfolio manager is leaving one fund to go to another. (A top-performing fund that loses its manager suddenly becomes an unknown quantity, because the next manager may use a different approach.) Advisors usually try to understand the nuts and bolts of how a fund portfolio is managed and they know who to call to get this information (it's not in the prospectus). But the most important service these advisors perform is helping you allocate your assets among the different types of funds so you'll be properly diversified. Sure, you can do this yourself, but an advisor's experience and access to industry information may provide an edge over what you are able to do on your own—even with all that mutual fund information available on the Internet. I personally feel this is one of my most important functions now that investors seemingly want to throw caution to the wind and diversification out the window.

An important part of the investing process is an exploration of your investment objectives. These are slightly different from your financial goals, although they do emerge from them. Investment objectives relate specifically to your time horizon, your tax situation, and your risk tolerance, and they determine how your investment portfolio should be managed. The most complicated of these is risk tolerance. A skilled advisor understands the complexity of this (and all its psychological underpinnings) and will probe beyond the simple questions found in risk questionnaires you see in magazines and on the Web. Nobody likes to lose money. That's a given. But an advisor can help you understand the different types of risk, the tradeoffs involved, when it might make sense to take on more risk than you're totally comfortable with (when you're a long way from reaching your financial goals), and when it makes sense to pull back and give up some potential gains in exchange for

portfolio stability (when you're clearly bothered by the market's volatility). Exploring risk tolerance is an ongoing process of give and take,
and a good advisor will encourage you to talk about your feelings and
expectations. A big part of my job is helping you feel comfortable with
your investments.

Edward and Janis were a married couple with very different views
of risk. Ed, who was 18 years older than his wife, wanted a higher complement of bonds and ultrasafe investments. It was my job not only to
develop a portfolio to meet their mutual needs but to help them both
understand what the tradeoffs were between bonds and stocks. If we
went with Ed's ideas, we wouldn't achieve the kinds of returns Janis
had in mind. On the other hand, the portfolio Janis wanted wouldn't let
Ed sleep comfortably. Fortunately we were able to come to a compromise with a well-constructed portfolio. (See Chapter 10 for more portfolio ideas.)

Advisors who specialize in portfolio management buy and sell individual stocks and/or bonds, rather like a mutual fund manager but
keeping your money separate from everyone else's. When you have your
own professional money manager, you can specify certain restrictions,
such as no tobacco stocks. Even more important, an individual portfolio manager will take your tax situation into consideration when managing your portfolio. This may mean keeping trading to a minimum and
performing special year-end maneuvers to reduce taxable gains. If you
need to take withdrawals from the account, your manager may plan
ahead in order not to have to sell securities at an unfavorable time. If
you want to know about the activity in your account, you can request
confirmations of every transaction so you'll know when stocks are purchased or sold. If you have a question or concern about your account,
you can usually talk directly to the portfolio manager, or at least to a
knowledgeable representative if it's a big firm. All this personal service
isn't available to everyone, however. Almost all money managers have
account minimums. $100,000 is about the lowest anyone will go; most
require $500,000 to $1 million or more.

As professional portfolio managers, we use very disciplined methods to select stocks and manage portfolios. Rarely do we hear about a
stock we like, check a few research reports, and then buy it, the way
most nonprofessionals do. We usually establish a list of criteria, like
revenues over a certain amount, an earnings growth rate of a certain

percent, and a strong brand identity. We set up screens to cull stocks meeting our criteria from the broad universe of stocks. Then we do much more research, reading the usual 10-Ks and annual reports, and sometimes doing a site visit to tour the facilities and talk with management. Often, we will follow a stock for months before deciding to buy it. This gives us an opportunity to study trading patterns and get a feel for how the stock behaves in the marketplace. We also have established sell disciplines that keep us from reacting emotionally the way most nonprofessionals do when their stocks rise or fall by a significant amount. If you were to compare a professional portfolio manager's disciplined approach to an online investor's trigger-happy style, you would see a world of difference. This doesn't mean you can't manage your own portfolio, but like the other services financial advisors perform, professional portfolio management can save you a lot of time and lend an expertise that takes years to acquire.

How to Find an Advisor

Although I do not wish to endorse any brokerage firms or investment products in this book, I'd like to mention Women's Financial Network (wfn.com) because it offers some very good guidelines for selecting a financial advisor. Wfn.com prescreens the advisors who participate in the program and also has them sign a code of ethics. The prescreening makes sure the advisor is properly registered and passes all the background checks. You can then interview advisors to find one whose services match your needs.

Getting Names

You can prescreen an advisor yourself. But first you have to determine who to screen. Your first step in finding a financial advisor might be to ask other professional advisors, if you have them, such as CPAs or attorneys. Other professionals are usually very discerning about the advisors they choose to work with, so you're more likely to find a qualified advisor this way. If you don't have other advisors, ask friends, family, and work associates for the names of their advisors. One caveat here, though: Just because your best friend loves his or her financial advisor doesn't mean that the advisor is right for you. The services you need may not be offered, and your friend may not have done much due diligence before choosing the advisor. Popularity is part of the selection process, but there's a lot more to it than that. If you strike out with friends and family, contact the Financial Planning Association at 800-322-4237 or <www.fpanet.org> for a referral to a financial advisor in your area. As a last resort, look in the phone book.

Making the First Call

When you make the first call, try to do enough screening to see if you and the advisor are even in the same ballpark with respect to being able to work together. You'll want to find out if the advisor offers the services you need, while the advisor will be wondering if you are qualified to be a client. The best thing to do is be up front about what services you're looking for and the amount of assets you have available to invest. Please don't take it personally if an advisor tells you that you don't qualify for services. Just move on until you find one who's willing to work with you. When screening for services, the main thing you'll want to know is whether the advisor has a planning orientation or an investing orientation as discussed earlier. If you're looking for a financial planner ask, "Do you prepare financial plans?" If you're looking for help with investments ask, "Do you manage investment portfolios for clients?" Or, you might just ask, "What services do you offer?" You'll want to get more details on these services once you get in front of the advisor, but for now your objective is to gather enough information about the advisor to decide if an appointment would be worthwhile. Before you get off the phone, in preparation for your background check, ask the advisor to send you some information about available services. Specifically, ask the advisor about licenses or registrations held. This information will give you clues as to how the advisor works, as well as enable you to check on certifications.

If the advisor is a Registered Investment Advisor (RIA), individual portfolio management is most likely offered with a fee based on a percentage of the assets. Ask the advisor to send you a copy of the Form ADV. This is the standard form all RIAs must file with the Securities and Exchange Commission (if they manage more than $25 million in assets) or with their state securities regulator (if they manage less than

$25 million). The Form ADV has two parts. Part I has information about the advisor's education, business, and whether they've had problems with regulators or clients. Part II outlines the advisor's services, fees, and strategies. Be sure you get both parts.

If the registration is with the National Association of Securities Dealers (NASD), ask which licenses are held. A Series 7 license allows the advisor to deal in securities and mutual funds. This suggests that the advisor works on commission because a Series 7 license authorizes acceptance of payments from the sponsors of investment products.

A Certified Financial Planner (CFP) generally has a financial planning orientation, but this does not tell you how the advisor is paid—it could be fees or commissions, or a combination of the two. This designation also means the advisor has taken extra courses culminating in a two-day, ten-hour exam covering the financial planning process, tax planning, retirement planning, estate planning, investment management, and insurance. The CFP license is governed by the Certified Financial Planner Board of Standards <www.cfp-board.org>.

A Chartered Financial Analyst (CFA) has completed in-depth coursework and passed a series of difficult exams focusing on the analytical aspects of individual securities and the investment process. The CFA designation is sponsored by the Association for Investment Management and Research <www.aimr.com>.

Finally, a Chartered Financial Consultant (ChFC) has an insurance orientation and you can count on some form of insurance being included in any recommendations offered.

If it appears you have a fit, at least on the surface, go ahead and set up an appointment. Make it clear, however, that you're considering several advisors and the purpose of this appointment will be to learn more about each other so you can decide if you want to work together. The advisor may ask you to bring copies of tax returns, bank and brokerage statements, and other financial papers. You may or may not feel comfortable doing this. You're certainly not obligated to reveal the details of your financial life at this initial get-acquainted meeting. However, I've found that having your statements with you saves valuable time. Sometimes a new client will describe an investment in great length, when one quick review of the most recent brokerage statement will tell me more specifically what I need to know.

Doing the Background Check

Hardly anybody does background checks, despite all the warnings in the financial press about scam artists and dishonest advisors who are out to take your money. That's because you can usually get a sense about a person from the way they talk, the questions they ask, how their office is appointed, the diplomas on the walls, and other signs of professionalism. I'm assuming here that you will not be doing business with anyone who calls you on the phone promising a big return on your investment if you'll just send a check for $30,000 to a P.O. box. You're looking for a financial advisor—a professional who works in an office, whom you can visit in person, who has other clients, and who's probably been in business for a number of years. Certainly, if your trusted CPA refers you to an acquaintance who is a financial advisor, you probably don't need to worry about background checks.

Still, they're easy enough to do. Just go to the Web site of the North American Securities Administrators Association <www.nasaa.org/regulator>—or your local phone book—and look up the securities regulator in your state. Call them and ask if there have been any negative reports on the advisor in question. (While you're at the NASAA site, go to Investor Education for a list of every scam known to man; on second thought, after reading it you'll be so paranoid you won't trust anybody.) To check up on a member of the National Association of Securities Dealers, go to <www.nasdr.com>. If an advisor tells you he or she is a Certified Financial Planner, you can verify it by going to <www.cfp-board.org>.

Interviewing the Advisor

Your goal in interviewing advisors is to find one who: (1) offers the services you need, (2) you trust, and (3) you like. If you go into your interviews with the idea that you are looking for a match—that this is not an inquisition but a get-acquainted meeting in which you are both learning more about each other—both you and the advisor will be more open and at ease. Even though you initiated the meeting and will have your list of questions in hand, be aware that the advisor will likely direct the meeting. This may be your first time meeting with an advisor, but they do this all the time. They know what questions people ask and usually have the answers prepared. You may run into a chicken-or-egg situation in which you don't want to tell the advisor about yourself until you find out what he or she can do for you, and the advisor will explain that help can't be offered until more is known about you. The best way around this is to give the advisor a brief rundown on your situation, detailing what services you are looking for. Ask the advisor to talk about the approach used when working with clients with your needs.

Finding an Advisor Who Offers the Services You Need

If you don't know exactly which services you need, that's okay. Remember, advisors are trained to help you discover needs you didn't know you had. But you should at least decide whether you want to focus more on financial planning or investment management. If you're young and have a whole lifetime to plan for, you'll probably want financial planning. If you recently came into a large sum of money, you may want to focus on investment management. For financial planning, the complexity of your situation will determine whether or not an advisor is qualified to help you. While most financial planners know something about taxes and estate planning, many of them are not prepared to do in-depth work in these areas. Small business planning is another area where advisors vary in their knowledge and experience. What to do with stock options or evaluating retirement plan distribution options is another. Do keep in mind that the value of working with a financial advisor grows over time. In other words, the better they get to know you (and you them), the more the advisor will be able to anticipate your needs and be proactive in recommending solutions. So when you're interviewing advisors think about the future and whether or not an advisor has expertise in the areas you're going to need later on. And don't be afraid to ask questions. I'm always impressed when someone has taken the time to prepare a list of what they want to ask before our meeting. Here are some questions to ask (you'll probably think of more).

Open-ended questions.

- What services do you offer?
- What are your areas of expertise?
- How long have you been in business?
- Will you tell me about some of your clients?

Financial planning questions.

- Do you have a sample financial plan I could look at?
- What do your retirement planning services consist of?
- Do you do estate planning? Tax planning? Small business planning?

Investment management questions.

- Who manages the money?
- What is your investment philosophy?
- Will you describe the process you would use to manage a portfolio for someone like me?

Finding an Advisor You Trust

Keeping in mind that most advisors are honest and ethical but that there are a few bad apples you'll want to avoid, assess the trust aspect throughout the entire interview. This means turning on your intuition and listening not only for the answers to your questions, but also paying attention to the million little signals like body language and eye contact that tell you more about a person's integrity than any certificate hanging on the wall. You must have a good feeling about this person or the relationship will never work. Yes, education and experience are important, but your gut reaction should have the final say. Here are some questions to ask.

During the interview.

- How do you charge? Will I know in advance exactly how much I'm paying?
- Do you ever run into conflicts of interest? How do you deal with them?

After the interview (ask yourself).

- Do I feel good about this person?
- Can I imagine opening up my financial life to this person and working with him/her for many years?

Finding an Advisor You Like

I put this one last because it's the last thing you should evaluate. It can be easy to get caught up in charm and personality and go with an advisor you get along with, but who may not have the expertise you need. So once you've found an advisor who offers the services you need and that you know you can trust, check for rapport. This may mean being politically incorrect and looking for an advisor of a certain age, sex, and race. Don't worry about that. Most of us like to think of ourselves as unbiased, but it's human nature to have an affinity for people who are like ourselves. Or maybe you're looking for a father figure or mother figure. Whatever. This is no time to examine any deep psychological motives. Just pick an advisor you feel comfortable with and can easily communicate with. Your questions here will be more personal—more along the lines of chit-chat.

- Do you have kids? Pets?
- What are your hobbies?
- What is your philosophy of life?

Working with an Advisor in the Internet Age

As I've tried to make clear in this chapter, investing in the Internet age does not preclude seeking the advice of an expert. In fact, the Internet has greatly aided advisors too, by giving them access to sophisticated tools and resources that enable them to better serve their clients. But I do see the Internet changing the advisor-client relationship somewhat, and in a very healthy way. As people become more self-reliant, they assume more responsibility for the outcome of their decisions—even if they delegate some of those decisions to a professional. Advisors still take a lot of heat when (1) the market goes down, or (2) Amazon.com goes up (and the client doesn't own it). That's why advisors spend so much of their time managing expectations and helping clients understand risk. The Internet has the potential to make investors better informed about what an advisor can and can't do. With better-informed investors, the advisor-client relationship can be elevated from one of dependency to a true partnership.

Here's What You Can Do

The key to working successfully with a financial advisor is knowing what you want the advisor to do for you and being open and communicative at all times. Although you will be looking to the advisor for guidance, you'll want to avoid transferring responsibility. A good advisor is like a good doctor who will educate you, inform you of your alternatives, and let you make the ultimate decision. Here are some things you can do to ensure a successful working relationship.

- *Gather information about your financial picture.* Compile tax returns, insurance policies, employee benefits statements, bank and brokerage statements, and listings of assets not found on statements, such as collectibles or real estate. Share these documents with the advisor, along with any questions or concerns you have about your financial situation.
- *Know what you want the advisor to do for you.* Tell your advisor what you hope to get out of the relationship. Set priorities if there are several things you want to accomplish.
- *Use the advisor as a resource.* Use the Internet and various other information sources to find your own investment ideas and then ask your advisor for a second opinion. The advisor may not be able to predict what any particular stock will do, but can evaluate the risk/reward merits and tell you how it fits with the rest of your portfolio.

Here's What Your Advisor Will Do

In addition to providing professional expertise, your advisor will offer a new perspective on your finances—a perspective that may be difficult for you to see on your own, but which can clarify issues you may be struggling with. Here are some of the things your advisor will do for you.

- *Help you see the big picture.* It can be easy to get so involved in specific issues that you fail to see the larger picture. Your advisor will help you understand investing as it relates to your overall life goals.

- *Help you articulate your goals and put numbers to them.* Once your goals are written down and quantified—that is, once you know what you want to achieve, how much money it will take, and when the money needs to be there (also factoring inflation into account)—you'll be able to establish a plan for achieving your financial goals.
- *Provide a disciplined plan for investing.* Without a plan, investing can be a very emotional experience. Your advisor will set up a disciplined investing program to help you avoid the emotionalism that often causes people to make decisions they later regret.
- *Serve as a resource.* Advisors can't predict the market or tell you the best time to buy or sell. They can provide insight into your own financial situation and help you make sense of all the information out there within the context of your individual goals and objectives.

PART FOUR

Investing in a New Economy

8 Technology Is Here to Stay

In late 1999, when concerns about Y2K were at their peak, Weight Watchers International did an interesting thing. They removed all electronic cash registers from the counters and instructed employees to handle transactions the old-fashioned way—with paper and pen. Rather than take a chance on the computers not working, they removed the questionable devices in order not to be dependent on a system that wasn't 100 percent foolproof. Now, this might be a good way for an organization that handles a few dozen transactions a day in each of its centers to deal with technological uncertainty, but imagine what it would do to the country if all airlines, banks, and department stores did the same thing. Talk about lines! Consumers would revolt. Productivity would plummet. Sales would disappear. Clearly, our world today is dependent on technology.

When you consider how pervasive technology is in our lives today, it's interesting to note that none of the legends profiled in Chapter 5 invest in it. Benjamin Graham wouldn't have, of course, because technology didn't exist when he formulated his theories about intrinsic value. Warren Buffett, Peter Lynch, and Sir John Templeton didn't need to go through the effort of trying to understand this newfangled sector because there were plenty of opportunities in other areas of the market. For the most part, their track records were all established before technology became such a dominant force in our lives. Yet despite their seemingly old-fashioned approach to investing, these legends are more venerated today than ever. I believe it's because they offer a sense of solid ground to investors lured by the appeal of technology stocks, especially the Internet sector, where there are few guidelines for investing and the sand is constantly shifting. The feeling is that if we can just go back and understand the concept of intrinsic value, maybe we can get a handle on today's technology stocks, which seem to offer tremendous opportunities but are awfully scary from a valuation standpoint.

What's a reasonable price to pay for a company with no earnings and little in the way of tangible assets? Graham would say no price is reasonable. Although we may be dissatisfied with his answer, we have him to thank for even inspiring us to ask the question. Does this mean we must deprive ourselves of the opportunities that abound at the dawn of the twenty-first century? No. It means we have to let go of some of these traditional measures of value—at least for the portion of our portfolio that we are willing to expose to some risk—and consider some newer, albeit untested ideas about what constitutes value. We can respect Graham et al. for everything they contributed to the collective wisdom, but now it's time to forge ahead and discover some of the new standards for investing that will begin to take hold as technology continues to pervade our lives.

The New Economy Is for Real

Ever since Alvin Toffler wrote *Future Shock* in 1971 and followed up with *The Third Wave* in the early 1980s, we've been hearing about a paradigm shift that will launch us into a whole new economy. The first wave, which lasted about 10,000 years, was an agrarian-based economy in which agriculture was the dominant economic activity. The second wave was the industrial revolution, lasting about 200 years, in which mass manufacturing via factory automation and assembly lines established new standards of productivity. The third wave is a knowledge-based economy that at this very moment is replacing the industrial revolution (which can hardly be called a revolution any more). In this third wave, entirely new laws of success are being formulated around the usage and flow of information. This third wave has experienced three waves of its own. The first was the mainframe computer. The second was the client-server model, or PC. And the third, which we are currently in, is the Internet stage. In the last decades of the 1900s, mainframes and PCs revolutionized the way we worked and made us far more productive than we had been in the past. But they didn't change the way business was fundamentally conducted. In the twenty-first century the Internet promises to change all that.

In the book *New Rules for the New Economy,* Kevin Kelly says this new economy has three distinguishing characteristics: (1) it is global, (2) it favors intangibles—ideas, information, and relationships, and (3) it is intensely interlinked. He says this new economy represents "a tectonic upheaval in our commonwealth, a far more turbulent reordering than mere digital hardware has produced." It turns many of the old economic laws on their heads and forces us to look at companies in a whole new way. Isn't it ironic, he says, that 40 years ago, when General Motors was the paragon of progress, the pundits looked ahead 40 years and imagined that all successful companies would be like GM. But now that the future has arrived, GM is the counter example. This may serve as a cautionary example to anyone today who sees Microsoft as the paragon of success and believes that 40 years from now all successful companies will be like Microsoft. According to Kelly, "the vanguard is not about computers. Computers are over. The new economy is about communication, deep and wide." And it ushers in some revolutionary notions about success, productivity, and value.

Fundamental Laws of Value Are Being Reversed

The most dramatic shift we are seeing today is a complete reversal of the law of supply and demand. In the old economy, the scarcer something was the more valuable it became. Every student of Economics 101 learned that as products diminish in supply, people are willing to pay more for them. In the network economy, it's plentitude that causes things (only we're not dealing with atoms here) to become more valuable. Think fax machines. The first fax machine cost millions of dollars to produce but was worth nothing when it rolled off the conveyor belt because there weren't any other fax machines to send documents to. Once the second fax machine was produced, the first one acquired value. But it wasn't until fax machines became ubiquitous, when exchanging fax numbers became as common as exchanging telephone numbers, that faxing became a valuable method of communication. The fax machines themselves didn't increase in price. In fact, their cost dropped from around $1,000 to around $200. But their value skyrocketed. Now, of course, faxing is being replaced by e-mail, proving that value changes with the creation of new technologies.

Another concept we need to redefine is the difference between cost and value. Some of the best things in life today really are free, partly because profit-motivated businesses are giving them away. Microsoft gives away Internet Explorer, its Web browser. Qualcomm gives away Eudora, the popular e-mail program. Cellular phone companies give away phones. Why do companies give away items consumers were once willing to pay for? Because the only factor becoming scarce in a world of abundance is human attention. Giving things away captures human attention, or "mind share," which eventually leads to market share. Kelly calls this the gift economy and he has a completely rational explanation for why startup companies go public before they are profitable: many of the components of the gift economy—attention, community, standards, and shared intelligence—have to be in place before cold-cash commercialization can kick in. The gift economy is a rehearsal for the radical dynamics of the network economy. If it seems that companies are starting up with little or no idea of how they'll make a profit, it's because the profits come later, after the customers—and, it is hoped, their undying loyalty—are acquired.

In the new economy, tangible assets aren't as important as they were when it took factories, machines, and delivery trucks to make products and bring them to market. In fact, today these assets are often considered liabilities because of the costs required for upkeep. More and more companies are going virtual, divesting their manufacturing operations and all those tangible assets so they can be more nimble in the marketplace. And new companies are able to get up and running fast, without the need for heavy financing, because they are able to outsource activities requiring costly plant and equipment. That's assuming we're talking about tangible products, of course. Many of the *products* being made today consist of electrons and are developed by the human mind. In this case, all that's needed to produce tremendous output are a computer, a chair, an intelligent human being, and a body of knowledge upon which to build.

Where Graham's theories of intrinsic value fail today is in the assumption that tangible assets are required for earnings generation. In fact, it is the investment in intangible assets like research and development that creates an apparent double whammy: it prevents companies from showing higher profits and at the same time doesn't add anything of value to the balance sheet. While it may appear on the surface that a company with no tangible assets and no visible earnings has nothing to offer, it's often because we don't know how to value those intangible assets, like human capital, intellectual property, and the ability to seize new opportunities in the marketplace, that we tend to overlook their tremendous potential. At the same time, we have to be careful. Just because a company has a neat idea and smart people on staff doesn't mean it has a formula for profitability.

The Internet Ushers in a New Way of Doing Business

While most people agree that the Internet has the potential to usher in profound changes in the way we live, work, and play, there is little agreement at this point about how the Internet will impact our economy—or to be more specific, how companies can make money from it. As Kevin Kelly suggests, some companies aren't bothering to explore the cold-cash commercialization aspects of the Internet yet. In the mad scramble to get eyeballs, followed by some semblance of customer loyalty, many companies are doing whatever it takes to establish a toehold in this (maybe) lucrative marketplace, usually racking up huge losses in the process. The daring entrepreneurs who are forging into new territory in pursuit of early dominance aren't alone in their efforts. They are supported by an army of venture capitalists who are throwing billions of dollars at risky ventures in hopes that a few of them will hit it big. Following the venture capitalists on the food chain are ordinary stock investors who will jump on any dot-com IPO (initial public offering) in order to get in on the ground floor of this amazing new phenomenon, even if the ground floor is a stock that's trading many times higher than its original offering price. And this is something every reader of this book should keep in mind. Much of the risk of Internet investing lands squarely on the shoulders of the investing public. As long as IPOs are greeted with high enthusiasm on the first day of trading, entrepreneurs and venture capitalists can be assured of cashing out early and profitably. I won't say they don't care what happens to a stock after it goes public, but it should be remembered that many of them have gotten the bulk of their investment back at that point. I'm also not saying that you won't make money if you pay $240 per share for a stock that went public at $30. All I'm saying is that you are assuming a tremendous amount of risk by doing so.

Still, the appeal of the Internet is undeniable, largely due to its potential magnitude. Unlike the local hardware store whose market is limited to the number of residents who physically occupy space in the surrounding area, the Internet is not bound by space constraints at all. Or distance. Or time. The same Web site can sell to people in Africa, Australia, Asia, Europe, and the Americas with equal ease, 24 hours a day, with no borders and no space or time constraints. The market for any Internet business is theoretically six billion people and an unlimited number of transactions. This is why valuations for the most promising Internet stocks have reached such astronomical levels. How does one value infinity, anyway? And compared to traditional business models, the cost to reach those six billion people and process that infinite number of transactions is practically miniscule—instead of costly storefronts, bare-bones warehouses can be built on inexpensive land, and with the right systems in place, a company doesn't even need to maintain inventory. It really is different now.

The *Internet Industry Almanac* forecasts more than 327 million Internet users by the end of 2000—more than triple the number at the end of 1997. At least 25 countries will have more than 10 percent of their population on the Internet. Almost half of the U.S. population will be on the Internet, compared to slightly over 20 percent at the end of 1997. Forrester Research predicts that business transacted over the Internet will explode from $43 billion in 1998 to $1.3 *trillion* in 2003. Retail dollars spent over the Internet will rise from about $8 billion in 1998 to $187 billion in 2004. Anyone who denies that the Internet is having a tremendous impact on our economy is simply not facing the reality of this unbelievable force, which is just beginning to make inroads into the global population. And if the Internet goes wireless, as it is starting to do, the speed with which it reaches the far corners of the earth will make our heads spin. This is not a bubble.

Still, we must keep in mind that some companies are overpriced and based on shaky business models. Many will fail. Many already have. There will be a tremendous shakeout over the next decade as we continue to define the Internet's role in our lives and as companies test various business models to find out what works. Some people compare the dawn of the Internet to the 1920s and 1930s, when the invention of the automobile led to a complete revamping of the way we move around in our world. At one point there were hundreds of car manufacturers. Most of them went out of business or merged with other firms. If you'd bought Ford or General Motors back then and held it for all these decades, you would have done very well. If you'd picked Packard or Studebaker, you wouldn't have been so lucky. On the other hand, if you'd sold your Studebaker stock somewhere along the line and bought IBM, you would have done better than if you'd held GM the whole time. The point is that you don't necessarily have to choose this era's ultimate winners today. Indeed, there will be lots of winners, and the winners will likely rotate. The goal is to be in the right stocks at the right time and to balance your quest for high investment returns with sensible risk-management strategies.

Parallel Universe: Internet Companies versus Non-Internet Companies

It is interesting to note that although the Internet promises to have a positive effect on virtually every business that takes advantage of it to reach more customers and process more transactions, the market seems to be dividing stocks into two groups: Internet companies and non-Internet companies. The Internet companies are those that have been formed for the express purpose of doing Internet-related business. The non-Internet companies are mostly those that existed before the Internet happened. Even though they may now be incorporating the Internet into their business processes, they don't hold the appeal of straight Internet businesses, because the mystique is missing. They are considered a known quantity. The Internet companies have much higher valuations because of the excitement and high expectations surrounding them, while the non-Internet companies, even though they may be based on a similar business model, are still valued the old-fashioned way. For example, Amazon.com and Barnes & Noble both sell books. Both use a business model based on the classic notion of buying wholesale and selling retail. This means their financial results depend on (1) how many books they sell, and (2) the difference between how much they pay for a book and how much they receive for a book, less the expenses of running the business. Using the same valuation ratios we looked at in Chapter 4, let's see how the market currently values Amazon.com versus Barnes & Noble (remember, lower numbers are better):

	Amazon.com	*Barnes & Noble*
Price/book ratio	61.50	1.72
Price/earnings ratio	n/a (no earnings)	11.31
Price/sales ratio	19.98	0.46
Price/earnings growth (PEG) ratio	n/a (no earnings)	0.23

Compared to the light and lively Amazon.com, Barnes & Noble's bricks and mortar have clearly dragged them down—from a valuation standpoint. That's why Barnes & Noble spun off its online division, which trades as a separate security. But guess what? It's also selling at much lower valuation levels than Amazon.com. It seems that any company that existed before 1995 has a built-in liability.

	Amazon.com	*BarnesandNoble.com*
Price/book ratio	82.50	3.19
Price/earnings ratio	n/a (no earnings)	n/a (no earnings)
Price/sales ratio	26.90	13.76
Price/earnings growth (PEG) ratio	n/a (no earnings)	n/a (no earnings)

Now granted, I am simplifying this explanation. But I'm doing it for a reason. When you strip away the hype, the two companies are not that different. Both sell books. Both use the Internet as a sales channel. Both are based upon the same business model of buying wholesale and selling retail. Do they really deserve such vastly different valuations? This is a rhetorical question, of course, and the answer is obviously yes. The marketplace is where such valuations are determined and the marketplace has spoken.

Let's look at a couple of other examples: Toys R Us and eToys. Both sell toys. Both are based upon the retail business model. Both use the Internet. The main difference is that Toys R Us has been around for awhile and has lots of toys on lots of shelves in lots of stores, whereas eToys was formed in response to the Internet and has toys, but no shelves and no stores.

	eToys	*Toys R Us*
Price/book ratio	9.47	0.99
Price/earnings ratio	n/a (no earnings)	10.13
Price/sales ratio	32.93	0.30
Price/earnings growth (PEG) ratio	n/a (no earnings)	0.74

And finally, let's look at two brokerage firms: Charles Schwab and Merrill Lynch. In this case, both have been around for awhile, but Schwab embraced the Internet early while Merrill Lynch only recently included it in its offerings. Here's how these two firms stack up:

	Charles Schwab	*Merrill Lynch*
Price/book ratio	15.25	2.61
Price/earnings ratio	61.10	15.97
Price/sales ratio	8.90	1.01
Price/earnings growth (PEG) ratio	1.00	0.28

No one can explain the extraordinarily high valuations being assigned to Internet companies these days. It's tempting to pass it off as a bubble, to the inexperience of novice investors who don't know any better, to the unbelievable media hype surrounding dot-com companies when they go public, to the stories of average Joes who are getting rich beyond their wildest dreams. It has to be more than that, though. The Internet is a very real phenomenon and it promises to have a bigger impact on business—perhaps even more than the telephone or computer. Why? Because it's changing the very nature of how companies do business. Although Amazon.com seems to epitomize the model of a successful Internet business today (if you count revenue growth, not earnings), it's really based on the standard retail business model. True, Amazon.com is using the Internet to improve upon the marketing and distribution systems of traditional retail operations, but other than selling from a virtual storefront, it's not that different from Barnes & Noble in its fundamental business proposition.

Looking Behind the Scenes for Investment Opportunities

What is even more exciting about the Internet's potential impact on business is what is going on behind the scenes. Most of us think of the

Internet as a collection of Web sites that we can call up at will to gather information, chat with friends, or buy things. But the Internet is much more than that. It's actually a *communications network* that we can't see from our desktop terminals but which has the capacity to transform our world in ways we can't even imagine yet. The companies that are exploring the potential uses of this network are the ones I'm excited about. They may be new companies formed for the purpose of creating a new Internet-based business model, or they may be existing companies that are daring to turn their backs on established methods and open themselves up to new possibilities. WalMart and Federal Express are good examples of traditional companies that have identified and positioned themselves to take advantage of the Internet and doing business.

So the next question is, who else is doing this? Aside from the Amazon.coms, the eBays, and the eToys, who are obviously incorporating the Internet into their business models, who else is either creating a whole new business or transforming an existing business to capitalize on the exponential growth that is possible through this vast communications network we call the Internet? Before I give a few examples, we as investors really need to understand the process one must go through to find companies that are doing exciting things. When you think about it, Benjamin Graham had it easy. All he had to do was look at a balance sheet to see if a company met his valuation criteria. But in a world that's as future-oriented as the one we're in today, we almost need a crystal ball to identify good companies to invest in. In Chapter 9, I will talk about some of the quantitative measures we can employ to take some of the guesswork out of stock evaluation. In the meantime, let's look at some of the more qualitative ways to identify today's up-and-comers.

First, do like Peter Lynch and keep your eyes and ears open for the next Hanes, the example he likes to give when his wife discovered L'Eggs. Keep in mind, however, that the next big thing will probably not appear on a rack in your local grocery store. The retail business model is maturing, so it won't be as easy to identify opportunities from our own shopping experiences. Instead, keep your eye on the business news, especially reports that talk about current and upcoming trends. Be aware of interesting things going on at work. Business-to-business activities are seen by many to be the next big thing in Internet opportunities, so watch what your own company is doing, especially the way it relates to customers and suppliers. Remember, it's the network that matters today—the interrelationships among all the people and entities that create products or services and bring them to market. Expansion of the network is a good thing, as is the quality and quantity of information passing through it. Be aware of how your company (and any other company you come into contact with) is building its network. Also be aware of the type of information flowing through it. Does the information come from many sources and is it integrated before it travels back out again so everyone can make intelligent use of the data? A business that operates with discrete departments that don't share information is old-world and out of date. But a business that unites all of its departments—and its customers' and suppliers' various departments—into a huge web with information zipping back and forth and all around is taking advantage of the latest communications technology to learn more about customers and their needs, suppliers and capabilities, and how to put everything together in a seamless, efficient, cost-effective, money-making model. What you're looking for, in essence, are companies participating in the new economy.

Trends That Suggest Tomorrow's Winners

Following are some current trends to help you identify investment opportunities. Please note that any specific companies mentioned here are for illustrative purposes only and are not meant to serve as stock recommendations. In this chapter, we are dealing with qualitative information only—business models, potential markets, and how companies are seizing new opportunities. The purpose of this section is to show how you might go about evaluating companies for possible inclusion in your portfolio. In Chapter 9, we'll look at some of the quantitative measures that can help you determine if a particular new-economy stock is priced fairly—now that we know none of them would pass Graham's intrinsic value screens. This approach is definitely a combination of qualitative and quantitative analysis in an effort to find promising companies without overpaying for them. In other words, try not to get so carried away by today's exciting stock opportunities that you fail to apply sensible valuation strategies as discussed in Chapter 9.

Trend 1: The Balance of Power Is Shifting toward the Customer

Blame it on competition, but reap the rewards. Anyone selling any-thing these days is forced to bend over backwards to please the cus-tomer or risk losing the business. That's why companies we buy from online remember our preferences and make it easy for us to find what we want. It's why in the near future vans will be circling our neighbor-hoods with groceries, books, CDs, and videos, bringing items we ordered just hours before up the steps and to our door. It's why we can even set the price for some of the things we buy. A company called NexTag pio-neered a novel approach where buyers say what they're willing to pay for a product and let competing merchants slug it out to see who will get the business. It makes its money by collecting a small percentage of each sale. Even without such services, you can obtain price compar-isons with just few clicks of the mouse and go directly to the merchant offering the best deals. Although consumers are clearly benefiting from this trend, in the business world the Internet is having an even greater impact on pricing. United Technologies, which used to spend months haggling individually with dozens of vendors for printed circuit boards, put one of its contracts out on FreeMarkets Online Inc., a Web market-place for industrial goods. Bids from 39 suppliers poured in—and the winners managed to slash $10 million off the initial $24 million estimate.

An up-and-coming business on the Web is that of information in-termediary, or *infomediary,* whose allegiance is with the buyer, not the seller, and whose function is to help the buyer get the best goods at the best price. Unlike the salesman of the past, whose success depended on how well he could schmooze and trick buyers into paying more with-out realizing it, infomediaries have put the customer in control by pro-viding product and pricing information from competing suppliers so the buyer has the upper hand. In the consumer market, Autoweb.com and other car-buying sites have completely reversed the dynamics of car buying and enabled consumers to avoid showroom haggling and go straight to the dealer offering the best price. In the business world info-mediaries are revolutionizing customer/supplier relationships and en-abling companies to save millions on supplies and raw goods. Three examples are National Transportation Exchange, which serves as a trucking spot market; GoFish, which lists the best prices for seafood for restaurants; and IMB Exchange, which provides an online marketplace for mortgage brokers to find loans.

Any business still setting firm prices and offering a take-it-or-leave-it proposition to the buyer is operating under the rules of the old economy. It will not survive in an era where buyers are used to calling the shots. To capitalize on this trend, invest in companies that put the customer in control, and that also use these new customer-dominated dynamics to reduce their own operating expenses. Customer control is a fundamental aspect of the new economy, so be sure it's present in any company you invest in.

Trend 2: E-business Outlays Will Boom

Any company that is not incorporating e-commerce into its business plan will soon be toast. That's why there's a mad scramble by businesses of all sizes to get up and running on the Internet and make the Web a meaningful sales channel. Due to the complex technology and the unique characteristics of Web-based sales, most companies are not able to do this themselves. Instead, they turn to companies like IBM, Oracle, BroadVision, and Hewlett-Packard, as well as myriad smaller companies that are set up to analyze a company's business and offer customized e-commerce solutions.

In Internet time, things happen at warp speed. In the past, a company might have spent months or even years contemplating a new business proposition. Once a decision was made to proceed, people would be hired and trained, policies would be drafted, and programs would be tested and perfected before the new proposition was fully implemented. Nobody has time for that today. First, it's become clear that e-commerce is not an option. Companies don't need to run focus groups or conduct market surveys to decide whether or not they should do business over the Web. It's a given that they must. Second, there's no time to hire the right people and train them. The move to e-commerce requires an extraordinary set of skills. It's faster, more efficient, and actually cheaper to find those skills among the many businesses already set up to move companies onto the Web.

Some companies outsource all Web-related activities, from initial Web design to hosting and ongoing maintenance. Others hire an outside firm to set up the Web site and then do ongoing maintenance in house.

Still others hire outside firms to do certain specific tasks, like handle
e-mail. And don't forget that once a sale is made over the Web, the order
must be filled and the goods delivered. Again, there are companies that
offer fulfillment services so a Web-based business does not need to hire
its own people and risk incurring high fixed expenses for a business that
may be seasonal. Delivery is not a problem either, with UPS, Federal
Express, and Airborne Express standing by with their fleets of planes
and trucks and their efficient sorting and tracking procedures already
in place.

As you can see, there is a whole host of companies that benefit
when businesses go online. You do not need to restrict your stock buying to the Amazon.coms and eToys of the world in order to capitalize
on e-commerce. In fact, take another look at the traditional retailers
who are moving onto the Web. It's unlikely that online shopping will
ever replace mall shopping, for the same reason catalog shopping never
replaced mall shopping. Shopping is still a touch-and-feel experience.
The key for retailers is integrating the Internet into their overall business plan so it complements store, catalog, and telephone sales, and gives
customers a real choice on how to interact with their company. Also
look at the many companies serving this market, from IBM and Oracle
to UPS, Federal Express, and the hundreds of smaller companies serving various market niches. Keep in mind that when automobile manufacturing was in its prime, there was money to be made in steel makers
and parts assemblers as well as the car companies themselves. The many
behind-the-scenes companies that serve the more visible e-commerce
businesses offer promising opportunities as well.

Trend 3: Net Connections Will Get Faster

The World Wide Wait will someday come to an end as Internet infrastructure companies work to quench our thirst for bandwidth. This is
a hot industry right now, with Cisco Systems leading the pack and companies like Juniper Networks, Foundry Networks, Broadcom, and
many others doing a ton of business building and enhancing the basic
infrastructure over which data travels. Some analysts believe this trend
will continue for awhile because in our data-hungry culture, bandwidth
is an addiction. The faster data travels, the more data we want to download (think fancy graphics, even motion pictures). As long as we insist

upon more data and faster downloads, these infrastructure companies will have plenty to do. Some analysts call this a multiyear, durable cycle of which we are still on the front end.

"There are the glamour companies, and then there are the companies that are building the new Net economy," says Edward J. Zander, president of Sun Microsystems, Inc. "We're the lumberyard of the Internet." A few years ago the Internet was a geeky communications link between scientists and universities. Now, it's on its way to becoming the world's central nervous system, and the companies building the underpinnings—the wiring, routers, switches, computers, software, and other gear—are cleaning up. And construction work appears to be far from over. U.S. companies are expected to triple spending on Internet equipment, to $203 billion, by 2002. Some believe we're only a third of the way along the road to building the Internet infrastructure.

Corporate data networking equipment purchased by big corporations is the biggest chunk of the Internet infrastructure business right now, but small and midsize businesses offer a significant market opportunity as well. In addition to Cisco Systems, companies like 3Com, Nortel Networks, Intel, and Alcatel are also cashing in on the demand for networking equipment. The next big thing in Internet infrastructure may be a convergence with telephone networks. Right now, voice travels over phone lines, which is more reliable but more expensive, while data travels over the Internet, which is less expensive but less reliable. It is believed that we are moving toward the best of both worlds and that the Internet will soon offer the reliability of the telephone network with the low cost of the Internet network. In 1999, Cisco Systems bought Cerent Corp., a telecom equipment maker, at what some thought was an outrageous price ($6.9 billion) in anticipation of this expected convergence of voice and data networks. As this trend continues, look for telecommunications companies like Lucent, Alcatel, Siemens, and Fujitsu to benefit.

Trend 4: The World Will Go Wireless

Even as Internet infrastructure companies are adding pipe and routers on the ground, wireless technologies are getting better at sending data through the air. Wireless communications technology and the Internet have been developing side-by-side for several years. Now, many

experts say the two will converge and the growth will be explosive.
Until recently, there were three problems with sending data (as opposed
to voice) using wireless technologies: (1) a lack of standards, (2) fragmented networks, and (3) a lack of applications. These problems have
been solved paving the way, as it were, for wireless connections to the
Internet. The three largest handset makers, Nokia, Ericsson, and Motorola, have already started putting microbrowsers in their digital phones.
The two major wireless carriers, AirTouch (a unit of Britain's Vodafone
AirTouch PLC) and Sprint PCS, link mobile subscribers to Internet
services through phones that function either as standalone devices or as
modems for laptops and hand-held computers. Web portal Yahoo! is
working on a product that will integrate a user's e-mail, online calen-
dar, and address book with other content available from Yahoo!'s site,
such as weather and horoscopes, and allow Sprint PCS customers to access them on mobile phones.

Along with new applications and new phones, the digital networks
themselves will speed up. The companies behind all three types of digital networks in the United States, GSM (global system for mobile
communications), CDMA (code-division multiple access) and TDMA
(time-division multiple access), will start upgrading the speed of data
services to between 100,000 and 170,000 bits per second. That's about
two to three times faster than the speediest conventional telephone
modem connection. Meanwhile, equipment makers are busy producing
hardware for local-area networks, or LANS, to enable computers that
are part of an in-house network to communicate without cables. Manufacturers of both communications and computer equipment have ral-
lied behind a new wireless standard that could create even smaller
networks. Called Bluetooth, the technology would permit high-speed
communication among devices within any 10-meter area, basically en-
abling a person's various devices—wireless phone, pager, Palm Pilot,
and computer—to talk to each other without wires.

In contrast to these very localized personal-area networks, are satellites circling the globe. It's been estimated that complex satellite systems soon will provide data links at speeds as high as 50 million bits
per second. And once these high-speed networks are deployed, the sky
is truly the limit for the kinds of applications that can be developed.
Among the possibilities: mobile videophones, videoconferencing, and
mobile video surveillance of homes and offices for security purposes.

But for many people—those who live too far away from urban centers to connect to high-speed phone or cable lines—wireless technology will serve as their only link to the Internet. Companies currently spending billions to get satellites ready for launch in 2003 or 2004 include Sky-Bridge, which is backed by France's Alcatel, and Teledesic, which is backed by Craig McCaw, Bill Gates, Boeing, and Motorola.

Trend 5: Software Will Move to the Web

Now that we've all become accustomed to buying shrink-wrapped software and installing it on our own computers, there is a trend toward "renting" software over the Web. The software resides at a remote location—on the server of an application service provider, or ASP—and travels over the Internet whenever we need to use it. An example of this already in existence is Microsoft's Hotmail. You go to a Web page, where you enter a password to access your account. Then you can compose a message, send it, and review your incoming messages, just as if you were using a standard e-mail program, except you're typing everything into a Web page. The server that holds the Web page does all the heavy lifting—storing your files and accessing them—so you don't need a very powerful computer to perform these functions. In this way, the Internet is essentially transforming software from a product to a service. If the idea catches on, we won't need to worry about upgrading our computer systems with more memory or faster processors because all the heavy processing work will be done by a megaserver located far, far away. All we'll need is an inexpensive appliance that enables us to hook into this rich source of data and functionality.

This idea has tremendous applications for the corporate world. No longer will companies need to keep large IT (information technology) departments in house. Instead, an ASP, which may range from GTE to a small startup company, will make sophisticated software as readily available as flipping on a light switch. With no need for heavy technology investments, the speed with which businesses may be started is truly mind-boggling. *The Wall Street Journal* told the story of LoanCity.com, an online mortgage company in San Jose, California, that set up shop in August 1999. The company, which arranges residential mortgages via its Web site, was starting out with zero revenue. But its plans were ambitious: to serve more than a million customers in a few years. Any online operation of that scale would require a sprawling computing center costing millions of dollars in hardware and software licenses, as well as a staff of as many as 20 engineers. Instead, LoanCity.com outsourced all of its technology functions by hiring an ASP to set up and run the various enterprise resource planning software packages that the company would need to handle in such areas as sales, accounting, and human resources. Jim Dybalski, chief technology officer for LoanCity. com, said, "I had six months to go from a mom-and-pop start-up to a world-class system. I don't think I could have done that myself."

Once this trend takes hold, shrink-wrapped software will become a thing of the past. Instead, we will see a new model of subscription software and services where new functionality and bug fixes are added continuously, not every six months. It makes computing more of a utility, like the telephone, where the technology behind the system is not visible to the user. According to Forrester Research, the market for such services could total $6.4 billion by 2001, up from less than $100 million last year. Frontrunners in this field are USinternetworking Inc. and Breakaway Solutions, Inc.; other companies include Exodus Communications, Citrix Systems, Futurelink Distribution Corp., and TeleComputing Inc. Software giants Oracle and Microsoft are getting into the field, too, as well as Sun Microsystems, the network software evangelist.

Trend 6: The Internet Is Saving Companies Billions

You wouldn't know it from all the dot-com hype, but companies in all industries are using the Internet to save billions of dollars almost behind the scenes. How? By turning to the Internet and using in-house computer networks to handle everything from customer inquiries to employee expense reports. According to Giga Information Group, companies save much more in internal and business-to-business e-commerce than in online retailing to individual consumers, which is five times smaller in volume. By 2002, it is expected that e-commerce savings from corporations around the world will total $1.25 trillion. Cisco Systems likes to serve as an example of a business that uses the Internet to streamline its business processes; nearly every facet of its operations, from manufacturing to inventory and finances, is electronic. Cisco Systems estimates it saves $500 million annually this way; it saved $8 million just by recruiting and accepting job applications online.

Another "manufacturer" that discovered how to use the Internet to save money is Dell Computer Corporation. Dell encourages computer buyers to design their own computer configurations online. It then puts those configurations together (or arranges to have them put together) and ships them to customers. Dell's ultrafast build-to-order approach allows the company to put a customer's money in the bank before it pays for parts and labor, generating a 160 percent return on invested capital.

The Internet is allowing even the lowest of tech companies to forge direct links between customers and factories, so that buyers—now mainly corporate customers—can tailor products the way they want them. It used to be that any company that made products saw itself as the center of a nucleus around which suppliers, distributors, and customers revolved. Now the customer is in the center directing everyone around him. The company and all of its suppliers and distributors must perform a carefully choreographed dance to produce what the customer wants and, even more important, deliver it on time and at the right price. The Internet actually enables custom manufacturing to be cheaper than mass production because of all the links it provides among suppliers, distributors, and customers. And by jobbing out many (or all) of the manufacturing operations to contractors, a company can save the investment in plant, equipment, and inventory and achieve a better return on invested capital.

In an effort to bring old-economy companies into the new-economy marketplace, Michael Dell of Dell Computer is even giving lessons to car manufacturers in Detroit. Today it takes weeks to get a customized car, because assembly lines are geared to turning out standard cars. Dell is teaching automobile companies how to develop links among manufacturers, suppliers, and dealers in order to scale more quickly, give customers what they want, and get things off their balance sheets that aren't their specialty. He's essentially showing them how to fill orders in Internet time by revamping—or even tossing out—the mass-production model developed by Detroit at the height of the industrial revolution. Both Ford and General Motors are saving billions by replacing an elaborate network of personal contacts and triplicate forms with a global electronic forum where deals can be done almost instantly. It is estimated that at a minimum, replacing some of their purchasing bureaucracy with online links will allow the auto makers to reduce the roughly $100 it now costs to process each of the hundreds of thousands of purchase orders they issue each year.

And the rest of the industrial world is sure to follow. GM spends about $87 billion a year, working with about 30,000 suppliers. Ford's purchases are only slightly smaller. (Only the U.S. government is a bigger buyer, industry executives say.) By dragging their vast networks of suppliers online, the auto makers will be plugging in a big chunk of the nation's economy. That could help catapult e-commerce to at least $1 trillion annually in just two or three years, says market researcher Dataquest. GM estimates that its company's site alone could be handling sales of as much as $500 billion within a few years—a staggering figure when you're talking about sales, not stock market valuations.

The most important thing to keep in mind about these or any other trends is that the investment opportunities are not always immediate or apparent. Some trends are just beginning to take shape. This means companies are still finding their way and jockeying for position. For example, the trend toward putting software on the Web is exciting and inexorable, but there are a lot of bugs that have to be worked out before it becomes fully established with winners and losers clearly defined. Within each trend are high-risk and low-risk companies you can invest in. For example, Juniper Networks is a small, nimble company with an infrastructure technology that some say surpasses that of Cisco Systems; but due to Cisco System's size and leadership position you'd have to consider it the less risky investment.

The main point of this chapter is to bring to light the impact of technology on our economy and to identify some—but certainly not all—of the trends that point to promising investment opportunities. At this pivotal point in our world, timing is everything. While there are tremendous opportunities at hand, there are also many risks; it is therefore essential to tread cautiously and not be afraid to pause and wait for clarity before subjecting our investing dollars to undue risk. You may not get in on the ground floor, but the third floor of an investment that is building toward towering proportions isn't bad.

9

The Ultimate Challenge: Valuing Technology Stocks

Just because the Internet has such vast potential doesn't mean all Internet stocks are great buys. As we get further along in this Internet boom, investors will become more discerning in their choice of Internet companies. Rather than jumping on every dot-com stock that comes along, investors will take a closer look at each company's business model and do a more realistic appraisal of its earnings outlook. This is difficult to do right now because nobody really knows what the long-term, money-making potential of the Internet is. So in the absence of clues suggesting who the eventual winners might turn out to be, the market is currently treating nearly all of them as potential winners. It's also overestimating the success of certain winners, assigning valuations no company could ever grow into during one person's lifetime. If a shakeout hasn't already occurred by the time you read this, you can count on one happening. Its timing and severity are impossible to predict, but like all market shakeouts, it promises to be painful for the people it touches. It will, however, provide valuable lessons for the future. The main lesson will be the folly of turning stocks into gambling vehicles and paying any amount of money for a company with questionable fundamentals.

We've been here before. In the early 1990s, biotechnology stocks were all the rage. They promised amazing medical breakthroughs and justified their lack of earnings by the need for extensive drug research. When earnings didn't materialize soon enough, the sector crashed. Only in the past few years has it begun to revive as biotech drugs have been approved for sale. A similar fate befell the technology sector in 1983.

Investors were right in seeing that the industry held great promise. They were just too early. Tech stocks crumbled and took years to recover. There were similar manias in jet-airliner stocks in the 1960s and in color-TV stocks in the 1950s. Any idea that's new and exciting has the potential to cause investors to get carried away. But people are seldom twice-burned. That's why older market participants, who have never forgotten the pain of losing money during one of the market's previous corrections, worry when they see dewy-faced kids driving up prices on Internet stocks. One of these days, when reason takes over and investors get tired of waiting for earnings promises to materialize, these over-priced stocks will fall. And then investors will see that momentum works on the downside, too.

This is not to say there isn't more money to be made in some of today's high-priced stocks. As we've been discussing, the rules of the game are changing due to this new economic order that is taking over business today. Who knows how much higher stocks can go before investors demand to see profits? Maybe they'll go a lot higher. Maybe everyone will soon be reciting the essence of this letter that appeared in the August 1999 issue of *Money* magazine:

> When a paradigm shift occurs in a field like technology, (a) never listen to anyone over 30; (b) never listen to anyone who says, "I have seen this before," (see a); and (c) disregard all blather concerning price/earnings ratios, price/book ratios, capitalization rates, etc. Apply due diligence, then go with your gut.

The letter writer then goes on to complain about value-oriented brokers who talked him out of following his intuition and caused him to see "meager growth of my equities." This under-30 person could very well represent the technology investor of the future. Like George Soros, he relies more on instinct than established guidelines. He formulates a theory and then tests it in the market. If he's right, he makes a bundle. If he's wrong, well, let's hope he didn't bet too much. Every investment opportunity is different because the market is constantly changing. The trick is to jump in and out of the right stocks at the right time. Although this brand of intuitive investing is derided by Wall Street professionals, it's not unlike the way companies run their businesses today: quick and nimble wins out over staid and unchanging. Therefore, I do not entirely discount this approach and would never say you're destined to lose money if you follow it. However, it is difficult to perform successfully on a consistent basis and requires a tremendous amount of time and energy. It also involves a high degree of risk. The whole point of this book is to show you how to take advantage of opportunities in high-growth sectors without exposing your money to excessive risk. That means paying attention to valuations.

Changing Ideas of Value

In researching different theories on how to value Net stocks, the same three words kept popping up time and time again: Nobody really knows. It seems every analyst and portfolio manager involved in Internet stocks has some sort of formula to determine whether or not a stock is overvalued. But virtually all admit that their formula is only slightly better than an educated guess. By combining certain known metrics—annual sales or number of customers, for example—with certain assumptions, such as the cost to acquire a customer, an analyst can eventually arrive at some sort of earnings estimate. But if the assumptions are off by even a small amount, the estimate can be wildly inaccurate. Analysts and portfolio managers would have a hard time explaining an intuitive style of investing to their bosses, but that's what many of them are employing anyway; they just create fancy formulas to justify what their gut is telling them to do. As one analyst put it, "You can ignore what is driving the stocks and opt out of the game. Or you can ignore valuation and stay in the game." That's pretty much what it boils down to.

One analyst who makes no pretense about not trying to apply standard valuation measures to a sector that refuses to accept them is Lise Buyer, an Internet analyst with CS First Boston. Having come from T. Rowe Price, where she was trained in traditional value methodologies that made use of price/earnings ratios and other such earnings-based methods, she found it impossible to apply the same standards to Internet stocks. Searching for a resolution to this dilemma, she went back to the source of intrinsic value, Benjamin Graham. She reread the book Graham wrote with his partner David Dodd, *Security Analysis* (as mentioned in Chapter 5), and found her answer in this quote:

Unseasoned companies in new fields of activity . . . provide no sound basis for the determination of intrinsic value. . . . Analysts serve their discipline best by identifying such companies as highly speculative and not attempting to value them. . . . The buyer of such securities is not making an investment, but a bet on a new technology, a new market, a new service. . . . Winning bets on such situations can produce very rich rewards, but they are in an odds-setting rather than a valuation process.

This passage essentially gives the reader permission to ignore the rest of the book when it comes to evaluating new and different kinds of stocks—as long as the reader understands that he's speculating. Ms. Buyer covers 13 Internet companies and in June 1999 had a buy rating on 11 of them. Yet she concedes, "I still can't make the math correlate with the stock prices." With the Graham and Dodd quote hanging on her wall, she has gathered the courage to abandon her valuation bias and recommend stocks that appear attractive despite their high prices. She applies the following four tests when evaluating an Internet company:

1. Does someone need what they are doing?
2. Do they have a sustainable advantage?
3. Is there a business model that will lead to profitability?
4. Is the management good?

When asked about the valuation of any particular company she says, "It is what it is."

The new paradigm style of investing has been explored by academia as well. "If the stock market provides a forecast of future events, then the recent dramatic upswing represents a rosy estimate about growth in future profits for the economy," wrote Jeremy Greenwood and Boyan Jovanovic, economics professors at the University of Rochester and New York University respectively, in a paper published in mid-1999. The professors tracked the market value of thousands of companies over a 30-year period beginning in 1968. They classified companies into two groups: (1) companies listed on the New York or American stock exchange as of 1968 (called the 1968 incumbents), and (2) smaller companies trading in the over-the-counter market (there was no Nasdaq Stock Market at that time) plus companies that went public after 1968. What they found was that the incumbents' market value fell from 80 percent of gross domestic product then to about 46 percent in 1996, as some companies went out of business and others declined. Meanwhile, the value of the younger group rose from 34 percent to 85 percent of GDP. The authors see this as evidence of another revolution equal to the rise of electricity and the internal combustion engine and note that young companies are "unencumbered by the ignorance, outdated capital and vested interests of their older brethren."

Two professors from the Massachusetts Institute of Technology determined that the stock market recognizes the benefits of information technology investment that don't show up in earnings statements. Erik Brynjolfsson and Shinkyu Yang looked at 1,000 companies' financial statements from 1987 and 1994 and concluded that the market values a dollar invested in information technology ten times higher than a dollar invested in conventional capital. What the market is saying is that technology investments are far more valuable in terms of their effects on productivity and long-term earnings growth than investments in tangible assets. They illustrate this by comparing Wal-Mart to Sears, indicating that Wal-Mart has invented a whole cluster of innovations that enables it to sell products more cheaply and efficiently and get them to customers more effectively. Even if Sears installed Wal-Mart's technology, it couldn't replicate all the systems and processes Wal-Mart has developed around that technology. That's why the market values Wal-Mart much more highly than Sears: "It's not because they own a whole bunch of valuable land in Arkansas. It's obviously the intangibles."

What these professors are saying is that the market is creating its own measures of value. It is ignoring certain aspects of corporate financial statements—like tangible assets that the market doesn't believe contribute to future earnings growth—and placing a very high value on other aspects—like intangible assets and certain kinds of spending. If investors are ignoring P/E ratios today, it may be because they don't trust the *E*—or many of the other accounting conventions that were developed when the world was different. Let's fire all the accountants and analysts, the market is suggesting, and make up our own ideas about what constitutes financial success. For one thing, the market seems to be realizing that when it comes to the Internet, heavy spending up front can pay huge dividends later on. Once software is written, databases are established, and brand identity is formed, it doesn't cost very much to acquire each additional customer. A tremendous amount must be spent to get the first customer, but after that spending is minimal. While this scalability is a significant part of the Internet's potential, it also presents the biggest risk. Many companies will spend enormous up-front sums and still fail. That's why risk-averse investors will wait for market leaders to emerge before investing in new companies.

Initial Public Offerings

The riskiest of all investments today are initial public offerings, or IPOs. Luckily for the investing public, it's very difficult to buy stock in the initial offering because only a limited number of shares are available and they are usually reserved for a brokerage firm's best clients. In fact, it's been said that the blatant exclusion of individual investors from the IPO process suggests that IPO should stand for initial *private* offering. It's just as well. The dynamics surrounding IPOs today make them treacherous for all but the most intrepid investors.

First, let's quickly review the process. Companies starting up today usually obtain private capital to get going, drawing from the entrepreneur's savings account or funds from friends, family, or so-called angels. At some point the company may take a more formalized approach and seek funds from venture capitalists. These are private investors who are in the business of providing capital to young companies they believe have the potential to provide a high, fast return on investment. As soon as the company can show several quarters of revenue growth, it contacts an investment banking firm to study the company's finances and prospects to determine how many shares it can expect to sell to the public and at what price. Over a period of several months, the company gets its financial statements in order and prepares an *offering memorandum* that tells investors everything they need to know about investing in the company, especially the risk factors as required by the Securities and Exchange Commission. About a month before the big day, the investment banking firm starts lining up buyers for the stock, often in conjunction with other securities firms. The bulk of the shares are allocated to institutional investors such as mutual funds, but participating brokerage firms also distribute shares for brokers to dole out to their best clients.

On the day the stock goes public, dollars and shares exchange hands. The company receives the net proceeds from the offering, less the investment banker's commission and other expenses associated with the offering, and a bunch of lucky (?) investors get stock at its initial public offering price. What does the company do with all this money? The offering memorandum spells out the use of the proceeds, which may include paying down debt, spending money on expansion activities, and/or cashing out the owners or venture capitalists. After the company gets its proceeds from the offering, it is not affected by subsequent trading in the stock—at least not right away. But it is in a company's best interests for its stock to go up in aftermarket trading because at some point—months or years hence—it will probably want to issue more shares, and the higher the stock price is at that time, the more money the company will get for its shares. This is why companies, venture capitalists, and investment bankers have an interest in preserving the mystique of the IPO process and in keeping shares in short supply. Despite the new rules for the new economy, the classic law of supply and demand is still alive and well and operating confidently in this arena.

One of the most dramatic IPO examples was VA Linux, which went public in December 1999 at an offering price of $30. Its first trade in the aftermarket was at a price of $299. By the time it closed that first day the price was down to $239, and four days later it was at $173.88. If you had listened to all the hype surrounding this IPO, you would have thought it was easy money. Simply buy it on the offering at $30 and sell it at the opening trade of $299. But unless you were a big institution or tight with a broker who had available stock, you would not have been able to get shares at the offering price. And if you'd entered a market order to buy the stock when it first began trading, you'd have paid $299 for a stock that was trading at $206.63 on December 31, 1999. Yes, trading in new issues can be very, very volatile. Enter at your own risk.

And then there is the lockup—literally. You'll want to keep that in mind when considering IPOs. It is becoming more common today for companies to grant stock options to their employees. This allows companies to keep wages relatively low yet still reward employees who contribute to the company's progress. But until a company goes public and the stock price climbs, these stock options are essentially worthless. It is every pre-IPO employee's dream to see the stock go public so he or she can cash in those shares and reap hundreds of thousands, even millions of dollars. But to prevent employees from dumping all their shares as soon as the stock goes public, there is usually a lockup period lasting anywhere from three months to a year during which company insiders are prohibited from selling their shares. But once the lockup period ends, look out. And it's not just the insiders who are selling when the lockup period ends. Many other investors sell in anticipation of this sell-off, compounding the decline. Let this be a caution to anyone considering buying stock in a company that's been public less than a year.

Other Risks of Internet Stocks

One of the most dangerous aspects of investing in Internet stocks is that the ground is constantly shifting. IPOs will be hot one month and cold the next. Internet portals will be all the rage for a while, and then the interest will suddenly shift to something else. If you're a momentum investor and very quick with the mouse, you can spot these twists and turns and react in time to avoid large losses. But if you're more of a buy-and-hold type investor (saving taxes and trading costs while preserving your sanity), your best bet is to avoid anything with the word *hot* associated with it because in this market nothing stays hot for long. Better to go with warm.

In the early days of the Internet, before e-commerce was viable or even practical, many companies saw advertising as a natural way to generate revenue. But as Web site visitors have learned to ignore banner ads, response rates have dropped suggesting that advertising may not be a reliable source of revenue on a long-term basis. Salon.com was one of the first Internet IPO casualties to be subjected to changing investor attitudes. It went public in June 1999 with nothing more than an online magazine and an idea to attract e-commerce partners. Nothing unusual about that; many other companies whose revenues depended on advertising or partnerships had completed successful public offerings during the first half of 1999. But right about the time Salon.com went public at $10.50, the market changed its mind about what it wanted in an Internet company. Salon.com closed its first day of trading at $10, and as of December 31, 1999 was trading at $5.

The problem with hot stocks is that the investors who follow them need a constant flow of exciting news to hold their interest. Once a company settles into the normal day-to-day activities of running the business, it loses its appeal. The momentum investors bail out and the long-term investors start looking for the usual attributes like higher revenues and even—gasp!—earnings. In the second half of 1999, the market started shifting its interest from consumer issues like America Online and Amazon.com to infrastructure companies like Cisco Systems and Sun Microsystems. Although there are a lot of good reasons why business-to-business infrastructure companies are a more sustainable investment, mainly because they're already showing profits and have a lot of work left to do to build the underpinnings of the Internet, there's no telling how long their reign will last or what will ultimately replace them as the Internet darlings of Wall Street.

Different Ways of Defining Value

Turn on today's news and you'll hear all about the stocks that captured investors' attention and dollars on Wall Street today. Turn on tomorrow's news and you'll hear about a different set of stocks. Next week, next month, next year, all kinds of different stocks will be making headlines. Hype attracts viewers and sparks short-term interest in the stocks being hyped, but for a sustainable investment that will serve you in the absence of media attention, you need a solid company with a viable business proposition that will continue to prosper whether or not it ever appears in the news again. And you'll want to avoid paying too much for it. This requires considerably more due diligence than just going with your gut. If you are disinclined to do your own stock analysis, just say so and invest in one of the many mutual funds devoted to technology or Internet stocks. But if you want to invest in individual companies, and you want to buy good long-term investments at reasonable prices, consider some of the current valuation strategies being employed by some of the experts in the field.

The purpose of these valuation strategies is primarily to avoid overpaying for a stock. Once you've found an interesting company with promising potential, you'll want to make sure it's not too expensive relative to its peers. When the Internet shakeout does occur, investors will be taking a closer look at each company in order to decide if it warrants its current market value. There will be a flight to quality and the buy-anything-with-a-dot-com-in-it-no-matter-what-it-costs mentality will come back to bite investors who fail to consider valuations. But if you invest in good, long-term companies and pay reasonable prices for them, you'll have little to fear from a stock market shakeout, providing you are prepared to weather the volatility and perhaps even buy more on dips. Do keep in mind, however, that valuation theories will change as the Internet sand continues to shift. So be open to new information and pay attention to the various theories coming out of Wall Street as analysts work to define this sector that presently seems to defy analysis.

One common theme among the various valuation theories is the idea of relativity, or comparing one stock to another within the same group. It doesn't do any good to compare an Internet stock with a steel stock because from a valuation standpoint the steel stock will win every time. It will have positive earnings, a low price/earnings ratio, and maybe even some earnings growth. The Internet stock will have no earnings and therefore no P/E ratio and no earnings growth. But if you compare two Internet companies, especially two companies within the same subsector, you can see which of the two is priced lower based on whatever metrics you're applying. Now let's look at some of the metrics Wall Street analysts are using to value Internet stocks.

Internet-Specific Metrics

Internet analyst Steve Harmon realized several years ago that traditional valuation methods wouldn't work for Internet stocks. So he invented new metrics, like dividing the market value of an Internet company by the number of times its Web site is visited in a month. Some people call this *monetizing eyeballs.* Other ratios he developed include: market cap divided by users; revenues divided by subscribers; market cap divided by ad views; and market cap divided by potential market share. What does he do with these rather odd ratios? He uses them to compare similar companies with each other to see which is the more undervalued stock. He compared Yahoo! with CNET when Yahoo! was deemed overpriced by practically everyone and determined that Yahoo! was actually an undervalued stock—relatively speaking, of course. Forrester Research <www.forrester.com> provides statistics relevant to the Internet sector, as does The Internet Analyst, which is part of Multex Research <www.multex.com>. You can also dig up some of these obscure numbers in a company's 10-K. Just remember that any analysis of this type is only relevant when it's done on a comparative basis; otherwise you end up with a bunch of numbers that have no meaning.

Revenue Growth

The problem with counting eyeballs is that it doesn't necessarily follow that Web site hits or potential market share will turn into actual revenues. While it's true that a company doesn't necessarily need to show profits due to the high costs of establishing an Internet-related business, revenues do need to be there. And the faster revenues are growing from one quarter to the next, the more likely the company is to establish a toehold in its line of business and eventually become profitable. This presumes, of course, that the company isn't digging itself into a hole and that it has a viable plan for producing positive earnings at some point in the future. In the meantime, before earnings arrive, revenue growth shows that there is a clear and growing market for the company's products and that business is thriving. In the old economy, revenue growth of 15 percent to 20 percent was considered pretty good. In the Internet age that's a snail's pace, as investors look for 50 percent or even a doubling or tripling of revenues year over year.

Price-to-Sales Ratio

Sales and revenue growth are only part of the equation. To find out if a stock is reasonably valued based on those revenues, some analysts divide the stock's market capitalization by annual sales (P/S), as discussed in Chapter 4. This is actually a very popular ratio today and has replaced the standard P/E ratio, especially for young companies, even if they have earnings. Sales are seen as a purer reflection of the company's progress, especially if it's already been determined how and when earnings are expected to materialize. Young, fast-growing companies usually deserve a higher price/sales ratio than more mature companies. Most companies that are ramping up fast in the early years are unable to sustain those astronomical growth rates for very long. So as a company matures, its P/S ratio should decline. When comparing P/S ratios of two similar companies, consider the ages of the two companies and the revenue growth rates; allow the younger, faster-growing company a higher ratio.

Discounted Cash Flow

Many analysts go back to the fundamental definition of an investment and consider that any investment is worth the present value of
future cash flows. Estimating future cash flows is the tricky part, of
course, which is why most value investors won't touch technology
stocks. Still, analysts can get an idea of future cash flows by looking at
revenue growth, customer growth, and other metrics suggesting a company's future cash flow. To provide wiggle room, analysts will often
assign a higher discount rate to high-risk Internet stocks than they use
for non-Internet stocks.

Gross Margins

Gross margin is the portion of each dollar of revenue that remains
after subtracting production costs. It does not include advertising costs.
The larger the gross margin, the more money a company has to work
with to strengthen its brand. Newly public companies often use offering proceeds to flood the airwaves and newspapers with ads in an attempt to become household names. But if public financing begins to
fizzle out (i.e., IPOs are no longer greeted with the hoopla they've had
over the past couple of years) companies will have to finance their advertising out of operations. Some analysts say that a company needs
gross margins of at least 40 percent or 50 percent if it is to survive.
Companies in competitive market segments with high marketing costs
generally have much smaller margins than that, which suggests their
future viability may be in question.

Variations on the Price/Earnings Ratio

With the P/E ratio having served investors well for so many years,
it's hard for some people to give it up. After all, it's the quickest way to
assess the price of a company relative to its earnings and lets you see at
a glance how expensive a stock is in relation to another. To apply the
same principle to Internet companies which have no earnings, analysts
estimate future earnings through a variety of methods and then divide
that number into the price.

Theoretical Earnings Multiple Analysis

Analyst Shaun G. Andrikopoulos, who follows Internet stocks for BT Alex. Brown, has come up with what he calls theoretical earnings multiple analysis, or TEMA. This measure projects future earnings by estimating revenue growth and the operating margins that the company would hope to achieve when it has matured. He then divides the stock price by this estimate of future earnings. He still comes up with awfully high P/E ratios, but believes that when you factor in the growth rate, those ratios are justified. He recommended Yahoo! when its P/E ratio, as determined by this method, was 124.

Practical P/E Ratio

Chip Morris, who runs the T. Rowe Price Science & Technology Fund, calculates what he calls a practical price-to-earnings ratio. This essentially converts a company's future promises into current prof- itability. He takes the ratio of price to projected sales (i.e., four times current-quarter sales) and divides it by his best guess of the company's prospective net margin when it gets around to making a profit. For ex- ample, Amazon.com trades at 21 times sales and could someday, maybe, have a sustainable margin of 7 percent. So its prospective P/E is 21 divided by 0.07, or 300—too rich for Mr. Morris. He says he might buy a Net company with a practical P/E of 150.

Working Backwards

The standard valuation strategy is to look at a company's revenues and earnings in relation to its price and decide if the stock is fairly val- ued. Then a decision can be made as to whether or not to invest. In this topsy-turvy Internet world, some analysts are taking the opposite ap- proach. They look at what a stock is selling for and determine what the company needs to do to grow into that valuation. For example, Rose- wood Capital, a San Francisco venture-capital fund specializing in In- ternet brands, selected eight e-commerce companies at random and calculated how much annual revenue was needed above and beyond their average annual operating costs to break even. The results were rather frightening. It determined that Garden.com, with estimated 1999 revenues of $14 million and margins of just 16 percent, would need to grow its revenues by 1,507 percent by 2002 in order to break even. Homestore.com, on the other hand, appeared to be in pretty good shape. This national real estate listing site has extremely high gross margins of 64 percent because it has locked up exclusive relationships with the largest real estate and homebuilders associations, which encourage their agents to use the site, saving the company marketing costs. Estimates show that Homestore.com needs revenues of $235 million by 2002 to make a 5 percent operating profit; the company is on track to produce revenues of $275 million by then. Whether you want to dig through a company's 10-K and do these calculations yourself or not, the main idea here is to gain some understanding of what a company needs to do to grow into its valuation. Some stocks today are priced so high that it would take an unbelievable feat for the company ever to meet investor expectations. Those are the stocks to avoid.

Economic Value Added

Economic value added (EVA) is a concept developed by Stern Stewart & Co., a management consulting firm. The idea behind EVA is that in the long run, it's not accounting profits—taking in one more dollar than you put out—but economic profits that matter. And simply put, a company earns an economic profit only if it has earned more than its cost of capital, which is not found on an income statement. The idea here is that the market value, or capitalization—the stock price times the number of shares—has two components. One, the current operations value (COV) is a measure of the worth of the company as it now operates. The second, future growth value (FGV), measures the company's expected growth. Once you determine the COV—and that's the easier of the two—you can figure out the implied future growth value. And once you know that, you can determine the implied revenue growth rate. Then you can make a judgment as to whether that growth rate is achievable. For example, EVA calculations showed that Amazon.com needed to reach sales of $63 billion in 10 years in order to justify its stock price. Can it do it? Who knows? This is where common sense and individual judgment come into play. Calculation of EVA is not something you'll want to do yourself. In fact, many of these calculations are better left to analysts. See Chapter 6 for information on where to find analyst reports.

Valuing Non-Internet Growth Stocks

One way to take advantage of the Internet revolution without assuming the tremendous risk associated with untested business models is to avoid the "pure play" Internet stocks and invest in more mature companies that are recharging themselves for the twenty-first century by incorporating the Internet into their business processes. Eventually, there may not be any Internet companies—*all* companies will be Internet companies because they'll all use the Internet just as they use electricity and telephones now. But some companies, more forward-thinking than others, are quickly taking advantage of opportunities to accelerate revenue and earnings growth in the years ahead. The nice thing about valuing more mature companies is that you don't need to rely on crazy metrics like eyeballs or make wild assumptions (guesses) about future events that no mortal could possibly foresee. You can deal with the here and now—plus some ideas about a company's future growth prospects, of course—and even rely on our old friend, the price/earnings ratio, to determine a stock's relative value. The growth comes in two ways: (1) through actual earnings increases, and (2) what analysts call multiple expansion or a higher P/E being granted to companies showing especially rapid earnings growth or very high-quality earnings. The market tends to be pretty efficient—that is, it already assigns high values to high-growth companies. So the key to making money in growth stocks is to find the little gems the market hasn't discovered yet. These are stocks that don't show up on the high growth screens because their best growth is yet to come, perhaps through the launch of an exciting new product or a technology that enables them to reach more markets.

During inflationary times, companies were able to grow just by raising prices. That's not possible today. In order to show real earnings growth (what is meant by quality earnings), a company needs to have unit volume growth. This means producing and selling more products or services and not depending on pricing or other financial gimmicks for part of its earnings growth. Industries that are believed to offer the best growth potential over the coming decade include health care (as baby boomers age) and financial services (as baby boomers retire). These are in addition to all the Internet and technology-related industries discussed in Chapter 8, such as telecommunications and software.

The key to analyzing any growth stock lies in the answers to these three questions:

1. How fast will the company grow?
2. How long will the growth last?
3. How certain is the company's future?

Companies with greater and longer growth are accorded higher P/E ratios, so if you can find them before this greater and longer growth is recognized by the market, you'll have a winner on your hands, both due to the increased earnings and the expanded multiple. But when evaluating growth stocks, don't necessarily search for stocks with the lowest P/E ratios. Look instead for high growth rates. A rapidly growing company will keep going up as long as its earnings are going up. It's only when the company disappoints the market by reporting lower earnings that it gets punished. Then the stock gets hit with a double whammy on the downside: lower earnings and multiple contraction (the opposite of multiple expansion) work in concert to push the stock price down.

In Chapter 4 we talked about the P/E ratio, which is the stock price divided by earnings per share, and the PEG ratio, which is the P/E ratio divided by the earnings growth rate. The PEG ratio is very meaningful for evaluating growth stocks because it allows you to compare two companies and see at a glance which stock is the better buy based on earnings growth. The P/E ratio is the numerator of the equation and the growth rate is the denominator. So let's say we want to compare two drug companies, Bristol-Myers Squibb and Merck. Bristol-Myers Squibb's P/E ratio is 36 and its growth rate over the next five years is expected to be 13.2 percent (according to analysts' estimates as revealed on Yahoo! Finance). So if you divide 36 by 13.2, you get 2.72. Now let's compare that to Merck. Merck's P/E ratio is 28, and its earnings growth rate is 12.5 percent. Divide 28 by 12.5 and you get 2.24. Merck's 2.24 is lower than Bristol-Myers Squibb's 2.72, indicating that Merck is the better buy. Now let's do the same with two financial services companies, Citigroup and American Express. Citigroup's P/E ratio is 24 and its five-year growth rate is 14 percent, giving it a combined PEG ratio of 1.71. American Express has a P/E of 29 and a growth rate of 13.5 percent, giving it a PEG ratio of 2.14. Citigroup's 1.71 is lower than American Express' 2.14, indicating that Citigroup is the better buy from a valuation standpoint.

A key aspect of analyzing growth stocks is accurately estimating a company's future growth prospects. Analysts use a number of different calculations to come up with estimated growth rates, using both qualitative and quantitative information. In addition to studying individual companies—talking to management and understanding what products are coming down the pike—they also study the industry in which the company operates in order to assess market size and the effects of competition. You can access much of this information via the Internet. (Go to <finance.yahoo.com>, enter a stock symbol, and click on Research; or visit <www.multex.com>, which offers research reports from some of the major investment firms.) You can also supplement analysts' number crunching with your own intuitive ideas about a company's future growth prospects.

One way to gain a better understanding about a company's future is to look at how much it is spending on research and development. This especially applies to technology companies. Michael Murphy, a technology analyst and author of the book *Every Investor's Guide to High-Tech Stocks & Mutual Funds,* puts a lot of stock in R&D spending because that is what drives new or significantly improved products, which in turn drives rapid sales growth. New products also carry higher profit margins because there is usually little competition when they are first introduced. Murphy looks for companies that spend at least 7 percent of revenues on R&D.

What to Do When Stock Prices Are Too High

Every investor wants to buy low, sell high. So what do you do if every stock you like has already made a gigantic run and is selling at or near its all-time high? There are two schools of thought on this. One is to refuse to buy stocks selling at their highs, to wait for a pullback, or find another stock to buy. It would have been crazy, for example, to buy VA Linux when it was selling near $300. The run-up was too far, too fast, and a pullback was inevitable. The other school of thought is to go ahead and buy anyway, especially if it's a solid company that's continuing to grow, like Cisco Systems. All during the 1990s, as Microsoft climbed higher and higher and higher, the people who said it's too expensive and refused to buy missed out on a tremendous opportunity. As we've seen, many good stocks just keep getting better and to wait for a pullback could mean missing the boat entirely.

Because this book is all about avoiding extremes and finding a middle ground, I'd like to offer a third option. If a stock you like is trading near its highs, buy some now and keep some cash available to buy more on a pullback. You can enter a limit order at a lower price and make it "good till cancelled." That way you won't miss out on a good opportunity that may only get better, and you'll also be able to reduce your average cost if the stock does pull back.

We are fortunate to still be on the front end of a revolution that offers so many amazing investment opportunities. Ten or 20 years from now, when the winners have emerged, we'll look back wistfully and wish we had invested early. By then it will seem obvious which stocks we should have invested in. We will have forgotten that when the Internet first began commercial operations back in the 1990s, there were hundreds of bright and promising companies that all had the potential to become winners. When reminded of this, we'll look back and wonder how we could have been so naïve and wildly optimistic about brand-new companies that had little more than a bright idea and a dream of making big money off the Internet. Yes, the honeymoon for Internet stocks is coming to an end. Investors are now beginning the earnest search for winners. Market participants are applying more rigorous standards for financial performance and shunning companies that do not have a solid plan for making profits. The most important thing we can do as investors is to watch closely as the drama unfolds and be ever more discerning about where we invest our money.

10

The Third Wave
in Asset Allocation

The audience is hushed as the CEO rises to the podium. He looks the part, dressed in jeans, black shirt, and matching dark tie. He has a youthful appearance despite his 32 years of age. After the obligatory opening joke, he proceeds to give his State of the Company address. It goes something like this. "It gives me great pleasure to tell you that we've had an extremely successful year. We lost more money this year than we did last year and if we can keep up the good work, I would anticipate this trend to continue into the foreseeable future. As you'll see in our business plans for 2001, we've developed several new services that we'll be offering free to our subscribers. Our subscribers pay no membership fees so it's definitely a win for them and the more customers we have, the better we look on Wall Street. Remember, our goal is not to *make* money but to *attract* money. Market capitalization is what counts, and we've clearly demonstrated our ability to boost our stock price. I'm here today to pledge that our superior management team stands ready, willing, and able to take this firm to the highest pinnacle of success." The audience breaks out in applause as those with wireless hand-held devices dial into the Internet and check the stock price: up 6½ points!

So why am I writing a chapter on asset allocation when all you have to do is pick a stock like this and make 6½ points in one day? Obviously, it's because this company is on shaky ground financially and its future viability is in question. But some people don't see that. All they see is a stock going up—never mind how or why—and that there's money to be made. I encounter clients all the time who hear about hot companies and want so badly to invest in them. They read about stocks doubling or tripling in price over a short period of time and they feel terribly left out. "Everybody's getting rich but me," they lament. "Why am I stuck in this stupid diversified portfolio when all the money is being made in just a few hot stocks? And while we're on the subject, why did you recommend bonds, anyway? Everyone knows bonds won't get you where you want to go financially."

One of my biggest challenges as a financial advisor is responding to hindsight bias (described in Chapter 2), which convinces clients beyond the shadow of a doubt that any dummy could have known that Qualcomm would turn out to be one of the best-performing stocks of 1999. (Okay, maybe this is a bad example because my firm did buy Qualcomm for clients before its meteoric rise in 1999; however, it's pretty unlikely that we'll be able to pick *next* year's big winner.) Despite my rational explanations to justify the theory behind asset allocation and diversification (which of course made perfect sense when we started the investing process), most investors have shown that they really don't want diversification. They want to be in the best-performing investments. This is creating tremendous conflicts for those of us in the financial advisory business as we attempt to give our clients what they want while recommending what's right for them at the same time. I would love to put 100 percent of my clients' assets into next year's best-performing stocks. The problem is that I don't know what those stocks are—and neither does anybody else. Given this inability to predict the future, I must recommend to my clients that they follow the next best course of action, which is to spread their assets around. Yes, this guarantees that they will not have all their money in the best-performing stocks. But it also reduces their risk of having it all in the wrong stocks. After all, if you lose 10 percent, you have to gain only 11 percent to get back to even. But if you lose 33 percent, you must earn 49 percent to get back where you started. And if you lose 100 percent, you have nothing left to work with. It's these kinds of truths that motivate financial advisors to recommend unpopular strategies to their clients, not unlike a parent telling a child to take her medicine.

At the same time, I definitely see some things wrong with the classic notion of asset allocation as it is currently being practiced by most financial advisors and portfolio managers. Talk to virtually any advisor, or open any financial magazine, and you'll get the standard pitch on asset allocation. First divide your money between stocks and bonds, varying the ratio to correspond with your age and risk tolerance. Next, take the stock portion and divvy it up by market capitalization: put some in large-cap stocks, some in mid-cap stocks, and some in small-cap stocks. Also divide the portfolio between growth stocks and value stocks. And don't forget to divide it between domestic and international. The belief is that if you slice and dice your portfolio all these different ways, you'll be sure to have all the bases covered. If large-cap stocks do well, you'll participate in the rally with at least some of your money. If value stocks sink, well, you can take heart in the fact that you didn't have all your money in that one sector.

When Harry Markowitz first developed modern portfolio theory, he based it on the idea of combining assets that were negatively correlated—that is, when one asset class is falling, another will be rising, as discussed in Chapter 4. But more and more, we are seeing that the standard approach to asset allocation—using market cap, growth/value, and domestic/international categories—doesn't provide much in the way of negative correlation. In other words, it doesn't ensure the belt-and-suspenders safety it was designed to provide because stocks often move together in response to interest rate changes and other economic events. This is not to say all stocks move in tandem. Quite the contrary, in fact. We're seeing that stocks within the same category, such as small-cap, will often produce widely divergent returns depending on industry conditions and the outlook for each individual company. And lots of people are wondering if having a perfectly balanced, negatively correlated portfolio is the right thing to do anyway. It forces you to accept mediocre returns because part of your portfolio is, by definition, in poor performing investments. So partly due to client complaints ("Why didn't you put more of my money in Qualcomm?") and partly due to sheer observation of the way the various sectors have been behaving, I realized that there has to be a better way to manage asset allocation so it reduces risk yet still takes advantage of some of the more compelling market opportunities. This is what inspired me to write this book.

Why Diversify?

First, I want to make it clear that I'm not throwing out the baby with the bath water. I still believe deeply in the concept of diversification— also known as asset allocation—because it's impossible to know in advance what the future holds. Yes, you can formulate some theories about which sectors or stocks will outperform the rest. And in fact the new asset allocation theory I am proposing does let you improve your odds by favoring certain sectors. But for an investor to put all of his or her money into the next big thing is anathema to a financial advisor whose responsibility is to save clients from excessive risk. Just think, if clients have a problem when I recommend sensible risk-management strategies that result in high, but not astronomical, investment returns, what would they think if I threw caution to the wind and recommended a risky strategy that caused them to actually lose money?

Those of us who are in the business of preaching diversification have had to change our explanations over the years as market conditions and investor sentiment have changed. Otherwise, people turn a deaf ear to our teachings. For example, the classic argument in favor of diversification is that it reduces risk. This argument works very well when the market is in a correction or prolonged decline and people are worried about losing money. Today, however, people are worried about not making enough money. Today's stock market is like a land grab (unless it has turned and headed south since this writing). The risk is not in losing money but in missing out on opportunities to make big money. Because the risk reduction argument doesn't carry much weight in this environment, I'll switch to the other argument in favor of diversification, which is this: it paradoxically lets you make risky investments that you otherwise might be afraid to make. How? When you have a sensible investment plan in place—one that's tailored to your goals and built on the always-sound concept of diversification—you can go ahead and take a few flyers in the market and not worry about losing it all because you won't be gambling with your entire life savings.

Here's what I mean. The opening of this chapter described a hypothetical CEO addressing an audience of shareholders who are clearly very excited about the company's ability to make them rich. I have 80-year-old clients who would love to get in on the excitement of today's high-tech investment opportunities. After all, 80-year-olds like to have fun with their money just like anybody else. But the problem with being 80 is that it's not so easy to make up any losses because most 80-year-olds are not working anymore. So a lot of older people (and younger people who also have an aversion to losing money) feel they must sit on the sidelines while all the brash, young players rake in the chips, so to speak. As you will see by reading the rest of this chapter, it is possible to design an asset allocation program that gives you some play money to invest in new opportunities while the rest of your assets are safely (or reasonably safely) tucked away earning returns consistent with your future financial goals. If you've had an itch to invest in some of today's high flyers but have been afraid to do so because you see it as an all-or-nothing proposition, this chapter will show you how you can have your cake and eat it too.

But more than giving you the opportunity to take a flyer every now and then, an asset allocation plan lends stability and balance to your overall investment program. Without it, you may be inclined to buy stocks on a whim, without regard for your long-term objectives. Soon you end up with a mish-mash of investments, an odd collection of stocks and/or mutual funds that do not complement one another and may even work against each other. By starting from the ground up with an asset allocation plan that specifies what percentage of your portfolio should be in the various assets or sectors, you can look for individual stocks or mutual funds to plug into those categories. This will keep you from buying another e-commerce stock when you already own three. It will discourage you from overweighting your portfolio in the stocks and market segments that generate the most hype. It will provide a comfortable framework for making investment decisions both now and in the future.

Asset allocation has earned a bad name in the last few years because the S&P 500 has done so well. Why bother buying anything else, the naysayers say, when you can put all your money into an S&P 500 index fund, get automatic diversification, and outperform most other investments? I must say to the naysayers that they are being very short-sighted. Whenever one investment does well for several years in a row people tend to think it will stay on top forever. And it never does. Remember real estate in the 1970s? Couldn't go wrong there. Good inflation hedge. They weren't making any more of it, etc., etc., etc. In the

1980s, it was Japan. For three years in a row, from 1986 to 1988, Japan had the best-performing market. Now that inflation has stayed low real estate isn't the deal it once was, and we all know what happened to Japan: the Nikkei index peaked at 38,957 in 1989; ten years later it's 53 percent off its high. Now, the thing that has boosted the S&P 500 over the past few years has been the strong U.S. economy, which is showing no signs of slowing. But there are indications that in the years ahead there will be some excellent opportunities in stocks other than the 500 largest U.S. corporations. The asset allocation plan that follows will allow you to take advantage of them.

Another reason for diversification's bad name is that most people don't do it right. They think diversifying means buying dozens of stocks or mutual funds—often without regard to which types of stocks or funds they're buying. They'll buy six large-cap growth funds think-ing they're getting good diversification when it turns out all six funds invest in the same stocks. Or they'll diversify into so many market seg-ments that even if they do pick a winning stock, its high returns are severely diluted by the rest of the stocks in the portfolio. A broadly di-versified portfolio will be relatively unaffected if one stock plummets, but it will also be unaffected if one stock soars. A study by Charles A. D'Ambrosio, CFA, showed that 8 to 12 stocks, whose returns were not highly correlated with each other, were enough to reduce the portfolio risk to approximately that of the marketplace in which they were traded. Morningstar has indicated that an investor can get adequate diversifica-tion with just three mutual funds. In addition to diluting performance, excessive diversification can also result in higher investment costs.

The First Two Waves in Asset Allocation

In the 1970s and 1980s, asset allocation was based on the concept of a pyramid. At the bottom of the pyramid—forming the foundation—were safe, stable investments like U.S. Treasury bills, money market funds, bank certificates of deposit, and savings accounts. In the middle of the pyramid were 30-year Treasury bonds, corporate bonds, and blue-chip stocks. At the top of the pyramid were risky investments like gold, small-cap stocks, commodities, futures, and options. The idea here was to have stable-value investments comprise the majority of the portfolio.

It was not until the foundation was built that an investor could comfortably layer on some of the more risky investments that are subject to principal fluctuation. Keep in mind that when this idea was first developed, many investors were still shell-shocked from the 1973–74 bear market, and some were still carrying childhood memories of the crash of 1929. Stocks were viewed as risky investments, suitable only for investors who could tolerate significant fluctuations in their portfolios—primarily young, well-to-do people. Retirees certainly would not invest in stocks except for maybe utility stocks which paid good quarterly dividends.

Then the high inflation of the late 1970s and early 1980s caught up with people. Suddenly investors found that these nice, safe, stable investments at the bottom of the pyramid weren't so safe after all. As interest rates rose, the value of long-term bonds fell. Retirees who had put all their money into one-year CDs paying 15 percent got hit with a big pay cut when they went to renew their CDs and found that rates had dropped to 12 percent, then 8 percent, then 6 percent, then 4 percent. In the meantime, stocks started going up. The bull market we're still enjoying started in 1982 after lying dormant for decades. Now those higher-risk investments in the middle of the pyramid, the ones that no respectable retiree would touch with a ten-foot pole, turned out to be less risky than the stable-value and fixed-income investments at the bottom of the pyramid. Those seemingly safe investments on the bottom had caused risk-averse investors to lose purchasing power and, in some cases, principal. Fortunately, most of these people also owned real estate, which was appreciating at a high rate due to the very same inflation that was decimating their financial assets.

So in the last half of the 1980s and in the early 1990s, the investment pyramid has morphed into a circle. Forget Treasury bills, money market funds, and bank CDs at the bottom of the pyramid. They don't keep up with inflation and for that reason can hardly be called investments. Also forget gold, futures, and options at the top of the pyramid because nobody ever invested in them anyway. Let's just concentrate on stocks and bonds. And to illustrate the balance between stocks and bonds, let's simply draw a circle representing a pie chart. One part of the circle will be stocks, the other will be bonds. Depending on the investor's age, risk tolerance, and time horizon, the stock part may be 60 percent, 80 percent or even 100 percent, with bonds making up the balance (if any).

Next, the stock and bond portfolios would be dealt with separately. The stock portion would be sliced and diced into the categories noted earlier—large cap/mid cap/small cap; growth/value; domestic/international—with percentages being allocated to each group based (again) on the investor's age, risk tolerance, and time horizon and using past performance as a guide to risk levels and potential returns. The bond portion would be sliced up by maturity and would include some short-term bonds, some intermediate-term bonds, and some long-term bonds. This method of strategic asset allocation has served investors well over the past 10 to 15 years. It has provided a good framework for investing and generally produced returns that exceeded inflation. Investors have enjoyed real growth in their assets and most people have been able to tolerate the volatility, which overall has been quite reasonable (especially because it's mostly been on the upside).

What is making investors restless today, and what suggests that we may be ready for a third wave in asset allocation, is the idea that the stock market is turning into a world of haves and have-nots. Certain sectors are doing extraordinarily well while others are not only languishing, they're declining in value at a time when economic conditions have never been better. Why classify stocks by market capitalization or by growth versus value when what really matters is what industry a company is in and what it's doing to build market share and gain dominance in its field? In today's borderless, global economy, why classify stocks by domestic versus international when everybody is doing business everywhere? The whole concept of asset allocation emerged from the idea that nobody can predict the market. But you don't necessarily need to spread your money across *all* market sectors in order to achieve adequate diversification. If you look at the stock market by industry sector instead of by market cap, investing style, or country, and if you apply information about upcoming trends for the new economy, you can get a pretty good idea of which sectors will do better than others in the decade ahead. For example, in 1999 the S&P 500 was up 21.0 percent. Not bad. But if you look at the index by sector, you see that transportation stocks and utility stocks were down 10.7 percent and 12.5 percent, respectively, while technology stocks were up 74.8 percent. If, instead of owning the whole S&P 500 index you had focused on technology to the exclusion of transportation and utility stocks, your returns would have been much better than the average. And it wouldn't have been that difficult at the start of 1999 to predict that technology stocks would outperform utilities and transportation stocks: that's just the way our economy is heading.

Now, sometimes sector rotation can fool you, which is why my asset allocation plan does call for investing part of your portfolio in a total market index fund because who knows? Transportation and utility stocks could bounce back again next year. But my point is that sector rotation is not entirely random. I believe that technology-related stocks have a long-term edge over basic industry stocks because the directives of the new economy suggest that this is so. And within the technology sector certain companies show more promise than others. These companies can be identified by the major trends discussed in Chapter 8 and by revenue growth and some of the other criteria discussed in Chapter 9. So why, if it's possible to identify certain characteristics of market winners, should we dilute our investment returns by sitting around in stocks that we're pretty sure won't perform very well?

The Third Wave in Asset Allocation

If the first wave in asset allocation emphasized stable-value investments, and the second wave emphasized stocks identified by market cap, investing style, and country, the third wave focuses on the individual characteristics of companies that make them good investments in an era denoted by profound economic change. This third wave in asset allocation starts out the same way the second wave did: by dividing the portfolio between stocks and bonds based on the investor's age, income, risk tolerance, and time horizon, and then goes on to provide a flexible way to capture above-average returns in a changing market. I won't say too much about bonds here, except to note that they are not as bad as some people think they are. They provide respectable, predictable returns, ranging from 6 percent to 8 percent, and can generate a steady source of income, which you can either take in cash or reinvest. If you are young, earning a good salary and willing to assume above-average risk, you may not want to put any money in bonds. But if you are older and want to have part of your portfolio invested in stable, predictable, income-generating investments, you'll probably want to allocate some percentage of your assets to bonds.

If it will help you to understand how bonds can provide a solid foundation to a risk-averse investor's portfolio, you might want to drag out the old pyramid as a visual aid. But instead of T-bills and money market funds on the bottom, you have a combination of short-term, intermediate-term, and long-term bonds that have been selected to co-incide with your financial needs. It's the predictability of bonds that makes them such a good foundation for an investor's portfolio. You know in advance how much income they'll be generating and when they will be maturing. This certainty can help offset the sometimes unsettling uncertainty of the stock portion of your portfolio and allow you to stay calm while the dot-coms are going wild. If this rational approach appeals to you and you do decide to invest in bonds, you have to promise one thing: you can't come back later and complain that your bonds didn't earn as much as your stocks. When you allocate part of your assets to bonds you know they won't earn as much as stocks—at least you hope so. What you really want is for stocks to earn high returns. But in case they don't, the bonds will serve as a safety net, producing current income and stability of principal. Also, if you do decide to invest in bonds, you may want to get help with this part of your portfolio because bonds can be very complicated. It's difficult to buy individual bonds on your own (the bond market is largely institutional), and bond mutual funds do not give you the same certainty with regard to yields and maturities that individual bonds do because the portfolio is always changing.

Okay. Now with the bond portion of your portfolio out of the way, we can concentrate on stocks. What follows is a rather radical notion of how to divide up the stock portion of your portfolio, but if you've gotten this far in this book, you'll see that it makes perfect sense. Here are the six assumptions that form the basis for this third wave in asset allocation:

1. Stocks in general offer an excellent opportunity for growth of capital, having earned an average of 12 percent per year over the past 50 years.
2. We are in a new economy, where many of the old assumptions about productivity and value are no longer valid.
3. Technology plays a key role in the new economy due to its exponential impact on productivity.
4. Companies that either produce technology or use it effectively are experiencing more dramatic growth than those that do not, and these stocks tend to be valued more highly in the marketplace.

5. The current paradigm shift will bring with it many dislocations and distortions over the next decade, offering excellent investment opportunities but also very large risks.
6. The best way to minimize risk while taking advantage of opportunities is with a diversified portfolio having a technology bias.

The third wave in asset allocation provides a framework for investing that is also very flexible. It gives you guidelines for choosing stocks or mutual funds and lets you adapt the guidelines to fit your individual objectives. It also allows you to change your portfolio as market conditions change—if you want. This plan allows active investors to move in and out of stocks and still work within the guidelines, while less active investors can establish their portfolio and basically forget about it. It all depends on which stocks or mutual funds you choose.

First, I'm going to give the basic framework, and then I'll spend the rest of the chapter describing the four categories and discussing ways you can employ this asset allocation plan to meet your objectives and investing style. Here is how I would divide the stock portion of an investor's portfolio:

- 30 percent total market index fund
- 30 percent core nontechnology stocks
- 30 percent technology stocks
- 10 percent emerging opportunities

If you are starting out with limited funds, you may need to layer the investments, starting out with the total market index fund and then adding the other categories as more savings become available. Unlike other asset allocation plans which call for a ready-made pie to be sliced up into the various stock categories, this asset allocation plan allows you to start with a foundation of one fund representing all stocks and then add the other categories one by one.

Thirty Percent Total Market Index Fund

Before you start tilting your portfolio toward technology, it's important to establish a solid, diversified base of stocks that you can set and forget. Why? Because nobody can predict the future. Yes, we *think* technology and tech-related companies will outperform utilities and transportation in the years ahead. But we don't *know* that. And we don't want to put all of our money into the newer sectors because they can be volatile and very risky. As we've pointed out, there will be a shakeout in the Internet sector in the years ahead as the winners emerge and the losers go away. While this drama promises to be fun to watch and, we hope, profitable to participate in, it will also be dangerous. For financial peace of mind, you will want to have at least 30 percent of your portfolio spread across all market sectors because nobody knows for sure what next year's (or next decade's) best-performing stocks or sectors will turn out to be. By definition, this part of your portfolio will earn average returns. And yes, the worst-performing sectors will drag down the returns achieved by the best-performing sectors. But again, this is necessary because you don't know what the worst-performing and best-performing sectors will turn out to be.

Although the S&P 500 has been the most popular index for index funds over the past few years, it does not represent the entire market of stocks. By definition it includes only the 500 largest U.S. corporations—and even that's misleading because much of the index's performance comes from a handful of stocks. While the S&P 500 has done very well over the past few years, I believe that smaller stocks will begin to catch up and may even outperform the blue chips in the years ahead. Certainly the outstanding performance of the Nasdaq Stock Market in 1999 (up 85.6 percent versus 21.0 percent for the S&P 500) indicates that a shift in market leadership may be emerging. Nevertheless, the reason for investing in a total market index fund is to avoid having to make calls like this. By owning a little piece of all stocks, you can benefit from a strong economy and a strong stock market without having to think about it very much. You can set up this part of your portfolio and basically forget about it, earning market returns without having to worry about which sectors are due to perform the best this year.

To participate in the entire stock market, you'll need to buy an index fund based on the Wilshire 5000. Unlike other indexes, which capture only a portion of the market, the Wilshire 5000 is the best measure of the entire U.S. stock market. Originally developed in 1974 with 5,000 stocks, it now includes over 7,000 stocks, comprising nearly 2,000 from the New York Stock Exchange and more than 5,000 from the Nasdaq Stock Market. As of September 30, 1998, the sectors comprising the Wilshire 5000 were as follows:

	Number of companies	Number of companies as % of Wilshire 5000	Market value of companies as % of Wilshire 5000
Capital goods	331	4.63%	4.62%
Consumer durables	251	3.51%	1.83%
Consumer nondurables	1,544	21.60%	26.68%
Energy	266	3.72%	5.36%
Finance	1,414	19.78%	15.98%
Materials & services	1,665	23.29%	9.01%
Technology	1,232	17.23%	25.23%
Transportation	157	2.20%	1.02%
Utilities	289	4.04%	10.27%

The following mutual funds are based on the Wilshire 5000 index:

T. Rowe Price Total Market Fund: 800-638-5660
Minimum initial investment: $2,500
Expense ratio: 0.40%

Vanguard Total Stock Market Index Fund: 800-662-7447
Minimum initial investment: $3,000
Expense ratio: 0.20%

Benefits of Index Funds

The main reason to invest in a total market index fund is so that part of your portfolio will cover all the bases no matter what happens in the economy and the markets. This is extremely important once you begin tilting your portfolio toward preferred segments like technology. The total market index fund serves as the foundation of your portfolio and will remain in place indefinitely, unless you decide to change your stock/bond allocation. The decision to invest more or less in stocks, however, would be based on your own personal objectives, not the outlook for the economy and the markets. Two circumstances that might call for a larger allocation to stocks are: (1) a willingness to assume more risk, perhaps due to a more stable financial situation; and (2) the need to achieve higher investment returns to meet a specific goal, such as retirement. Two circumstances that might call for a smaller allocation to stocks are: (1) retirement or other lifestyle change that dictates the need for lower risk and/or higher current income; and (2) significant growth in assets so you no longer need to achieve high returns in order to reach your goals. Barring any change in your stock/bond allocation, your total market index fund will not require any attention on your part except to add a portion of new savings as they become available and to periodically rebalance your assets as described at the end of this chapter.

As noted, the main reason for investing in a total market index fund is to gain exposure to all stocks for this part of your portfolio. But it's also worth noting that index funds have two important advantages over actively managed funds. One is tax benefits. The other is lower costs. An index fund seeks to provide returns that match the index on which it is based. It is managed by a portfolio manager, yes, but the manager's job is not to seek the highest returns possible. Rather, the manager works to maintain the portfolio so it matches the index as closely as possible. Rather than buying and selling stocks all the time as regular fund managers often do, index fund managers seek to maintain a static portfolio, making changes only when there are changes in the index itself. This lack of portfolio activity keeps trading costs down and also results in little or no taxable distributions.

Thirty Percent Core Nontechnology Stocks

Once you've built the foundation of your stock portfolio with a total market index fund, you can add a selection of core nontechnology stocks that you think have the potential to outperform the broader market averages in the years ahead. These stocks will provide a measure of concentration, giving you the opportunity to outperform the averages by focusing on those sectors which are expected to benefit from the major economic and demographic trends that are taking shape today. One huge trend, which was not covered in Chapter 8 because it's not purely technology related, is the aging of the baby boomer population. Due to its sheer size, this group of cohorts born between 1946 and 1964 has always had a major impact on the national economy, from the construction of new schools in the 1950s, to the acceleration of real estate values in the 1970s and 1980s. What's next for the 76 (or so) million boomers who are now entering their 50s and preparing for empty nests, a life of leisure, and, as much as they hate to admit it, age-related health issues?

First, the economy and the markets should remain strong as boomers continue to spend money and invest in the stock market over the next couple of decades. Harry Dent, author of *The Roaring 2000s,* has done extensive research showing that a person's spending typically reaches its peak at age 46. He uses this information to predict that the economy will stay strong as boomers roll into that magic high-spending age over the next 15 years. If I may add my own intuitive opinion to Mr. Dent's well-researched thesis, I believe boomers may keep spending long past the age of 46. As they enter their 50s and 60s, they'll be in their peak earning years. With their nests empty of college-educated children, they'll have vast amounts of disposable income burning a hole in their collective pocket. Boomers have always been good at spending. Just because housing, education, and other family-related costs have dropped doesn't mean they won't find other things to spend money on. Let's see now. Where do you suppose all this boomer money will go?

Health care is a biggie for aging boomers. But keep in mind they're not sick yet—and never will be, if they have anything to say about it. Wellness care, preventive medicine, nutrition products—anything that will help boomers stay well and feel good—will capture a large portion of the boomer wallet in the years ahead. Companies offering products and services designed to keep boomers healthy are worth watching, as are those making strides in pharmaceuticals and medical technology. Later on, as boomers face the inevitable physical declines that come with old age, look into companies providing products and services designed to assist with daily living, including special types of nursing homes and new, creative forms of housing/health care arrangements. For the next several decades, however, boomers should remain well and healthy for the most part. Like the generations before them, they will likely take this opportunity to travel. Boomer travel may differ from that of their elders, however. Cruises and RV travel will likely be less popular as boomers explore more exotic forms of travel such as safaris and spiritual pilgrimages. Look for companies offering travel and entertainment services that cater to the boomer sense of adventure and activity. As you explore investment opportunities to capitalize on these demographics, keep in mind that boomers have always charted new territory when it comes to lifestyles. This means you can't just look at what older people are doing now and extrapolate it out for a larger population. For example, boomers are currently redefining retirement by not conforming to a single mode of behavior. Some are retiring early, in their 50s, while others will keep working well into their 70s. Some are retiring early and then starting whole new careers. Many will work part-time and play part-time, striking a nice balance between work and leisure that can go on indefinitely. When contemplating investment opportunities, keep your eye on companies that are spotting trends related to boomer aging and are seizing opportunities to offer relevant and meaningful products and services to this large, affluent population group.

Whatever money boomers aren't spending on themselves (and their grandchildren) will find its way into investments. As a group, boomers have been very poor savers. They are just now starting to recognize this and are making up for lost time by pouring money into mutual funds and brokerage accounts. Over the next several decades, they will also be inheriting trillions of dollars from their parents. When evaluating financial service companies, again look for the ones that are tailoring their products and services to meet the demands of a newly affluent generation. Look for financial service companies that offer a blend of education, advice, and services allowing them to transact business quickly and efficiently.

The main thing to keep in mind when choosing stocks for the core nontechnology portion of your portfolio is that you are beginning to concentrate on stocks that have a good chance of outperforming the market averages, but that do not carry as much risk as the more volatile and highly valued technology sector. This category can also provide the negative correlation to technology that will keep your portfolio on an even keel—some sectors will zig while your technology stocks zag. At the same time, you can buy nontech companies that are using technology to achieve huge productivity gains, for example, Federal Express and Wal-Mart. Think of the core nontechnology category as an extension of the base that began with the total market fund—slightly more concentrated to provide exposure to certain desirable sectors but still relatively low risk. For this reason, you will want to focus on strong, stable companies that will be around a long time. Choose from the following four sectors: (1) health care (especially drugs), (2) financial services, (3) consumer durables, and (4) utilities. Look for household names that have consistent earnings growth and reasonable valuations, and buy stocks you'll feel comfortable owning for many years. This category isn't quite as "set and forget" as the total market fund base, but it's close. Save your energy for the next two categories.

Thirty Percent Technology Stocks

As recently as a few years ago, it would have been considered extremely risky to put 30 percent of your assets into technology stocks. But as technology has assumed a greater role in the economy, and as market capitalizations have mushroomed, the sector has come to represent a much larger share of the overall market than it did in the past. Anyone who owns an index fund based on the S&P 500 index does, in fact, have nearly 30 percent of his or her assets invested in technology stocks.

The most important thing to keep in mind when investing this segment of your portfolio is the wide range of risk you could be facing in the technology sector. Larger stocks like IBM and Microsoft can be considered blue chips and may therefore serve as core holdings, while newer, smaller companies may be extremely volatile and in danger of going out of business. These high-risk stocks will need to be monitored closely or avoided entirely. When considering technology companies, refer to some of the valuation methods discussed in Chapter 9, such as price-to-sales ratios and PEG ratios, and use these ratios to compare stocks in the same sector. This will allow you to pick the better buy, just as you do when comparing prices on refrigerators or new cars.

An interesting phenomenon taking place in business today is a winner-take-all mentality that is heaping huge rewards on companies perceived as the best performers in their fields (this includes nontechnology sectors as well). In a book called *The Winner Take All Society,* Robert H. Frank, an economics professor at Cornell University, argued that the very best performers, even if just marginally better than their competitors, were enjoying a huge and widening gap in financial rewards. Although the book was written in 1995 when the Internet was just emerging, this thesis certainly has played itself out in recent years as companies like Cisco Systems and Amazon.com have left their rivals in the dust in terms of market capitalization. The winner-take-all theory makes sense as it applies to the Internet because success and brand recognition feed on themselves, resulting in more customers and more business, and making the strong stronger and the weak weaker. Stock market participants, who are keenly aware of the impending shakeout in high-priced Internet and technology stocks, will be madly searching for winners as time goes on. They will actually be doing much of the work separating the wheat from the chaff, assigning higher valuations to those companies they believe will be the ultimate winners. Does this mean we should all buy stocks with the highest valuations on the theory that the market has figured out that these companies are the winners? Not necessarily. Sometimes high valuations are the result of hype and misguided opinion.

This brings us to the second most important thing to remember when building this part of your portfolio. There's no rush. Technology will be around for a long time. The productivity gains that are possible through technology should keep our economy growing stronger for the foreseeable future. There will be plenty of opportunities to buy good stocks and achieve sizable investment returns. Michael Murphy, the technology analyst referred to in Chapter 9, likens your position to that of a baseball batter without a ball and strike count—you can wait and wait until you get the pitch you want. If you don't feel comfortable swinging the bat quite yet, just stand there and get a feel for the kinds of pitches coming your way. After you've watched a number of pitches go by, you'll be in a better position to identify the good ones. So start your foray into technology investing by making a list of stocks to watch. Include stocks from several subsectors, such as biotechnology, computer hardware, computer software, Internet infrastructure, e-commerce, networking, and others. Although the economy is strong now, prepare for a slowing economy by including some medical technology stocks on the theory that people will always need medical treatments even when the economy isn't booming. Also consider the size of the companies; because the technology sector is so nebulous and subject to so many unknown factors, you'll want companies with a market capitalization of at least $200 million. Microcap companies much smaller than that are simply too lean to have enough reserves to make it through tough times. Make your list manageable enough that you can really get to know the companies and be able to follow them on a regular basis. Become familiar with their trading patterns and read analysts' reports so you'll know what the market is expecting from the companies in terms of future sales and earnings. If their prices seem too high right now, set target prices at which you would be willing to buy. Then watch and wait.

Keep in mind that you don't need to buy dozens of stocks to get adequate diversification. Eight to 12 should be enough—fewer if you're leaning toward the larger companies and waiting until the clear winners emerge. And you don't need to buy them all at once. Remember, your total market index fund is allowing you to participate in market returns (including the technology sector), so it's not as if you are standing completely on the sidelines while you are deciding what to buy. Choose carefully. What you are searching for are technology's biggest winners— those companies that are on their way to achieving near-monopoly status, such as Cisco Systems, Dell, Intel, Nokia, and MCI Worldcom. Exercise patience and due diligence and you'll be handsomely rewarded as the strong get stronger in the years ahead.

Ten Percent Emerging Opportunities

The conventional wisdom for conservative investors has always been to buy good long-term holdings and then hold them long term. Generally, this is good advice, but the problem with it is that: (1) the world is changing too fast for anyone to know what the future holds, making it impossible to really plan long term, and (2) a 100 percent set-and-forget portfolio means you'll miss out on the many interim opportunities that come around. By allocating about 10 percent of your portfolio to what I call emerging opportunities, you can feel free to play in various areas of the market while knowing that 90 percent of your portfolio is sensibly invested in accordance with your long-term goals. By the way, the term *emerging opportunities* is not to be confused with emerging markets, which is a standard investment category that has been denigrated over the past decade due to poor performance (until it took off in 1999), although at some point you may indeed choose emerging markets as your latest emerging opportunity.

This category can comprise just about anything you want to include: IPOs, some microcap company your brother-in-law works for, some Latin American stock your friend told you about, or even a mutual fund that invests in a market niche which capitalizes on one of the very latest trends. The idea here is to seize short-term opportunities offering the potential for large gains. Because you'll be risking no more than 10 percent of your portfolio, you can take a chance on a flyer every now and then without disturbing the rest of your portfolio. In fact, you may want to keep this money in a special account to avoid mixing it with your serious investments. Start by putting the money into a liquid account. Then, depending on how active you want to be, you can either trade in and out of stocks or let the money sit until you find just the right opportunity.

Investment Vehicles

The preceding discussion has assumed the purchase of individual stocks for the actual investments, but you can also implement this asset allocation plan with mutual funds. You'll have to shop carefully, however, to avoid overlapping sectors. For example, if you were to buy a standard growth mutual fund for your core nontechnology category, you would be hard-pressed to find a fund that does not invest in technology stocks. If you were to then invest in a pure technology fund for your technology category, you would be overweighted in technology. The solution may be to combine the two categories and invest in one mutual fund that invests up to 50 percent of the portfolio in technology stocks. This would give you the technology bias you're trying to achieve, but it may be hard to find a fund that meets this requirement. While it's always a good idea to examine a mutual fund portfolio before you invest in it, the fact remains that you have no control over which sectors the fund will be investing in the future.

Another way to implement your asset allocation plan is through sector funds, also called specialty funds. Sector funds are just what the name implies: they invest in a specific sector of the market and are generally prohibited from straying into other sectors. Buying sector funds enables you to stick to your asset allocation plan without worrying about researching and choosing individual stocks, and without worrying that the portfolio manager will load up on stocks outside the specified group. There are sector funds available in the following categories: communications, financial services, health, natural resources, real estate, technology, and utilities. Some sector funds are further broken down; for example, some technology funds invest only in Internet-related stocks. The advantage to using mutual funds is that you are essentially hiring someone else to do your research and investing, and for this you will pay an annual fee. Sector fund expenses tend to be on the high side— 1.5 percent or more—compared to index funds which have expenses of 0.4 percent or lower. The rationale is that sector fund investing requires a great deal of research and expertise; if you'd just as soon not do this yourself, you may be glad to pay someone else to do it for you.

One other consideration to remember is taxes. If you buy and hold individual stocks, your gains are not taxed until you sell. Mutual funds, however, often buy and sell stocks without regard to tax consequences, forcing shareholders to accept taxable distributions whether they want them or not. In the end, your decision to invest in mutual funds or individual stocks (or a combination of the two) will probably depend on how involved you want to be in managing your investments. Mutual funds do make investing awfully easy. An alternative, if you have at least $100,000 to invest, is to hire a professional money manager who will honor your asset allocation plan and tax situation and manage your portfolio according to your needs.

Examples of Asset Allocation Plans

The beauty of this third wave in asset allocation is that it can be tailored to meet your individual objectives while still providing a framework for investing. As you move through the various stages of your life—accumulating more assets, acquiring more financial knowledge, and changing your risk tolerance—you can alter the individual investments while adhering to the basic plan. Figure 10.1 illustrates some examples of how the program can be altered for various life stages and temperaments. Please note that the examples in Figure 10.1 deal with the equity portion of an individual's portfolio only. More risk-averse investors will also have some money in bonds.

Managing Your Asset Allocation Plan

After a while, your perfect 30-30-30-10 allocation will get all out of whack. That's because market movements will cause some investments to grow more than others. You may be tempted to let your win-

FIGURE 10.1   Sample Asset Allocation Plans

Twenty-Something Investor with $50,000
Limited investment knowledge, moderate risk tolerance

Equity Portfolio—100% of assets
    $15,000 Total market fund
    $15,000 Core nontechnology stocks
        $5,000 Health care sector fund
        $5,000 Financial servies sector fund
        $2,500 Utilities sector fund
        $2,500 Real estate investment trust (REIT)
    $15,000 Technology stocks
        $5,000 Technology sector fund
        $5,000 Global telecommunications fund
        $2,500 Biotechnology sector fund
    $5,000 Emerging opportunities
        $2,500 Internet fund
        $2,500 Emerging markets fund
        $2,500 International small-cap fund

Forty-Something Investor with $300,000
High risk tolerance, moderate investment knowledge, little time to devote to investments

Equity Portfolio—100% of assets
    $90,000 Total market fund
    $90,000 Core nontechnology stocks
        $30,000 Health care sector fund
        $30,000 Financial services sector fund
        $30,000 Leisure sector fund
    $90,000 Technology stocks
        $45,000 Global telecommunications fund
        $15,000 Internet fund
        $30,000 Technology sector fund
    $30,000 Emerging opportunities
        $15,000 Small-cap international fund
        $15,000 Biotechnology fund

Sixty-Something Investor with $1,000,000
Low to moderate risk tolerance, high investment knowledge, likes individual stocks

Equity Portfolio—60% of assets
    $300,000 Total market fund
    $300,000 Core nontechnology stocks
        $50,000 Citigroup
        $50,000 Merck
        $50,000 Wal-Mart
        $50,000 General Electric

$50,000 Procter & Gamble
$50,000 CBS/Viacom
$300,000 Technology stocks
$50,000 MCI Worldcom
$50,000 Intel
$50,000 America Online
$50,000 Sun Microsystems
$50,000 Cisco Systems
$50,000 Nokia
$100,000 Emerging opportunities
$50,000 Asia-Pacific fund
$50,000 Latin America fund

ners ride, but there's a very good reason to periodically rebalance your portfolio by selling investments in one category and moving the money to another category. Here's why. Let's say you're starting your investment program with $30,000. You take your 10 percent emerging opportunities money and buy what turns out to be the year's best-performing stock. It increases sixfold, turning your $3,000 into $18,000. Let's also say that the rest of your portfolio increases at an average rate of 15 percent, so that the $27,000 invested in the total market fund, core nontechnology stocks, and technology stocks is now worth $31,050. If you hang onto your emerging opportunities stock, you'll have $18,000, or nearly 40 percent of your total assets, in one stock. And after a sixfold increase in one year, there's a pretty good chance the stock will take a breather the following year. So as much as it pains you to bail out on a stock that was so good to you, the prudent thing to do would be to sell part or all of that wonderful stock and restore your original asset allocation by transferring money into the other three categories.

Here's what your asset allocation plan would look like at the start of the year:

Total portfolio: $30,000

Category	Assets invested	Percentage of portfolio
Total market fund	$9,000	30%
Core nontechnology stocks	$9,000	30%
Technology stocks	$9,000	30%
Emerging opportunities	$3,000	10%

Here's what it would look like at the end of the year:

Total portfolio: $49,050

Category	Assets invested	Percentage of portfolio
Total market fund	$ 9,315	19%
Core nontechnology stocks	$ 9,315	19%
Technology stocks	$ 9,315	19%
Emerging opportunities	$18,000	37%

Here's what it would look like after rebalancing:

Total portfolio $49,050

Category	Assets invested	Percentage of portfolio
Total market fund	$14,715	30%
Core nontechnology stocks	$14,715	30%
Technology stocks	$14,715	30%
Emerging opportunities	$ 4,905	10%

To accomplish the rebalancing, you would sell enough of the emerging opportunities stock to bring your investment in this category back to your original 10 percent allocation, and place the proceeds in the other three categories. For the sake of simplicity we are assuming that the three other categories all appreciate at the same 15 percent rate, but that would not be the case in real life, of course. You'll need to get your calculator out to determine how much you'll need to place in each category to restore its 30 percent allocation. I can't emphasize enough how important it is to restrict your aggressive investments to 10 percent of your portfolio. I know that it may seem as if you are playing with the house's money at this point, so what harm does it do to leave it where it's doing so well? The harm is that this is your riskiest category and to have as much as 37 percent of your assets exposed to high risk is simply not a prudent thing to do. Rebalancing runs counter to the conventional Wall Street wisdom of cutting losses short and letting profits run, but when your goal is to earn consistent returns with limited risk, rebalancing forces you to follow another Wall Street axiom, which is to buy low and sell high.

11 Strategies for Success

The asset allocation plan described in Chapter 10 is designed to serve as a framework for your investment decisions. It ensures diversification while also allowing a measure of concentration, so you can minimize risk and still take advantage of market opportunities. If you've been using a strict asset allocation formula that calls for a mix of large cap and small cap stocks as well as growth and value styles, you'll note that this new approach—the third wave in asset allocation—allows you to focus more on industry sectors and provides much more freedom with regard to the other criteria. You can still include a mix of sizes and styles, but your focus will be more on the type of business a company is in and what it is doing to succeed in its market niche. After all, when you invest in stocks, you are investing in living, breathing companies. Focusing more on a company's business operations than size or financial ratios helps remind you of that. On the other hand, if you've never used asset allocation before and have tended to base your investment decisions on breaking stories of hot stocks, you'll appreciate the structure it provides when putting a portfolio together. You'll also appreciate the discipline and reduced risk it provides when a market correction hits. This third wave in asset allocation ensures that you won't become overweighted in certain sectors and gives you some guidance for stock selection, which can be helpful when you're facing a universe of about 7,000 stocks and 10,000 mutual funds.

What the asset allocation plan does not provide is specific advice on how to choose stocks or mutual funds. That's intentional. For one thing, everyone is different. Some people like to trade fairly often, others like to buy and hold. Some people like to reduce risk by sticking with large, well-established stocks, while others like to place early bets on unproven companies and are willing to accept the risks inherent in this strategy. Some people can tolerate high volatility, others can't. Another reason for making the asset allocation plan intentionally vague in the area of stock selection is that you may want to vary your strategy depending on economic and market conditions. When the market outlook is very positive, you may want to be aggressive; when it's negative you may want to pull back and be defensive. So, the purpose of this chapter is to identify some of the strategies you can employ depending on your investing style and the outlook for the markets.

What Kind of Investor Are You?

Throughout this book I've been referring to buy-and-hold investors versus those who like to trade. Now it's time to put a little clarification on these two different investing styles and suggest that the best approach may not be one or the other, but a blend of both. The conventional wisdom is that buy-and-hold is better, that market timing doesn't work, and that frequent trading results in high trading costs and gains taxed at the higher short-term capital gains rate. This is all true. But boys will be boys, as they say (because most active traders are male), so rather than echo advice which you may have heard and chosen to ignore, I'd like to acknowledge that there can be some benefits to active trading and offer some ways to make it work. At the same time, if you are a dyed-in-the-wool, buy-and-hold investor, don't feel as if you need to change. You've got to have the right temperament and motivation to actively buy and sell stocks, and if you don't have it you probably won't be very successful at it. Stick with mutual funds or buy long-term stocks instead.

What I would like to suggest is that people who do want to be actively involved in their investments can vary the risk/reward characteristics of their portfolios by buying some core stocks that they put away, while making other investments on a more short-term basis. I don't mean day-trading or even switching in and out of stocks on a weekly or monthly basis. I do mean paying attention to the news and the economic outlook and varying some of your investments as market conditions change. I'll explain this further in a minute. But the most important thing to understand is that the strategies for long-term and short-term investing are very, very different. So if you're applying a mix of both, you'll need to keep the strategies straight for the kind of investing you're doing. For example, let's say you're worried about the market and want to retreat to Benjamin Graham's value approach on the theory that you can never go wrong buying low-priced stocks which are trading near their intrinsic value. By definition, you would be engaging in a long-term investment strategy. The whole idea behind value investing is to buy stocks nobody wants and then wait for the market to recognize their value. The wait can sometimes be years. So if you buy value stocks hoping to see a quick pop, you'll be sorely disappointed and will likely end up selling out and incurring unnecessary trading costs without ever seeing a profit. I'll be discussing more of these long-term/short-term differences in the strategies that follow.

Strategies for Investing in Stocks

The premise of this book is based on the fact that our economy and markets are undergoing significant change, that some of the old ways of investing aren't working anymore, and that we need to explore some new methods of investing while still retaining much of the wisdom that has served investors for decades. The strategies that follow will allow you to take advantage of opportunities ushered in by the new economy without becoming a wild-eyed, mouse-wielding, day-trading, dot-com maniac. All you need to do is settle on a risk level and choose the strategy that's right for you. If you're not sure about your risk tolerance, that's okay too. In fact, it can be a sensible strategy to vary the risk characteristics within your portfolio as an additional form of diversification.

When to Buy

Low-risk strategy: Wait for leaders to emerge.
High-risk strategy: Take a chance on companies with emerging technologies.

If you are looking to capitalize on trends mentioned in Chapter 8, a key question is when to buy into the companies that are most likely to benefit from these trends. The advantage to getting in early is that if you pick the right companies, you can make a ton of money. For example, my firm began buying Qualcomm in December 1995 because we felt there would be a surge in wireless usage over the next several years. Qualcomm had developed a new and promising technology called CDMA (code-division multiple access) and would start manufacturing phones with this technology. We knew that Qualcomm would be a huge beneficiary of royalties for every phone made. Although we like to buy the leaders in an industry, we bought Qualcomm even though it was one rung down. Good move. Qualcomm was up 3,250 percent during the four-year period ending December 1999 and was up 2,621 percent in 1999 alone. This is a good (though unfortunately not typical) example of buying early and reaping huge rewards.

Normally, however, we will wait for leaders to emerge, especially when it comes to trends that are not so clearly established and where there are lots of players jockeying for position. Even though a trend may be inevitable, its timing can't always be predicted, and often it takes longer to fully take hold than most people realize. Past experience with the emerging biotech and software trends in the 1980s has shown that one of the biggest mistakes investors can make is to buy too early. What generally happens when you're too early is (1) you pay too much for the stock because all the hype surrounding the trend has pushed its price up beyond normal valuation levels, and (2) once the hype dies down and the stock falls in price, it trades in a narrow range for what is often years, before beginning to move back up again. Meanwhile, you're sitting on a loss and tying up money in a stock that's going nowhere. This is the downside of buying too early (just in case the Qualcomm story had you seeing dollar signs and ready to throw caution to the wind and put all of your money into a company with an emerging technology).

What to Buy (Quantitative Criteria)

Low-risk strategy: Look for solid fundamentals.
High-risk strategy: Look for rapid growth.

Use some of the financial ratios discussed in Chapters 4 and 9 to determine if a company is on solid footing financially and is reasonably valued compared to its peers. If you are buying stocks to hold long term, look for a strong balance sheet and a history of earnings growth.

For the core nontechnology part of your portfolio, you can use some of the more standard measures of value, like P/E ratios and PEG ratios to compare stocks in the same industry. Many of the newer technology stocks, as we've discussed, don't conform to these methods so you'll have to look at other metrics such as revenue growth. Generally, fast-growing companies carry more risk and also have more potential reward. Their high growth rate is already reflected in the stock price and as long as their financial performance doesn't disappoint, the stock price can keep going up as the company's revenues grow. However, be prepared for high volatility around the time the company reports earnings. Investors tend to be trigger-happy when dealing with high-growth stocks because if earnings come in below expectations by even one penny, the market can be merciless in trouncing the stock.

What to Buy (Qualitative Criteria)

Low-risk strategy: Look for management with clear vision and good execution.
High-risk strategy: Look for a great idea and innovative technology.
One thing you will find among virtually all market leaders is a CEO and/or management team that knows exactly where the company is going and how to take it there. Both elements must be in place. John Chambers of Cisco Systems, Jeff Bezos of Amazon.com, and Larry Ellison of Oracle all have an amazingly direct vision of where their companies are going and they are executing that vision with clarity and confidence. In fact, we've seen so much evidence indicating that talent at the top is one of the most crucial elements in a company's long-term success, that you can almost skip the boring stock research and read biographies of the executives. The major business magazines all feature executive profiles periodically, and these can provide great insight into companies worthy of your investment. Also look for best-places-to-work winners because retaining top talent is key to surviving and succeeding in a knowledge-based economy. Quality of customer service can also reveal a company's strength and commitment to achieving dominance in its field. Let your own experiences with various companies' service departments provide valuable clues into how the company is run as a whole.

For your high-risk stock picks, look for a company that has some outstanding invention or truly innovative approach to making or selling products or services. It's hard to separate the wheat from the chaff here because there's always a lot of hype surrounding companies with new technologies. The technology may be wonderful but the company may not know how to make a business out of it. Or the whole story may be exaggerated. I remember a stock called Fingermatrix back in the 1980s. It pioneered electronic fingerprinting, which of course had all kinds of applications for ATMs and building security access. It seemed to be a wonderful technology. When I first became aware of the stock it was trading around $12. Since then it has filed for bankruptcy and is now trading at about $.40 a share—despite the fact that it still holds 19 patents covering this revolutionary electronic fingerprinting technology. On the other hand, the recognition of Qualcomm's new technology worked out for us, so clearly it is possible to identify innovative companies and make money from them. Keep your eyes and ears open for ideas: read the business press, especially magazines like *Fast Company* which are on top of emerging trends, read trade magazines, talk to friends and associates, and always, always beware of hype.

When to Sell

Low-risk strategy: Reason for buying stock has changed.
High-risk strategy: Stock has reached your target price.

Knowing when to sell is one of the most difficult aspects of investing. Remember when I said that strategies for long-term investing and short-term investing are very, very different? Nowhere is this more apparent than in the sell decision. I have taken the liberty of equating low risk with long term and high risk with short term because usually the two go hand in hand (although they don't have to). A low-risk, long-term strategy would be to decide at the time you are buying a stock why you like it and to write down or document those reasons so you won't forget. Then periodically evaluate the stock and compare its performance against your criteria. If the company is still doing what you expected it to do, keep holding onto the stock. If any of the reasons for buying it have changed, consider selling. The thing you do *not* want to do if this is a low-risk, long-term investment is sell in response to market movements. By documenting your reasons for purchase, you are more likely to avoid the panic selling that is so often detrimental to returns. Sometimes even the best companies report disappointing earnings and experience a sell-off in the marketplace. If it's a company you like, resist the urge to sell into the weakness and even consider buying more. Long-term holdings should only be sold if the fundamentals change significantly (several quarters of earnings disappointments or some big shift in business operations), never because of stock price changes.

On the other hand, short-term holdings can be sold in response to market movements. This is what stop orders and limit orders are for. When short-term investors buy a stock, instead of writing down their reasons for buying it, they write down their price targets—both on the upside and the downside. Let's say you buy a volatile stock at $25. To limit your losses, you may want to set a downside price target of $20. To lock in your profits you may want to set an upside price target of $40. If the stock hits either of those prices, you're out, with either a small loss or a decent gain. Sometimes short-term investors keep raising their price targets if the stock is in a clear uptrend in order to eke out a few more points. I must emphasize again that you need to have the temperament, attention, and energy for short-term investing if you're going to be successful at it. It can be emotionally grueling and if you're not careful, your emotions can lead you into bad decisions (fear and greed are powerful influencers and can take over without your even being aware of it). Be especially watchful of investing costs because they are not apparent at the time you are trading. It's only later, when you total up your investment returns, that you find that commissions and taxes have eaten up as much as 40 percent of your profits.

Economic and Market Conditions

We've had such ideal conditions for investing over the past few years that it's hard to imagine anything else. Good economic growth, low inflation, low interest rates, and a positive outlook for stocks all bode well for the stock market and give investors permission to jump right in and enjoy the wealth-building power of stocks. It's important to keep in mind, however, that such ideal conditions may not always prevail. And although it's certainly possible for individual stocks to go against the grain—rising in value even when the overall outlook is negative—you must be an expert stock picker to identify those companies. "A rising tide lifts (or sinks) all boats" is a popular Wall Street saying meaning that all stocks are subject to general economic and market conditions, regardless of what sector they're in or how great a company is. This doesn't necessarily mean you should bail out of all your stocks at the first sign of negative news—some storms are worth riding out—but it does suggest that you may want to vary your investment strategy should economic conditions change. A positive outlook calls for a more aggressive strategy, while a negative outlook calls for a more defensive strategy. Following are some of the economic and market conditions you may encounter in your investing lifetime.

Economic Outlook

Condition: High to Moderate Growth, Low Inflation

Strategy: Ideal conditions for stocks; buy growth stocks in growing sectors like technology and financial services.   Because this is the prevailing economic condition at the time this book was written, all of the recommendations in this book apply to an economy having high to moderate growth and low inflation. In fact, it is because economic conditions are so good that I felt it was time to revise traditional asset allocation theories in order to benefit from some of the high-growth sectors of the economy—to be slightly more aggressive, if you will, because defensive strategies don't appear to be necessary and are resulting in significant opportunity costs. Still, it's important to keep in mind the bifurcation of the market as described in Chapter 3—also known as the separation of the haves and the have-nots—and to understand that the rising tide theory may be losing steam as we're seeing many stocks languish despite near-perfect economic conditions. Whether this is a temporary phenomenon or a fact of life in the new economy remains to be seen, but for now at least it brings up the importance of choosing good stocks in growing industries and minimizing exposure to sectors that are in decline. So dart throwing will have to give way to research and careful selection. But as long as the current economic conditions last, circumstances are ideal for making money in stocks.

Condition: Slow Growth, Low Inflation

Strategy: Buy defensive stocks such as utilities and consumer staples (foods, textiles, household products).   If the economy ever starts to slow down for a prolonged period of time—and this can happen for a variety of reasons such as a sustained drop in consumer spending—those high-growth stocks that performed so well when times were good won't look so attractive anymore, and valuations will decline in a response to investor pessimism. Throughout history, economic cycles have been a fact of life: periods of expansion are followed by periods of contraction, and that's just the way the economy works. When the economy is in contraction investors hunker down and switch their money from growth stocks to defensive stocks on the theory that people will always need to eat no matter what the economy is doing. In times like this it's hard to make money at all in stocks because recessions are often accompanied by bear markets. However, it's worth pointing out once again that we are in a new economy. Perhaps technology has influenced our world in such a positive way that we are no longer subject to traditional economic cycles. Time will tell.

Condition: Slow Growth, High Inflation

Strategy: Worst of all worlds; buy real estate and stocks that benefit from rising prices (energy, natural resources).   The last time we saw slow growth accompanied by high inflation was in the 1970s, when it was termed *stagflation.* The economy was in a funk yet prices were rising almost out of control. Growth in corporate profits—what little there was of it—came mostly from price increases, not higher output. The scars from this period are still with us, and in fact are what drive Alan Greenspan, chairman of the Federal Reserve Board, in his relentless pursuit of low inflation. Greenspan has done an admirable job of tweaking interest rates just enough to allow the economy to grow but without becoming overheated to the point where inflation sets in. Whenever the Fed raises interest rates a smidgen, or even whispers that it is thinking about doing so, the market acts somewhat like a spoiled child who knows his father is doing the right thing in the long run but whines that he is taking the fun out of everything. The market does not like higher interest rates, but it worships Alan Greenspan for keeping our economy on an even keel. The odds of stagflation happening again are pretty slim, but it's worth keeping this bit of economic history in mind—to appreciate what we have now, if nothing else.

Condition: High Growth, High Inflation

Strategy: Buy stocks with good unit-volume growth (i.e., earnings growth is due to higher output, not price increases). With Alan Greenspan at the helm of the Federal Reserve Board for the next few years, I really don't think we need to worry about high inflation. Sometimes the market worries about it, such as when the labor report shows extremely low unemployment suggesting that wage increases may be eminent. But then sometimes the market worries about everything. I find it amusing that one day stock prices will fall on fears of interest rate increases, and the next day they'll rise on the expectation that those very same interest rates will continue to stay low. This is the kind of noise that whipsaws short-term investors who pay too much attention to market sentiment on any given day.

Market Outlook

The economic outlook and the market outlook usually go hand in hand. Obviously, when the economy is doing well, corporate profits are rising and stocks are very popular. But because the stock market is anticipatory, sometimes market sentiment will shift before changes show up in the actual economy. So we can have an economy that's rolling along just fine, when the market starts to interpret certain leading indicators to mean a recession or higher inflation may be on the horizon. These fears will cause stocks to fall, maybe for only one day, maybe for months on end. Now, it's very important to note that the market is not always right about such things. A popular saying on Wall Street is that the market has predicted 12 of the last 8 recessions. This is why you never want to act too soon. What appears to be abject pessimism one day could shift to manic optimism the next. Assessing market sentiment requires just the right balance of long-term and short-term thinking, along with the willingness to react rationally and without urgency.

Market outlook really only affects your short-term investments anyway. Long-term investments should never be touched in response to market movements because it can play havoc with your long-term goals. A long-term strategy presumes that over time stocks will outperform other investments and that interim volatility doesn't matter because you won't be needing to liquidate your investments. It sees volatility as a fact of life and that it's better to leave the money fully invested rather than try to call interim market turns. The biggest risk with taking your long-term money out of stocks in reaction to market movements is that you never know when to get back in again. And you certainly do not want to be sitting on the sidelines when the market turns around for a prolonged bull run.

When it comes to short-term investing, however, you may indeed want to invest aggressively or cautiously—depending on the outlook for the markets. This requires vigilance and a keen eye for reality versus illusion. It is very easy to get whipsawed by the market, which is why day traders have such a hard time producing real profits. Short-term investors with a longer time frame, however, can stand back and give price trends a chance to develop before taking action. When I talk about the market outlooks that follow, I'm not referring to the day-to-day sentiment that causes stock prices to rise or fall; rather, I'm referring to price trends that are developing which suggest stocks are likely to head higher or lower over the near term. One other caveat belongs here, although it may seem obvious: Market outlook refers to the whole market and is based on the rising tide philosophy. Obviously, the stocks you own (or are thinking about buying) may behave quite differently from the general market.

Condition: Outlook Is Moderately Positive

Strategy: Invest aggressively.   Once again, this is the situation that's occurring as this book is being written. The outlook for stocks is generally very positive, and the fact that it continues to climb a wall of worry is the best news of all. Yes, many investors are wildly positive (see the next condition). Paradoxically, this is what makes other investors nervous. As long as at least some people are nervous about the market, it will have the element of skepticism needed for a healthy bull market.

Condition: Outlook Is Wildly Positive

Strategy: Invest cautiously.   Once the wall of worry comes down, stocks are sure to follow. This goes back to the idea presented at the beginning of this book: when *everyone* thinks stocks will go higher, then presumably *everyone* is already fully invested. With no more money available for stocks, there's only one direction the market can go: down. Actually, I'm not so sure this long-held theory is valid anymore because of increased participation in the market by individual investors (as opposed to institutions). After all, people are still working and contributing part of their wages to their 401(k) plans; this money at least will find its way into the markets (and in fact this phenomenon is part of what has propelled the bull market over the past decade). Still, when market participants are overly optimistic they tend to bid stock prices up too high, creating perfect conditions for a fall.

Condition: Outlook Is Moderately Negative

Strategy: Go to cash or invest cautiously.   If the outlook is moderately negative, it means market participants expect stock prices to decline. Usually it means prices have been going down for a while and the downtrend is expected to continue (as opposed to making a sudden turn from positive to negative). During this difficult time, short-term investors usually lay low in cash, waiting for stocks to bottom out. This is one of the most difficult conditions to evaluate because a correction can last anywhere from a few days to a few months before the market resumes its uptrend, while a true bear market can last for years. In assessing market sentiment, listen for the longer-term view: are market participants assuming this is a brief correction and will be over soon, or do they think economic conditions are now so negative that it will be a long time before stock prices recover? If it's the latter, be especially cautious.

Condition: Outlook Is Exceedingly Negative

Strategy: Remain cautious, watch for upturn.   The old saying about it being darkest just before dawn applies to Wall Street, too. When everyone is so negative about stocks that it seems prices will never go back up again, a glimmer of light begins to appear on the horizon. The rationale is the same as for market tops: if *everyone* thinks stocks will go down, then presumably *everyone* is holding cash; with all this cash available for investing, people will soon start to buy stocks. This is especially true if stocks have declined to the point where they are selling near their intrinsic value—investors simply can't resist a bargain. Maybe we'll be lucky enough not to encounter this situation in the decades ahead, but if we do, be careful. If there's been an extended decline, wait for the price trend to turn positive before jumping back into the market.

Global Investing

We Americans tend to think of our country as the center of the universe. And indeed, our economy is the most powerful in the world right now. Investors could easily ignore the rest of the world and do very well buying American-based companies, especially when companies having multinational operations are included. But because this book is about looking ahead and finding opportunities in places other than the obvious, I'd like to suggest that you not limit your investing universe to the United States, especially when it comes to technology and telecommunications stocks. Fifty percent of the planet's total market value lies outside the United States. Doesn't it make sense to at least take a look at this expanded arena?

On the whole, world stock markets in the 1990s did not perform as well as ours—until 1999, when they emerged from their slumber and turned in outstanding performance. Finland was up 153 percent (in U.S. dollars); Brazil, 152 percent; Mexico, 80 percent; Hong Kong, 68 percent; France, 51 percent. Emerging markets, a category that had investors pretty excited a decade ago but had pretty much been written off due to many years of poor performance, began to, well, emerge. Costa Rica was up 60 percent; Greece, 102 percent; India, 63 percent; Indonesia, 70 percent; Israel, 62 percent. At least one analyst has noted that the world's emerging markets can be equated to the United States in 1900—not a bad place to be if you have a long time horizon.

But the same point I made earlier in this book about indexes masking underlying market activity applies to international stocks as well. You must look at individual sectors and individual companies because performance is all over the map. And you have to be careful because other countries do not have the same accounting standards and disclosure requirements that we have in this country. Still, if you stick with big, well-known companies like Nokia of Finland, Ericsson of Sweden, or SAP of Germany, you can get the same quality and at least as much technological prowess as you'll find in their U.S. counterparts, Motorola, Lucent, and Oracle.

There are two approaches to investing overseas. One is to look at the country. The other is to look at the sectors. For your core nontechnology and technology categories, sector analysis is the best approach because any company that's in the right business will do well no matter where it's located. In fact, I prefer to look at international investing as a natural extension of U.S. investing because the larger companies are doing business everywhere anyway. The idea is to pick a sector and find the best company or companies within that sector regardless of where their headquarters are based. So when you're choosing stocks for your core nontechnology and especially your technology sectors, don't limit your universe to the United States; consider the whole world. At the same time, don't go overseas just for the sake of diversification because you won't gain much negative correlation if you're dealing with multinationals. Just pick the best companies regardless of where they are. If doing all that research seems daunting, consider investing in a good international technology fund. Dresdner RCM Global Technology Fund (800-726-7240) scours the globe looking for tech industries having the most attractive growth prospects. Then it looks for companies that are growing their earnings by at least 25 percent per year. It so happens that at year-end 1999 the fund was only 30 percent invested overseas, having found most companies meeting their criteria located right here in the U.S. But the fact that they examine the whole world gives them an edge over technology funds that limit their portfolio to U.S. stocks.

Emerging markets are another story. Due to the high risks and unpredictable nature of some of these little markets, these stocks belong in the 10 percent of your portfolio that's devoted to emerging opportunities (but please don't put all 10 percent into one emerging market). And because it can take years—even decades—for emerging markets to really get going, tuck them away and consider them long-term investments, just as John Templeton did when he invested in Japan long before its 1980s heyday.

General Investment Advice

As a financial advisor, I am, obviously, in the business of giving advice. Normally, this advice is customized to the needs of my clients. In fact, it can be difficult to give blanket statements regarding what a person should do because everyone is different. If you've noticed that this book has covered different perspectives on certain issues, that's why. First, nobody can predict the future, so any forward-looking statements must be tempered with the caveat that no one really knows what the future holds. Some futurists and economists may feel comfortable going out on a limb and making firm predictions, but they're not laying their clients' money on the line. One of the main points I've tried to get across in this book is that investing is all about the future; but because you can never know for sure what the future holds, you must design an investment program that will protect you in case what you think will happen doesn't. The second reason for covering different perspectives is that what is right for one person may not be right for another. Investing is an extremely personal matter; it depends on your financial goals, your age, your time horizon, your tax situation, your risk tolerance and temperament, your willingness to be actively involved in your investments, and many other factors. That said, here are some advisory points that apply to everyone.

Consider the Tax Impact of Your Investment Decisions

You've heard this before, but I can't emphasize it enough. Here's why. If you're like most people you think about taxes once a year: sometime between January and April when you gather your papers together and prepare your annual tax return. But by then it's too late to do anything to reduce your tax bill. The taxes that you pay in April are based on financial transactions that occurred between January and December of the previous year (with a few exceptions such as IRA contributions). So once December 31 has passed, it's too late to make any investment decisions affecting the previous year's tax bill.

Why does this matter? Because taxes can take a huge bite out of your investment profits. If you are in the 28 percent marginal tax bracket, you lose 28 cents on every dollar of profits from securities held less than one year—more if you also pay state income tax. You get a slightly better break on profits from securities held more than a year. The long-term capital gains rate is 20 percent (or 10 percent for investors in the 15 percent tax bracket). But the most important thing to remember is that the only time you pay tax is when you sell—when you actually realize a gain. So if you buy 100 shares of a stock at $25 and sell it at $35 before the end of the year, your $1,000 gain will be diminished by $280, leaving you an after-tax gain of $720. In percentage terms, this cuts your rate of return from 40 percent to 29 percent. But if you hold onto the stock, there's no tax due at all. Your unrealized gain is still $1,000, or 40 percent. Eventually, you'll have to pay the piper, of course, but for now you're saving $280 in cold, hard cash. As you make investments throughout the year, keep in mind that every sell decision will trigger a tax consequence. Figure out what the tax will be and ask yourself if it's worth it.

Now, some sell decisions can actually reduce your tax bill. These are the ones that nail down losses. The IRS doesn't totally share your pain when you lose money on investments, but it does let you offset gains with corresponding losses. This serves to reduce the taxes on your gains. Let's say you have the same $1,000 short-term gain noted above, but you also have a short-term loss of $800 in another security. You can subtract $800 from $1,000 and report a net short-term gain of $200. Now you're paying only $56 in taxes ($200 × 0.28) instead of $280. Some people have a real aversion to taking losses because it forces them to admit they made a mistake. But it can be a very prudent thing to do taxwise, and gives you a good reason to purge your portfolio of losers. (Remember that it has to be done before December 31.) This discussion doesn't begin to cover all the tax ramifications of investing, but the main point I want to make is that you need to think about taxes every time you make an investment decision—not later, when you file your taxes.

Consider Transaction Costs

Here's another hidden expense that investors don't think about at the time they are making investment decisions, but trading commissions and mutual fund fees can eat into your investment returns the same way taxes do. Now, when it comes to mutual funds and investment advisory fees that you pay to a professional money manager, you'll probably want to view the costs as fees for services rendered. If a mutual fund or money manager can save you the work of researching investments, and if the manager earns his fee by getting you above-average investment returns, then it's probably worth it to you. But if you're investing on your own and paying a commission every time you place a trade, those are the expenses to watch out for. Let's say you find a discount broker who charges $10 per trade. This doesn't seem like much on a $2,500 transaction, but if you place 100 trades a year—two a week—you'll spend $1,000 on commissions alone. Be sure to subtract that amount from your year's gains when toting up your investment returns. You may discover you didn't make as much money as you thought you did.

Over time, trading costs can really make a difference. A $100,000 portfolio that earned an average annual return of 12 percent over 20 years would net $900,406 if trading costs averaged 1 percent, but just $604,024 if costs were 3 percent—a difference of nearly $300,000!

Keep Long-Term and Short-Term Strategies Straight

I mentioned this earlier in the chapter, but it bears further discussion because people often mix them up—sometimes with disastrous results. Here's an all-too-typical example. Let's say you buy a stock based on short-term criteria; the stock has good momentum and high volume, but you know virtually nothing about the company's underlying fundamentals, which aren't so important when your investment decision is based on price trends. Well, let's say something goes wrong and the stock turns around and heads south. The correct action at this point would be to bail out and take your loss; obviously, the hoped-for price increase didn't materialize so the natural next step would be to close out the position. However, some people, in an effort to avoid admitting a mistake, decide to convert this short-term strategy into a long-term strategy and hold onto the stock. Now you have a stock in the long-term part of your portfolio that you know virtually nothing about. And how will you know when to sell it if you don't even know the long-term reasons for buying it?

It works the other way, too. Let's say you're investing the long-term portion of your portfolio. You do your research and find an excellent company like Qualcomm mentioned earlier: it has outstanding technology, a solid business model, and is experiencing rapid growth. You buy the stock with the intention of holding it for years. Then lo and behold, the market falls in love with the stock, drives its price up, and you can't resist selling the stock and taking your profit. Now, in addition to a whopping tax bill, you have to go out and find another extraordinary stock to replace the one you just sold. And to make matters worse, two years later the stock is selling at four times what you sold it for and you're kicking yourself for having sold.

Pay Attention to Investment Returns

This may seem exceedingly obvious, but studies have shown that most people really have no idea how their investments have performed. A recent study by Don Moore of Northwestern University and Max Bazerman, who teaches at both Northwestern and Harvard, surveyed a group of 80 mutual fund investors and found that 88 percent had exaggerated their returns, believing their portfolios had far outperformed the S&P 500. More than a third of the investors who thought they had beaten the market actually lagged it by at least 5 percent, and a quarter of all the self-described market beaters finished at least 15 percent behind the S&P 500. Another survey by *Money* magazine and Rosewood Capital revealed not that people were unaware of their performance but that Internet investors' returns were far worse than the media hype would have you believe. The survey asked 1,338 Web users about their finances. Two-thirds were investors, and a quarter of those held dot-com stocks. Of the Net investors, only 15 percent reported gains of 50 percent or more on the Net holdings. Over half said they had returns under 10 percent, and 29 percent of them *lost money.* Let this be a word to the wise.

Decide whether You Want to Be an Active or Passive Investor but Always Stay Involved

Active investors pay attention to the news, read the business publications, have a watch list of stocks they follow closely (in addition to their own portfolio), and spend anywhere from 5 hours to 20 hours (or more) per week attending to their investments. If this does not sound like your idea of a good time, admit it and hire someone else to manage your investments. Buy mutual funds or hire a money manager, and let the professionals handle the minutia of researching and selecting stocks and bonds. Even as a passive investor, however, you'll need to stay on top of things by making sure your assets are allocated appropriately and that the managers you have selected are doing a good job.

Review your portfolio once a quarter and see where you stand compared to where you want to be. Clarify your financial goals and check your progress along the way. Plan ahead for major financial events such as college and retirement. And never forget that financial success is not the ultimate goal in life: it's one of the means by which you attain happiness, security, and comfort in this world.

I hope this book has given you a new perspective on investing. If you're a new investor, I hope some of the historical perspective has encouraged you to develop realistic expectations and that you will take to heart some of the conventional wisdom that may seem outdated when stocks are doing very well, but that may prove useful when the markets are acting troubled and unpredictable. If you are a longtime investor, I hope you will let go of some of the beliefs that may be preventing you from fully taking advantage of current opportunities and open your mind to the fact that we are in a new economy with new rules. Paradigm shifts are never easy. There's a lot that is new, but much of the old stays with us too. When automobiles were invented, railroads didn't disappear. When TV came along, radio didn't go away. The Internet promises to enrich our lives in unimaginable ways, but it will not take away anything that is truly useful to us. The key to investing in an age of major change is to be open to new possibilities and to remain rational and thoughtful in the face of conflicting information and emotional extremes. I wish you much success as you seize new opportunities to achieve your investment goals in the years ahead.

Index

C

D